LITERACY, SEXUALITY, PEDAGOGY

LITERACY, SEXUALITY, PEDAGOGY

Theory and Practice for Composition Studies

JONATHAN ALEXANDER

UTAH STATE UNIVERSITY PRESS
Logan, Utah
2008

Utah State University Press
Logan, Utah 84322–7800

ISBN: 978-0-87421-701-8 (paper)
ISBN: 978-0-87421-702-5 (e-book)

Portions of chapters three and four of this work were previously published, respectively, as
"'Straightboyz4Nsync': Queer Theory and the Composition of Heterosexuality," in *JAC*, and
"Transgender Rhetorics: (Re)Composing the Body in Narratives of Gender," in *College Composition and Communication*. These texts have been revised and are reprinted here with permission.

Manufactured in the United States of America
Cover design by Barbara Yale-Read

Library of Congress Cataloging-in-Publication Data

Alexander, Jonathan.
  Literacy, sexuality, pedagogy : theory and practice for composition studies / Jonathan Alexander.
    p. cm.
  Includes bibliographical references and index.
  ISBN 978-0-87421-701-8 (pbk. : alk. paper)
  1. English language–Rhetoric–Study and teaching–Social aspects. 2. Authorship–Study and teaching
(Higher)–Social aspects. 3. Gender identity. 4. Sex. I. Title.
  PE1404.A44 2008
  808'.0420711–dc22

                              2008001335

For
MARGARET M. BARBER
and
WILL HOCHMAN

my first colleagues,
a sister and a brother in the art of writing instruction

CONTENTS

ACKNOWLEDGMENTS

As I was working on this book, colleagues and friends would ask me about the project, wondering how I was spending my sabbatical days. Invariably, and for some shock value, I'd say I was writing a book called "Writing Sex," one of the original titles for the project. Just as invariably, people would hear "Writing *Sucks*" as the title. I'd patiently correct them and say, "No, 'Writing *Sex.*'" Now I must admit that a book entitled "Writing Sucks" sounds intriguing, especially for someone who has taught writing for over fifteen years. But the writing of this book has been anything but "sucky." Indeed, *Literacy, Sexuality, Pedagogy* has been a labor of love, and often a sheer delight on which to work.

That delight is due in no small part to the many supportive colleagues and friends I have had during its authoring. First and foremost in my *personal* world, Mack McCoy, my partner, husband, best friend, and constant companion, has seen me through the many difficult times surrounding the writing of this book. First and foremost in the *scholarly* world, my editor at Utah State University Press, Michael Spooner, has offered keen insight, diligent support, and firm guidance—when such was needed. He knew precisely how to sift through the anonymous reviewers' comments—which were always generous, fair, and smart—and focus my attention on what was most important. This book is a far better one for his patient editorship of it.

Colleagues and friends at my former academic home, the University of Cincinnati (UC), provided both moral and scholarly support. Early on in my work, my writing group in Cincinnati—dear friends Lucille Schultz, Russel Durst, and Laura Micicche—were encouraging and supportive, providing thoughtful and insightful commentary in the early stages of my writing. Leland Person, my department head at the time, granted me a slightly extended sabbatical, allowing me a very rare opportunity to take my time with this text and mull it over carefully. The UC Faculty Development Council (FDC) provided financial support toward the end of that sabbatical for me to attend the National Sexuality Resource Center's Summer Institute at San Francisco State University during the summer of 2006, where I met a host of wonderful colleagues and friends who not only inspired but encouraged me when I was grappling with thorny theoretical material. I thank Wayne Hall for his support and encouragement as coordinator of the FDC. And Kristi Nelson, vice provost for academic planning at UC, provided much-appreciated additional research support in partial compensation for my work as interim director of general education.

Two other dear colleagues and friends at the University of Cincinnati, Michelle Gibson and Deborah Meem, were with this book in spirit much of the way. I have worked with both of them on a variety of projects, and Michelle and I were among the first to write about "queer composition"; I owe her much for challenging my thinking, particularly in the material in the last chapter on student resistances. In many ways, my collaborative thinking with Michelle permeates this volume, and I include in this book, with Michelle's permission, some of the work we put together for a conference presentation on teaching Dorothy Allison's *Bastard out of Carolina*. But moreover, Michelle, Deb, and I were also working on another book, *Finding Out: An Introduction to LGBT Studies*, while I was writing and revising this book, and I cannot help but think that *Literacy, Sexuality, Pedagogy* is a stronger text now because I was working with Deb and Michelle on a project about queer sexuality more generally. At the very least, our work together has provided me with much inspiration, many good times, and the dearest of friendships. Indeed, I miss all of my University of Cincinnati colleagues very much.

But perhaps the most importantl inspiration at the University of Cincinnati, where I worked for nine years, were my students, who were willing to talk to me frankly, openly, and probingly about their views on gender, sexuality, sexual politics, and the sociocultural and discursive dimensions of intimacy. Almost all of the pedagogical experiences I describe and analyze in this book come from my work with my students at UC, so I owe them a tremendous debt. And at times, students not my own were eager to participate in my research. My colleague and movie buddy Gary Weissman allowed me to interview him and his students, whose work enlivens chapter 5, and I am most grateful to Gary and his excellent class for challenging my thinking about marriage as both a deeply personal and profoundly complicated sociopolitical issue.

Nationally, several colleagues whom I have worked with over the years have offered their scholarly wisdom, intellectual support, and unfailing comradeship. David Wallace, Martha Marinara, Samantha Blackmon, Will Banks, and I were all working on projects at the time of my writing that made me stop, think, and rethink some of my basic claims in this book. Our CCCC 2006 presentation on LGBT content in composition textbooks and readers was crucial in helping me think through this book's third chapter, and I am grateful for our work together on these topics. David Wallace in particular has become a good friend, and our work on two articles that we wrote near the end of my work on this project came at an important time in the revision process. As always, my dearest friend and nonsexual lifemate, Karen Yescavage, provided constant comradeship and creative rigor in my thinking about sex, sexuality, and queerness. Two other collaborators and friends, Jackie Rhodes and Keith Dorwick, were great academic companions as we worked on other projects during the years I was working on this book. I appreciate their good humor and support, and I'm delighted to now live so close to Jackie, who is among my dearest friends in the larger groves of academe.

Many other academic colleagues whom I do *not* know personally—some I do not know at all—have shaped this work. They are the various reviewers and editors who have published earlier work from which I have drawn some of the material included here. I thank them sincerely for their guidance and advice. In particular, Lynn Worsham, who published "'Straightboyz4Nsync': Queer Theory and the Composition of Heterosexuality," in *JAC: A Journal of Composition Theory* (the basis of chapter 3), and Deobrah Holdstein, who published "Transgender Rhetorics: (Re)Composing the Body in Narratives of Gender," in *College Composition and Communication* (the basis of chapter 4), were both encouraging and appropriately demanding as editors. These texts are reprinted with permission. (Full citations for these texts is in the bibliography.) I also thank Gail Hawisher and Cindy Selfe for providing me with an opportunity to explore the world of "gay gamers" in a chapter for their collection *Gaming Lives in the Twenty-first Century*, and while I ultimately decided not to include that work in this volume, I nonetheless learned a great deal about queerness online from working with that project. Three book reviews I wrote were also influential in prompting me to think about two texts I ultimately found to be very important in my work. The first was a review of Bruce McComiskey's *Teaching Composition as a Social Practice* that I wrote for *Academic Writing*. Bruce's book showed me what a rich critical pedagogy could look like. The second was a review for *GLQ*, the preeminent journal on gay and lesbian studies, on Deborah Cameron and Don Kulick's fabulous book *Language and Sexuality*—an assignment that came at the right time in the development of this project. And finally, a review I wrote for the (alas, now defunct) *Lesbian Review of Books* on *Inside the Academy and Out* was immensely helpful early in my career in prompting me to think through what a "queer pedagogy" might look like. I thank the editors of all of these journals for allowing me to revise material from those much earlier works in these pages.

Finally, Will Hochman and Margaret M. Barber, my first colleagues in composition at the University of Southern Colorado (now Colorado State University, Pueblo), have inspired me from the beginning of my career, and their careful mentoring of me as a compositionist has taught me more about writing and teaching—and life—than I can adequately render here in my own paltry words. Will gave me my first job as a writing instructor, and Margaret shared an office with me through my first years as a full-time "comp jockey." Since those early years in the mid-1990s, both have stayed with me as colleagues and friends—a brother and a sister—sharing professional and personal lives in rich, rewarding, and profound ways. I have authored other composition and writing studies texts, but *Literacy, Sexuality, Pedagogy* owes more to them than does any other work I have published, for Will and Margaret were the first—and most persistent—in nurturing my combined interests in writing instruction and sexuality studies. For that, as well as for many other personal and professional reasons, I dedicate this book to them.

LITERACY, SEXUALITY, PEDAGOGY

INTRODUCTION
Toward Sexual Literacy

Sex and sexuality, and the complex personal and political issues surrounding them, are a powerful part of our daily lives. They form part of the most intimate moments we share with one another. But moreover, far from occupying a purely personal dimension in our lives, they saturate our public conversations and permeate the media. They lie at the core of some of our most pressing sociocultural and political debates, substantively informing how we think of ourselves and our identities, how we understand ourselves to ourselves. A brief scan of CNN.com on any given day at any time of the day will reveal that at least one (and usually two or three) primary news item is explicitly about sex or sexuality. Newsworthy topics include issues of gay marriage, sexual predation, reproductive issues, sex education, gays in the military, and sex among the famous. Debates about marriage, in particular, cut to the core of any number of intersecting issues, such as the meaning of marriage as a personal, social, and political institution. Without a doubt, sex and sexuality are key components of how we conceive of ourselves personally, organize ourselves collectively, and figure ourselves politically.

More significantly for us as writing and literacy specialists, *sexuality*—or the varied ways in which narratives of intimacy, pleasure, the body, gender, and identity become constructed and disseminated personally, socially, and politically—is itself a complex literacy event, evoking narrations of self, connections with others through complex discourses, and political formations mediated through ideological investments. Anthony Giddens, in his highly influential work *The Transformation of Intimacy: Sexuality, Love, and Eroticism in Modern Societies*, defines sexuality as "something each of us 'has,' or cultivates, no longer a natural condition which an individual accepts as a preordained state of affairs. . . . sexuality functions as a malleable feature of self, a prime connecting point between body, self-identity and social norms" (1992, 15). That connecting point—between our most personal, deep-seated senses of self and the "social norms" that organize democratic societies—is often story, narrative, and ideological discourse. In basic ways, when we talk about ourselves, when we define ourselves, we almost invariably use gendered and sexualized language. We are men or women, gay or straight, married or single. We make and take such declarations at face value, but they always already occur in thick social contexts, rooted in both shared and contested discourses and ways of classifying the world.

Noted theorist David M. Halperin argues in *One Hundred Years of Homosexuality*, much as do Michel Foucault and the queer theorists, that "sexuality is a cultural production: it represents the *appropriation* of the human body and of its erogenous zones by an ideological discourse" (1990, 25). Decades of feminist scholarship have demonstrated that the concepts male and female, masculinity and femininity, are much more than biological markers; they are intensely socially inflected constructs that mediate ourselves both to ourselves and to others. Interpolated with gender is a complicated nexus of desires that we attempt to label in order to "mark" us; identifications of gay and straight, for instance, are crucially significant labels in self-understanding, as well as being sites of contentious debate about citizenship and "normalcy." Indeed, the seeming ubiquity of sexuality within our cultural landscape and the multiple tensions surrounding it may be due in part to the close correlation in the contemporary West between sexuality and identity; in many ways, we define ourselves—and are defined by others—in terms of both gender and desire. And how we define ourselves and how we become defined, as men/women, gay/straight, married/single, become important dimensions of our sense of normalcy, of our agency (or not) within our society, and of our experience of justice and citizenship.

Learning how to talk fluently and critically about sex and sexuality composes a significant part of becoming literate in our society. Being able to address sexuality issues intelligently, critically, and even comfortably is vital if we are to participate in some of the most important debates of our time. At the most basic level, then, if our students are to learn how to navigate the wealth of information and media that grapples with issues of sex and sexuality, they need to become comfortable in dealing with such material in a mature, reasonable, and rhetorically savvy fashion. But of all the issues addressed directly and explicitly in college-level composition classrooms, sex and sexuality are probably among the least mentioned, the least discussed, the least analyzed and debated over any extended period of time. Indeed, despite the connection between sexuality and discourse, the complex languages we use to define and construct our experiences, intimacies, and desires, how often do we as compositionists explore with our students the powerful ways in which sex and sexuality are culturally produced through discursive practices, through specific kinds of literacy practices, through the normalizing stories we tell to sanction some behaviors, proscribe others? Learning how to navigate such questions and explore such discussions should be a crucial component of any literacy education, and yet it is not.

To fill this need, some organizations have called for greater literacy about sexuality. San Francisco State University's National Sexuality Resource Center (NSRC), directed by renowned anthropologist Gilbert Herdt, has recently begun publishing an online magazine, *American Sexuality*, which offers a "unique opportunity to disseminate scholarly research in a widely read, internationally accessible medium aimed at informing academics, the general public and community based advocates on the critical gaps in sexuality research and Policy" (http://www. americansexuality.org/). This effort arises out of a strongly perceived need to close the "gap" between sophisticated scholarly and academic knowledges developed about sex and sexuality and conceptions of sexuality as they circulate in the public sphere, in often very unsophisticated ways. Recent evidence suggests attempts by some politicians and textbook companies to *limit* information about sex and sexuality in the public school system. The following excerpt from a recent online petition protests such limitations, calling attention in particular to a case in Texas: "In November 2004, under pressure from members of the Texas State Board of Education, Glencoe/McGraw-Hill publishers, together with Holt, Rinehart and Winston publishers, changed language in health texts for Texas middle and high school students. The revised texts now stipulate that marriage is a union only between a man and woman, promote an abstinence approach to sex education, and omit information related to contraceptive use" (http://www.petitiononline. com/mh2004sm/petition.html). This case is particularly significant in that Texas comprises a substantial share of the nation's textbook market, so companies that produce textbooks for Texas are likely to market the same books in other states as well, regardless of whether those states limit education and knowledge about sex and sexuality in quite the same way as proposed in Texas.

Such debates suggest not only the contentiousness with which sexuality is discussed but also its centrality to important conceptions of ourselves as individuals and as citizens in a pluralistic democracy. In terms of sexuality and citizenry, Dennis Altman argues persuasively in his recent book, *Global Sex*, that "[s]exuality is an area of human behavior, emotion, and understanding which is often thought of as 'natural' and 'private,' even though it is simultaneously an arena of constant surveillance and control" (2001, 2). A significant part of that "constant surveillance and control" arises out of sexuality's complex intertwining with culture, politics, and even economics. Altman argues that it is imperative that we examine and understand sexuality "in the context of larger socioeconomic factors which create the conditions within which sexual acts and identities occur." Specifically, he notes the following: "These factors include the *economic*, as growing affluence allows—and forces new ways of organizing 'private' life, and as sexuality is increasingly commodified; the *cultural*, as images of different sexualities are rapidly diffused across the world, often to be confronted by religious and nationalist movements; and the *political*, in that state regulation plays a crucial role in determining the possible forms of sexual expression" (34).

Certainly, in thinking about the preceding example, the crafting of textbooks to promote particular kinds of sexual practices suggests a desire to promote a certain kind of citizen, a particular way of *being*. As a *compositionist*, I see in such examples and in Altman's analysis not only sexuality's connection to economics, culture, and politics, but also its powerful connection to literacy. How we talk about, define, and discuss the private versus the personal; how images and representations of sex and sexuality are constructed, written, and disseminated; how the state, the collective "we," defines sex and sexuality and controls information about it—all of these are *literacy* events that deserve attention and analysis. In terms of education, it is becoming increasingly apparent that how one learns about sex and sexuality in this culture is complexly wrapped up in notions of citizenship; put another way, how one develops a literacy about sexuality is crucial to one's understanding of important public debates, and hence participation in the democratic project.

As this brief foregoing sketch demonstrates, *sexuality and literacy are densely connected in contemporary Anglo-American culture*. At one level, literacy about sexuality as a highly significant personal, social, and political topic is crucial for students to understand some of the more important debates and issues of our time. But at another level, it is not the case just that we need more literacy about sexuality—which we do—but that we also need to recognize how our understanding of literacy itself is intimately bound up with the sexual, with sexuality. Put simply, the stories that we tell about sexuality are part and parcel, even *central* at times, to the stories we tell about ourselves, individually, collectively, and politically. As such, being literate in our society—that is, being able to work knowledgeably, engagingly, and critically with some of the dominant stories that organize our lives, individually and collectively—must necessarily take into consideration an understanding of the complex ways in which sexuality plays a significant role in our personal and public self-definitions, in the ideologically valenced stories we tell about our lives. I call this particularly kind of literacy *sexual literacy*—the knowledge complex that recognizes the significance of sexuality to self- and communal definition and that critically engages the stories we tell about sex and sexuality to probe them for controlling values and for ways to resist, when necessary, constraining norms.

My writing of this book has emerged out of two interlocking convictions: first, in Anglo-American culture, literacy and sexuality are intimately intertwined, even if that intertwining is not always acknowledged or understood; second, we as compositionists, those charged with forwarding and developing literacy among students in higher education, have done surprisingly little to understand this intertwining of literacy and sexuality, much less articulate and process such a nexus with our students. I believe the time has come when it is imperative both to understand the interrelationship of sexuality and literacy *and* to think more fully and critically about how we as literacy specialists can—and *should*—address this relationship in our composition classes.

It is time to develop a critical *sexual literacy*.

If we are invested in working with students to develop a critical understanding of their places—and their possibilities—in the world, then we must consider issues of sexuality as central to the development of contemporary literacy. With race, gender, and religion, sexuality must be acknowledged as crucial in forming contemporary Western senses of literacy. Therefore, I believe it is time for us as literacy experts and pedagogues to take up this intertwining, as a significant subject for both scholarly and pedagogical exploration. In the remainder of this introduction, I would like to consider how recent trends in composition studies have created a space in which to begin thinking critically about how we can address the connection between literacy and sexuality. Given this connection, I will then forward the notion of *sexual literacy*, which I believe should be a central concern in the teaching of writing. Then I will briefly outline how the remaining chapters of this book (1) develop theoretical approaches to understanding the connection between sexuality and literacy; and (2) situate those approaches in classroom-based

pedagogies that demonstrate the development and efficacy of a powerful and critical sexual literacy.

COMPOSITION'S SOCIAL—BUT NOT QUITE SEXUAL—TURN

Despite the potential significance of issues of sexuality in the development of literacy and literacy skills, very little research in our discipline
exists on the intersections between the two. And while some attention
has been paid in the last decade to composing practices and issues of
lesbian and gay students, no study analyzes how students, regardless of
sexual orientation, grapple with sexuality issues or what such a critical engagement says about the development of their literacy skills and
practices. Put another way, composition has, for lack of a better term,
"flirted" with the connection between sexuality and literacy, even as
it has often eschewed a more thorough investigation of it. Reviewing
some of the major themes of scholarship about socially minded composition pedagogies will demonstrate how sex and sexuality are often
overlooked, as well as showing the movements within composition that
gesture powerfully toward how they might be examined productively
by both teachers and students. Indeed, I believe that work in critical
pedagogies and feminist pedagogies, as well as the emerging work of
queer compositionists, have opened up spaces for us to begin considering sexuality and sexual literacy as significant components of a socially
conscious, critical pedagogy in composition studies. I will spend some
time with this background because I see my own project in this book as
arising out of and extending this work.

The "social turn" in composition studies has, without a doubt, significantly transformed how many of us understand, theorize, and practice
writing instruction. We know now that language, discourse, and literacy
are always already political, and that language use is complexly tied
to possibilities for—or constraints on—personal and political agency
within our culture. James Berlin was among the first of cultural studies
compositionists to take the political dimensions of language use seriously as a way to reconceive composition curricula. In the introduction to
the edited collection *Cultural Studies in the English Classroom*, Berlin and
coeditor Michael J. Vivion posit: "Cultural studies . . . deals with the production, distribution, and reception of signifying practices within the
myriad historical formations that are shaping subjectivities. These range
from the family, the school, the work place, and the peer group to the
more familiar activities associated with the cultural sphere, such as the

arts and the media and their modes of production and consumption. In other words, wherever signifying practices are shaping consciousness in daily life, cultural studies has work to do" (1992, ix).

The connection of such work to "English studies" and the teaching of writing lies in the conviction that "all texts are involved in politics and power: all tacitly endorse certain platforms of action. Language . . . is always a program for performance." As such, "English classrooms [can] provide methods for revealing the semiotic codes enacted in both the production and interpretation of a wide range of textual practices, practices including but not restricted to the medium of print" (Berlin and Vivion, 1992, xi).

Borrowing from such insights, other movements in the field of composition—including critical pedagogies, feminist pedagogies, and multicultural pedagogies—have offered us a rich sense of the connections among class, race, and gender differences and how people see themselves as *literate*, as being able to participate actively in a complex society by telling their own stories about their lives, or by having that participation hampered by controlling and sometimes silencing gestures of classism, racism, and sexism. Such work clearly envisions writing and literacy skills development as a cultural and political intervention. These pedagogies invite students both to see the sociopolitical dimensions of writing and to view their own writing as potentially interventional in sociopolitical processes and debates. Indeed, in a much-reprinted essay from 1988, "Rhetoric and Ideology in the Writing Class," James Berlin discusses his idea of a "social-epistemic rhetoric" that attempts to highlight for students the deep connections between politics and literacy. Citing a number of fellow "spokespersons," including Kenneth Burke, Richard Ohman, Kenneth Bruffee, Lester Faigley, David Bartholomae, and Patricia Bizzell, Berlin says that social-epistemic rhetoric forwards a "notion of rhetoric as a political act involving a dialectical interaction engaging the material, the social, and the individual writer, with language as the agency of mediation" (1997, 692) and that "social-epistemic rhetoric attempts to place the question of ideology at the center of the teaching of writing" (697). More pointedly, Berlin argues in "Composition and Cultural Studies" that "[t]he intention of forwarding this method is frankly political, an effort to prepare students for critical citizenship in democracy. . . . We are thus committed to teaching writing as an inescapably political act, the working out of contested cultural codes that affect every feature of our experience" (1991, 51).

Several other scholar-teachers throughout the field have taken up this call. Following the lead of Paolo Freire, the Brazilian critical pedagogue, Ira Shor's *Empowering Education: Critical Teaching for Social Change* extends Freire's work to argue for an "[e]mpowering education . . . [which] is a critical-democratic pedagogy for self and social change. It is a student-centered program for multicultural democracy in school and society. It approaches individual growth as an active, cooperative, and social process, because the self and society create each other. Human beings do not invent themselves in a vacuum, and society cannot be made unless people create it together. The goals of this pedagogy are to relate personal growth to public life, by developing strong skills, academic knowledge, habits of inquiry, and critical curiosity about society, power, inequality, and change" (1992, 15).

The multicultural sensitivity that Shor advocates in this passage has resonated with many in the field of English studies who want to help elaborate and interrogate the multiple ways in which literacy itself is a product of culture. Indeed, our differences—often systemically defined and constructed along lines of race, ethnicity, gender, and class—impact our ability to speak for ourselves, tell our own truths, and make common cause with others. Some literate acts, just as some social positions, are more valued than others, and many of us outside of the normative mainstream have been compelled, through racism, sexism, and classism, to remain silent about who we are and what we hold to be true and valuable. A critical *multicultural* pedagogy seeks to make a space in which *different* truths cannot only be articulated but can assume *critical* efficacy—a space in which differences become the lenses through which to examine the structures that keep us separate, isolated, and often powerless. bell hooks has argued compellingly: "Multiculturalism compels educators to recognize the narrow boundaries that have shaped the way knowledge is shared in the classroom. It forces us all to recognize our complicity in accepting and perpetuating biases of any kind. . . . When we, as educators, allow our pedagogy to be radically changed by our recognition of a multicultural world, we can give students the education they desire and deserve. We can teach in ways that transform consciousness, creating a climate of free expression that is the essence of a truly liberatory liberal arts education" (1994, 44).

Along such lines, compositionists have experimented broadly with curricula and pedagogies that attempt to highlight for students the multiple connections among culture, literacy, and participation in the democratic project. In particular, composition scholars invested in understanding connections among racial and ethnic experiences and literate practices have produced powerful work that shows us how racial and ethnic differences shape literate practices and often support rich literacy traditions that, while not shared by the mainstream, are nonetheless critical and insightful. In fact, their "outsider" relation to the mainstream, to "standard" or "marketplace" English usage, accounts for some of their critical power in that they can highlight how the experiences of those outside the dominant culture bear witness to systemic oppressions based on race and ethnicity. While I cannot recap all of this work in such a short space, I can point to the work of scholar-teachers such as Keith Gilyard, Jacqueline Jones Royster, Scott Lyons, Adam Banks, and Morris Young as emblematic of the kind of critical work paying attention to race and ethnicity as important shapers of literacy and the experience of literacy. For instance, Young's recent award-winning book, *Minor Re/Visions: Asian American Literacy Narratives as a Rhetoric of Citizenship,* examines "the ways literacy and race intersect in American culture, in particular, the ways the perception of a person's citizenship is overdetermined because of competing ideological constructions about literacy and race. The processes of reading and writing literacy narratives is one means for people of color to develop and articulate their negotiation of citizenship" (2004, 7). Young draws important connections between being able to tell one's story, articulate one's truth about racial experiences in our culture, and experiencing a sense of agency within that culture.

In a similar vein, the rich work of feminist compositionists speaks challengingly to the ways in which *gendered* experience is just as important in understanding literacy. Over the last three decades, many feminist scholar-teachers have undertaken an examination of how gender is a multivalent construct whose identity- and community-shaping power needs interrogation in our classrooms, our teacherly performances, and our students' writing.[1] In "Feminism in Composition: Inclusion, Metonymy, and Disruption," Joy S. Ritchie and Kathleen Boardman take a long, historical view of feminism in composition, noting: "The explicit recognition of composition's lack of attention to women's material lives has led women in anger, frustration, and recognition to tell the stories of their coming to awareness" (2003, 17). In so many ways, telling the *story* of women's experience has been at the heart of many feminist projects in composition. A significant number of early feminist compositionists worked in this vein, asking if men and women *fundamentally* write the stories of their lives in differently gendered ways. Elizabeth A. Flynn's landmark essay, "Composing as a Woman," originally published in *CCC* in 1988, asked a seemingly straightforward question: "Do males and females compose differently?" (2003, 245). Seeking to extend and complicate this discussion, Patricia A. Sullivan addressed a number of related issues in her 1992 essay, "Feminism and Methodology in Composition Studies," such as "considering the influence of gender on the composing process" (2003, 125), "tak[ing] issue with the assumption that discourse is gender neutral" (126), "seek[ing] to generate new knowledge about the relationships between gender and composing that can help us counteract the androcentrism that leaves women's modes of thinking and expression suppressed and undervalued" (132). Sullivan's work thus questioned the simplicity, even naiveté of wondering if men and women write differently at a fundamental level; rather, she argued that gender is a multivalent force that impacts composing in both subtle and profound ways, and she maintained that we should turn our attention to an examination of that impact.

Other feminist scholarship in composition has picked up on this theme and examined a variety of pedagogical strategies for understanding and interrogating with students the ways in which gender functions in our lives, both personally and politically. In the opening pages of "Genders of Writing," for instance, David Bleich discusses homophobic responses among students, and he links such responses to the privilege that men in general have in our society: "All authoritative social roles are held by men—in politics, medicine, law, religion, science, art, and, of course, the academy. It should come as no surprise that the style of thought developed by these men in the name of all people should correspond with the structure of social relations that sustains their social privileges." At the same time, Bleich counters such privilege with the assertion that "[neither] I nor anyone else can actually advocate some fixed taxonomy of gender. What I and many others do think, however, is that the flexibility and permeability of gender boundaries must be recognized and accepted by all" (1989, 13). For Bleich, recognizing the potential "permeability of gender boundaries" might help weaken the connection between a perceived sense of unassailable maleness and corresponding "social privileges."

To critique the patriarchal "social privileges" reinforced by static notions of gender, some writers discuss pedagogies attempting to multiply the voices in the classroom that can question such linkages between gender and power. Susan Romano's "On Becoming a Woman: Pedagogies of the Self" is a rich essay in which Romano looks at a number of pedagogical practices, including pseudonymous online discussion. For Romano, the goal in using such practices is clear; she's invested both "in expanding the range of students' discursive options, and in producing equitable discursive environments" (2003, 453). In a similar vein, Gail Hawisher summarizes even more broadly what she sees as the common goals of much feminist-inspired composition pedagogy: "[E]ven as we disagree as to the forms a feminist pedagogy might take, the goals of that pedagogy remain remarkably similar. They seek to elicit in students a critical awareness of that which was once invisible—to provoke in students through reading, thinking, writing, and talk a sense of agency, a sense of possibility. They aim to forward, through teaching, a feminist agenda that probes the dominant discourses of sexism, gender preference, and . . . racism and classism" (2003, xvii). The emphasis here is on creating spaces in writing classrooms for women's stories to be told and their voices to be heard, considered, and appreciated—with the ultimate goal, perhaps, of both (1) engaging a "critical awareness" of the relationship between gender and the sociopolitical matrix; and (2) promoting agency among those who wish to undertake such an analysis.

As I survey this work, I find many important places in which considerations of sex and sexuality may begin to play an important part in understanding how we come to be literate. When Berlin and Vivion describe the necessity, for instance, of examining with students the richly rhetorical and ideological dense constructs of "family, the school, the work place, and the peer group," I cannot help but think about how sexuality touches on each of those domains; we learn about sex and sexuality from family, through peer interactions, in sex education classes, and workplaces are often hotbeds (pardon the pun) of sex talk, of sharing sexual stories, even of sexual encounters. Throughout these domains, sexuality is an important, if often vexed and vexing, dimension of human relation, interaction, and knowledge. Moreover, as many feminist compositionists maintain, if gender is a powerful construct through which people's lives are conditioned and possibilities for freedom are constrained and then potentially resisted, then all the more so is sexuality such a construct, since it is through sexual desire that gender identity is most often articulated: we are straight and gay because of whom we desire, but we are also straight and gay because of whom we identify with as gendered people. Indeed, "straightness" is characterized by identification with one gender and desire for another, which is why homosexuality often troubles the hetero-normative in its confusion of identification and desire. Put another way, the queer troubles the dominant story of how we are to identify, how we are to desire. And it is at just this juncture that we can broach the small "sexual turn" in composition studies, through the work of queer compositionists, who bring us the closest so far to understanding the potential importance of sexual literacy.

THE QUEER TURN: TOWARD SEXUAL LITERACY

In a forthcoming article, David Wallace and I explore what we call the "queer turn" in composition scholarship, or the small but growing body of work that attempts to bring the insights of queer experience in general and queer theory in particular to bear on the teaching of writing (Alexander and Wallace forthcoming). Such work consists of Harriet Malinowitz's groundbreaking study, *Textual Orientations: Lesbian and Gay Students and the Making of Discourse Communities* (1995), Zan Meyer Goncalves's *Sexuality and the Politics of Ethos in the Writing Classroom* (2005), and a scattering of essays, some collected in special journal issues, such as a "special cluster" on queer theory that I coedited with Michelle Gibson for *JAC*, a special issue of *Computers and Composition* I coedited with William P. Banks (2004), and an issue of *Computers and Composition Online*, edited by Jacqueline Rhodes. Much of this work, like early articles by Allison Berg et al. (1994), Allison Regan (1992), and Scott Lloyd DeWitt (1997), argues for the importance of challenging homophobic responses in student writing and creating safe spaces in which queer students (in class, in their writing, and in online forums) can articulate their truths, tell their stories, and explore the development of literate practices that describe what their sexuality means to them. Increasingly, attention paid to the needs of queer students as well as growing tolerance for nonnormative sexualities (at least in some parts of the country) have made composition classes a much "safer" place for queer students.

Pushing this envelope, other scholar-teachers attempt to use insights from the experiences of LGBT people in ways that are rhetorically capacious by recognizing how stories of sexual identity are political and not just personal narrations. I would characterize both Malinowitz's and Goncalves's books as part of this movement, and their texts offer rich examples of how being attentive to and honoring the experiences of lesbian and gay people can enliven the composition classroom. In particular, Malinowitz's illuminating study connects her interest in critical pedagogy with an analysis of writing classes she taught focused on lesbian and gay topics and issues. In her rich case studies, she describes the particular insights that queer students bring to the classroom—and to their writing—about their experience of heteronormative social structures and ideological forces. Malinowitz argues powerfully for the value of paying attention to lesbian and gay students and the stories they tell about their lives for the critical energy that such stories bring us in questioning and querying dominant narrations of heteronormativity. Extrapolating from this experience to the field of composition as a whole, Malinowitz writes, "The sort of pedagogy I am proposing would entail thinking about the ways margins produce not only abject outsiderhood but also profoundly unique ways of self-defining, knowing, and acting; and about how, though people usually want to leave the margins, they *do* want to be able to bring with them the sharp vision that comes from living with friction and contradiction" (1995, 252). This "sharp vision," Malinowitz maintains, can help all students see their world differently and more critically. Along similar lines, Zan Meyer Goncalves's *Sexuality and the Politics of Ethos in the Writing Classroom* "challenges writing teachers to consider ethos as a series of identity performances shaped by the often-inequitable social contexts of their classrooms and communities. Using the rhetorical experiences of students who identify as lesbian, gay, bisexual, and/or transgender, she proposes a new way of thinking about ethos that addresses the challenges of social justice, identity, and transfer issues in the classroom" (http://www.siu.edu/~siupress/GoncalvesSexualityandthePoliticsofEthosintheWritingClassroom.html). Using an LGBT "Speakers Bureau," in which queer individuals share stories about their lives, Goncalves shows specifically how we can bring some of the "sharp vision" of queerness to question dominant narrations of normalcy that feed systems of inequity. For instance, paying attention to the romantic narrations of gay couples queries the "story" of marriage as the union of a man and a woman, and underscores how some are excluded from participation in social structures because their particular stories don't match those of the hetero norm.

Malinowitz's and Goncalves's work, though vitally important, focuses primarily on issues of gay and lesbian identity, drawing energy from the narrations of lesbian and gay students. Although the advantages of their pedagogical approaches for queer students are clear, it is important to keep in mind that they are not the only ones who can benefit from grappling with sexual orientation in particular and sexuality in general. William Spurlin, in his introduction to *Lesbian and Gay Studies and the Teaching of English*, notes that his contributors all "theorize, to varying degrees, queer difference as a lens through which to read, interpret, and produce texts, or as a way of reading the classroom and indeed the world." At the same time, Spurlin notes that including queer voices and texts is "in itself . . . not sufficient to move us toward a more critical pedagogy" (2000, xix). Likewise, I believe it is also time to start thinking *beyond* inclusion and begin grappling with a wide variety of ways in which sexuality and literacy intersect.

To engage this kind of critical pedagogical enterprise, some of us have turned to the insights of queer theory, which we will explore in the first chapter much more fully. In general, queer theory is designed to provoke consideration of the construction of *all* sexualities in our culture as sites of identity, knowledge, and power. In exploring these connections, I have been fortunate to work with a number of colleagues on two special issues of major journals in our field—*JAC* and *Computers and Composition*—to explore broadly the importance of considering sexuality in the composition classroom and to consider specifically the potential uses of queer theory in the teaching of writing. Michelle Gibson and I, in our introduction to the "Special Cluster: Queer Theory" in *JAC*, argue: "Queer theory moves us *beyond* the multicultural task of accepting and validating identity and moves us *toward* the more difficult process of understanding how identity, even the most intimate perceptions of self, arise out of a complex matrix of shifting social power. In this way, we believe queer theory has uses and applications for self-understanding that engage *all* students as they narrate their identities for us, tell us who they are, and give us—and themselves—the stories of their lives, past, present, and future" (2004, 3). Essays in this issue of *JAC*—by Jan Cooper, Robert McRuer, and Connie Monson and Jacqueline Rhodes—explore the necessity of, in Jan Cooper's words, "queering the contact zone" of composition and the composition class-room as a site in which the narration of identity, subjectivity, and norma-tivity is disciplined, particularly as the self is ushered into "adulthood," "career," and "professionalism" (23).

Certainly, we want to promote tolerance for difference, but we also want to promote a capacious interrogation of self and subjectivity.

And since sexuality is a key component of subjectivity—if not *the key index of how we define our identities*—then a critical understanding of sexuality and the stories we tell about it is vital to understanding the stories we tell about ourselves and our culture. Michel Foucault has argued provocatively that "[s]exuality must not be thought of as a kind of natural given. . . . [Rather, it] is the name that can be given to a historical construct: not a furtive reality that is difficult to grasp, but a great surface network in which the stimulation of bodies, the intensification of pleasures, the incitement to discourse, the formation of special knowledges, the strengthening of controls and resistances, are linked to one another" (1990, 105–6). For instance, how we present ourselves sexually and as beings with sexual interests is subject to our own fashioning *and* the interpretation of others—both modes that are shaped within the matrix of cultural codes that inform our understanding of what the "sexual" is. As such, learning to "read" that "great surface network" and become acquainted with the discourses of sexuality—what one can and cannot say about the sexual, how one can speak about it, what knowledges about sexuality are prescribed, proscribed, or held as taboo—are significant components of becoming *literate* in our culture.

Such thinking brought me to the idea of sexual literacy as I was working on a special issue of *Computers and Composition* that I guest edited with Will Banks, entitled "Sexualities, Technologies, and the Teaching of Writing." In the introduction to that issue, Will and I formulated the connection between sexuality, ideology, and language as linking sexuality directly to important issues of literacy, even to literacy itself:

> The consequences of thinking about sexuality in terms of literacy extend far beyond potential benefits to LGBT/queer students. What we are suggesting is that instructors interested in approaching the topic of sexuality in their writing courses consider their approach not from the standpoint of including queer voices, but as the possibility of ushering all students into an understanding of sexuality in its sociopolitical dimensions and of becoming literate about sexuality. . . . Ignoring critical inquiry into . . . connections [between sexuality and literacy] runs the risk of enabling, perhaps even furthering students' ignorance about the strong connection in our culture between sexuality and identity.

Considering sexual literacy, then, not only promotes a complex rhetorical awareness of an issue of great personal and political importance, but it also promotes students' understanding of how sexuality is used to enable participation in the democratic project for some, while constraining it for others. (2004, 287-8)

My own work as a queer and feminist compositionist has benefited greatly from such theorizing. For the last several years, I have been using a number of classroom activities and technology platforms—ranging from listservs to Web sites to synchronous communication programs—to do such work and to expand on it (see Alexander 1997; Boardman et al. 1999). I have sought to prompt students to query the ways in which sexuality and sexual identity are constructed, narrated, represented, and contested in many American cultures. My aim has largely been a rhetorical one of the James Berlin variety, a critical pedagogy, in which I have used texts and Web sites with queer content to provoke students into thinking about the many ways in which gender and sexuality are represented in our society. I have wanted to prompt students to think more critically about how the languages we use to describe and define our seemingly personal identities are inflected by and interpolated within pervasive ideologies about manhood, womanhood, and "appropriate" or "normal" sexuality. Transgender-themed Web sites, for instance, such as Leslie Feinberg's transgenderwarrior.com, provide provocative insights into how sexuality and gender are narrated, but also how their more "traditional" narrations can be resisted and reconfigured in pursuit of different personal, social, and political ends. I have also assigned and analyzed with students essays by Susan Bordo, who has done tremendous and eminently accessible work in her book *The Male Body: A New Look at Men in Public and in Private* (1999), taking insights from feminist thinking and sexuality studies to examine the construction of male bodies and masculinity in our culture—constructions that are often held up as ideal and desirable. She points out in pedagogically useful essays that straight men are subject to the same kinds of gender role conditioning that women are. In many ways, this is the work of *queer theory*—a "queering" that interrogates our sexualities and their construction from the inside out.

For me, these have been not just *attentive* pedagogies but also *critical* pedagogies—ones not invested only in a willingness to grapple with sexuality issues when they "emerge" in the classroom, but willing to approach explicitly the connection between sexuality and literacy, the intertwining of sociocultural narration, identity, and power. With that in mind, the part of Shor's *Empowering Education* that I have been drawn to most over the past few years is the discussion of "desocialization," or "critically examining learned behavior, received values, familiar language, habitual perceptions, existing knowledge and power relations, and traditional discourse in class and out." Put another way, it is "questioning the social behaviors and experiences . . . that make us into the people we are" (1992, 114). I believe it is increasingly imperative to create pedagogical spaces to desocialize sexuality issues—if only because so much social control is exerted through sexual orientation identities, restriction of information about sexuality, and our socially constructed views of sexuality. As we will see throughout much of this book, sexuality *is* often a very tricky subject to deal with in the classroom. But it permeates so many aspects of our culture's (often terribly conflicting and conflicted) ideologies that I find it hard to miss in discussions about a variety of discourses and discursive fields, from popular culture to politics. As noted, and as I shall explore in a later chapter, just talking openly and honestly about marriage can lead productively to discussions of how sexuality and identity are bound up with who gets privileged in our society—and why. Indeed, the marriage issue is hardly only a "gay issue," for that matter; single women with children and those who choose not to marry also have much to say about the place of marriage in our society as a social marker of privilege. Again, discussions of sexuality and intimacy are part and parcel of the stories of self and society told by *all* of us. In this way, so much of becoming usefully and productively literate in our society—in being able to understand, partake of, and participate in significant contemporary social discussions—depends on becoming *sexually literate.*

THE CHALLENGE OF SEXUAL LITERACY

Given the close intertwining of sexuality and literacy in our culture, then, I propose that sexual literacy become a key component of first-year composition instruction—specifically, of a socially conscious critical pedagogy. I see this work as forwarding and complicating social-epistemic approaches to composition and writing instruction. Sexual literacy, in other words, asks us to take seriously the sexual and sexuality as significant dimensions through which we can understand the relationship between literacy and power.

I see two primary goals for writing instruction and writing studies scholarship if we are to take seriously the call to interrogate the interconnectedness of literacy and sexuality in our culture. First, we need

methods for writing instruction that allow *all* students—gay, straight, bisexual, or those refusing an identification—to articulate, understand, and critique the ways in which sexuality and literacy impact one another in contemporary Anglo-American culture. Such includes paying attention to and exploring how sex and sexuality are constructed and figured in literacies about gender, intimacy, relationships, and marriage. Second, we as scholars and teachers need to recognize how some students are already undertaking such analysis in their own extracurricular literacy practices, as well as how our own pedagogies might benefit productively from such an analysis.

This book is deeply invested in forwarding both of these goals.

While exploring what exactly sexual literacy might mean will be the primary focus of the next chapter, I believe that some initial definitions and clarifications are in order, given the largeness of my claim and my use of the word "literacy." Anthropologist Herdt and his colleagues at the National Sexuality Resource Center, for which Herdt serves as director at San Francisco State University, are profoundly concerned with investigating the notion of "sexual literacy." For Herdt, sexual literacy is "the knowledge you need to protect and advance your sexuality." Concomitant with this definition are the assumptions that "sexuality touches each of our lives and is essential to our well-being" and that "accessible information and resources are essential for healthy discussions, education, and decision-making about sexuality" (http://www. sexliteracy.org/). I believe that defining sexual literacy, as Herdt does, as the knowledge needed to advance and protect one's own sexual health and well-being is useful in that it offers a much-needed sense of personal agency and empowerment vis-à-vis one of the most complex and often misunderstood (and sometimes misused) aspects of our humanity (Herdt et al. 2006). At the same time, this definition leaves unaddressed a sense of how "literacy" plays a part in that sexual agency and self-understanding. Herdt uses the term "literacy" in its broad sense of "knowledge about" or "expertise with."

I believe, though, that "sexual literacy" should be much more than just *knowledge* about sex and sexuality; it should also be an *intimate understanding of the ways in which sexuality is constructed in language and the ways in which our language and meaning-making systems are always already sexualized.* In this regard, I have learned much from scholars in the New Literacy Studies (which I explore in the next chapter), such as Brian Street's understanding of literacy "as inextricably linked to cultural and power structures in society" and his belief that "literacy practices [are wrapped up] in reproducing or challenging structures of power and domination" (433–34). While the word "literacy" is certainly overly used at times, I believe it is the correct one in this context. As we will see in the discussion in the next chapter, "literacy" implies not only fluency with discourses but an ability to think critically about them and use them to explore possibilities of agency. If sexuality is a dominant construct of identity, of how people understand themselves and one another, then it is a construct of power; learning how to articulate a *critical* understanding of that construct, then, provides greater self-understanding and potentially greater agency in changing the construct, or at least resisting it when necessary. But moreover, so many of our most pressing social issues are wrapped up in the power/knowledge complexes of sexuality that participation in our democratic project necessitates a fluency with discourses of sex and sexuality. Attention to *sexual literacy* provides such fluency.

When I use the term "sexual literacy" in this book, then, I want to evoke a sense of how understanding sexuality is vital to one's literate practice in the West today—and vice versa. Indeed, as we will see in the next chapter on theoretical approaches to sexuality, the insights of sexuality studies broadly and queer theory especially are designed to enliven critical thought about the construction of sexuality in our culture as a dominant—and often dominating—set of tropes and narrations that organize desire, intimacy, and identity. Development of a sexual *literacy*, then, is development of fluency with the very *narrations* through which so much cultural and political work is accomplished, and through which our identities themselves are often achieved. As such, a critical approach to sexuality as a *literacy*—as a topic, a set of controlling narrations, and a site of contested meanings—seems not only a wise and useful subject of composition studies but a compelling one. As social historian and sexuality scholar Jeffrey Weeks eloquently puts it, "Struggles around sexuality are . . . struggles over meanings—over what is appropriate and not appropriate—meanings which call on the resources of the body and the flux of desire, but are not dictated by them. This approach fundamentally challenges any idea of a simple dichotomy between 'sex' and 'society.' Sex and sexuality are social phenomena shaped in a particular history" (1985, 178).

Turning our attention and our students' attention to sexuality as an intense site of meaning making should enhance their critical abilities to investigate, explore, and question some of the dominant stories we tell about our lives and identities. As such, the concept of *sexual literacy* may be useful in helping us unpack the connections among sexuality, discourse, and their construction in language.

At this point it may be crucial to differentiate what I am advocating from what is more traditionally understood as "sex education." In their introduction to *A Dangerous Knowing: Sexuality, Pedagogy, and Popular Culture*, Debbie Epstein and James T. Sears usefully differentiate between what they call "sexual pedagogies": those that consist of "formal sex education" and those that examine the "production of sexual identities." They explain the differentiation this way:

> We are taking "sexual pedagogies" . . . to include, at one end of the continuum, formal sex education and teaching in schools aimed at sustaining or undermining hetero/sexism and patriarchal gender regimes; at the other end we are concerned with the production of sexual identities in conditions not of our own choosing and always related to other "differences which make a difference." We are interested in tracing the means by which borders are policed . . . on the one hand, and people interpellated into dominant forms of heterosexuality through seductions of, for example, the popular media on the other—and always recognizing that these may be happening simultaneously. (1999, 2–3)

Epstein and Sears want to move our understanding of "sexual pedagogies" from the basic and often rather mechanical "sex education" to more nuanced understandings of how knowledges of sex and sexuality are produced and disseminated. Inevitably, as I will discuss at length in the next chapter, such knowledges—from the deeply personal to the broadly collective—are negotiated and even constructed through a variety of language and literacy practices. As such, it makes sense to me to think about sexual literacies, or the ways in which constructions of and discourses about sex and sexuality come into existence to circulate in our societies.

Moreover, some scholarship suggests that gender and sexual politics are actually becoming more complicated, as one might expect at a time when discourses about sex, sexuality, and gender permeate our culture. For instance, in *Covering: The Hidden Assault on Our Civil Rights*, Yale lawyer and legal scholar Kenji Yoshino argues that "[w]e are at a transitional moment in how Americans discriminate," particularly in terms of issues of sexuality and sexual orientation. He maintains that sexual minorities are increasingly tolerated by and accepted into mainstream American society if they can successfully "cover"—that is, if their difference is not readily noticeable from mainstream norms. Yoshino borrows the term "covering" from sociologist Erving Goffman and explains his position as such: "In the old generation, discrimination targeted entire groups— no racial minorities, no women, no gays, no religious minorities, no people with disabilities allowed. In the new generation, discrimination directs itself not against the entire group, but against the subset of the group that fails to assimilate to mainstream norms. This new form of discrimination targets minority cultures rather than minority persons. Outsiders are included, but only if we behave like insiders—that is, only if we cover" (2006, 21–22).

For example, straight-acting gays can successfully "cover," while gays who are too effeminate are deemed less acceptable and consequently face much more discrimination. To work against this tide, Yoshino suggests, in a very Habermasian fashion, the need for open, widespread, and reasonable discussion about discrimination:

> I am troubled that Americans seem increasingly to turn toward the law to do the work of civil rights precisely when they should be turning away from it. The real solution lies in all of us as citizens, not in the tiny subset of us who are lawyers. People who are not lawyers should have reason-forcing conversations outside the law. They should pull Goffman's term "covering" out of academic obscurity and press it into the popular lexicon, so that it has the same currency as terms like "passing" or "the closet." People confronted with demands to cover should feel emboldened to seek a reason for that demand, even if the law does not reach the actors making the demand, or recognize the group burdened by it. These reason-forcing conversations should happen outside courtrooms—in workplaces and restaurants, schools and playgrounds, chat rooms and living rooms, public squares and bars. They should occur informally and intimately, where tolerance is made and unmade. (2006, 194–95)

While we could argue the relative usefulness of such "reason-forcing conversation" in effecting material political and cultural change, I believe that Yoshino's main claim—the need for a move toward rational, open, and mature conversation about difficult topics such as sexuality and sexual literacy—is not only valid but absolutely essential if we are to become more literate as a culture about sex, sexuality, and their relationship to how we think about ourselves, both individually and collectively, and the stories we tell about ourselves, both individually and collectively.

ENCOUNTERING RESISTANCES

Of course, some compositionists, and some students, will resist this call to think more critically about sexuality. They will not understand its connection to literacy and see it rather as either superfluous to their writing or as an overtly political intrusion on the instructor's part. I will detail and address such resistances throughout this book, particularly in the final chapter. For now, though, let me state that it is difficult to write about sexuality as a literacy specialist and not hear the voice of Maxine Hairston, as given to us in her essay "Diversity, Ideology, and Teaching Writing" (originally published in 1992). In this controversial piece, Hairston critiques a model "that puts dogma before diversity, politics before craft, ideology before critical thinking, and the social goals of the teacher before the educational needs of the student" (2002, 117). In the process of undertaking her critique, she takes several prominent scholar-teachers to task, including David Bleich, James Berlin, Lester Faigley, and Dale Bauer. Hairston suggests that greater student diversity, as well as a desire to make English composition a "sexier" course, probably drove the "social turn," at least in part. In contrast to "politicized" pedagogies, she maintains that "students' own writing must be the center of the course. Students need to write to find out how much they know and to gain confidence in their ability to express themselves effectively" and that "as writing teachers we should stay within our area of professional expertise: helping students to learn to write in order to learn, to explore, to communicate, to gain control over their lives" (125). With such values in mind, she resists the urge to put "multicultural issues" at the center of writing courses. At the same time, however, she maintains that "we can create a culturally inclusive curriculum in our writing classes by focusing on the experiences of our students" (129). Put more bluntly, she maintains that "[r]eal diversity emerges from the students themselves and flourishes in a collaborative classroom in which they work together to develop their ideas and test them out on each other" (130).

Certainly, there are blind spots and limitations to such a formulation. Not all students are going to feel safe or secure enough to let their diversity "emerge" from them. For instance, closeted students—whether closeted due to sexuality issues, past abuse and trauma, ongoing battles with mental illness, or the possibility of religious bigotry and misunderstanding—may hesitate to "work together to develop their ideas and test them out on each other," particularly when the ideas they may most want to explore and write about might elicit bias, fear, or loathing. In some ways, though, I agree with Hairston when she says that "students' own writing must be the center of the [composition] course." But what if that writing just happens to be about sexuality? And why *shouldn't* it be about—and grapple with—issues of sexuality? And why shouldn't it acknowledge that sexuality is wrapped up in complex ways with what it means to be literate in our culture?

Interestingly, an article by Richard E. Miller published just two years after Hairston's tentatively takes up such questions, showing how sexuality can seemingly "erupt" in a composition classroom context. The essay, "Fault Lines in the Contact Zone: Assessing Homophobic Student Writing," which originally appeared in *College English*, discusses a very controversial student essay (entitled "Queers, Bums, and Magic") and an instructor's attempt to work with the student and the extremely homophobic content of the essay. In fact, the piece insinuates that the student writer had been involved in a homophobic attack on another person. Miller's intention in recounting this essay is to note that we in composition are often ill equipped to deal with such "touchy" material, particularly material dealing with sexual and sexuality issues. He notes the following: "To sum up, then, these two lines of response to the student essay—the one recommending the removal of the offending writer from circulation, and the other overlooking the offensive aspects of the student text in order to attend to its surface and structural features— taken together dramatize how little professional training in English studies prepares teachers to read and respond to the kinds of parodic, critical, oppositional, dismissive, resistant, transgressive, and regressive writing that gets produced by students writing in the contact zone of the classroom" (2000, 240).

Miller rightly suggests that such student writing is probably highly uncommon in classrooms, which leads him to assert that "[t]his, surely, is a testament to the immense pressures exerted by the classroom environment, the presentation of the assigned readings, the directions included in the writing assignments, and the range of teaching practices which work together to ensure that conflicts about or contact between fundamental beliefs and prejudices do not arise" (2000, 245). As such, the classroom is not often, in Mary Louise Pratt's words, a "contact zone," "where cultures meet, clash, and grapple with each other, often in contexts of highly asymmetrical relations of power" (34).

At times, though, "difficult" subjects *will* emerge. And I would argue that, in an era increasingly comfortable with talking about sexuality in the public sphere, and when easily accessible news reports, media programs, and Internet sites readily circulate information, opinion, and discussion about sex and sexuality, it is likely that a variety of sexuality topics will emerge in the writing classroom with greater frequency. How should we handle such? Miller suggests that "[t]he most promising pedagogical response lies . . . in closely attending to what our students say and write in an ongoing effort to learn how to read, understand, and respond to the strange, sometimes threatening, multivocal texts they produce while writing in the contact zone" (2000, 251–52).

Beyond paying attention to and knowing how to respond responsibly to such "threatening" texts, some scholar-teachers argue that we *must* approach difficult and challenging subjects with our students. In *Beyond the Culture Wars*, Gerald Graff considers how some of the most significant debates about culture and politics are not critically examined in higher education pedagogies. In particular, he suggests that multicultural issues, a heated realm of debate in the public sphere, are infrequently addressed with students as debates or points of contention and cultural tension. As a result, he argues, students aren't being exposed to what an academic approach to such debates might offer; so he proposes instead that we actually "teach the conflicts," or acknowledge areas of cultural debate and actively process them with our students: "Teaching the conflicts has nothing to do with relativism or denying the existence of truth. . . . Acknowledging that culture is a debate rather than a monologue does not prevent us from energetically fighting for the truth of our own convictions. On the contrary, when truth is disputed, we can see it only by entering the debate—as Socrates knew when he taught the conflicts two millennia ago" (1992, 15).

Graff does not consider issues of sexuality in his book, but I believe that his basic premise—the necessity of "teaching the conflicts" in our classrooms—applies directly to "teaching the conflicts" about *sexuality* that currently range (and rage) throughout our culture. Moreover, turning our attention to how students "talk" about sex and then actively inviting them to talk and write critically about sex is in itself an act of critical pedagogy. Put another way, opening up a space for them to write about their concerns simultaneously invites them to bring their own sexual knowledges into academic discourse about sexuality *and*, potentially, to influence the direction those debates and discussions take.

Indeed, I believe that our students are already grappling with such "threatening" material. As we will see in the third chapter, many of our students are already considering sex and sexuality in some complex and revealing ways in the writing they do outside of our classrooms. Numerous online forums, such as blogs, Facebook, Friendster, role-playing games, and many other social networking platforms in which many of our students actively participate show them discussing and debating a variety of sex-related topics, such as reproductive issues, the availability of reliable information about sex and sexuality, and how sex is treated in the mass media. In other ways, some of our students are also already writing more explicitly and critically about sex and sexuality not only outside the composition classroom but *in it* as well. This is in part due to the development of socially engaged curricula over the past few decades. Many undergraduate composition classes across the country have students explore and write about a variety of themes, many of them concerning issues of social importance. For instance, the composition curriculum at the University of Cincinnati, where I served as composition director for four years, had students compose pieces on issues such as gun control, school violence, censorship of the Internet, and the sociocultural and political goals of higher education. At times, some students, usually on their own, considered issues of gender and sexuality as they pertain to these themes and issues. For example, some wrote about issues such as sex education in the public school system, the availability of contraception on campuses, censorship of sexually explicit material on the Internet, sexual orientation nondiscrimination policies, and teen/single-parent pregnancy issues as they affect college students and others. Being attentive to such issues can help us find critical ways of working with students to develop sexual literacies.

Perhaps it's time for us to catch up.

THINKING LITERACY AND SEXUALITY TOGETHER: WHAT THIS BOOK WILL DO

With such thoughts in mind, the chapters in this book examine three specific questions:

How do students write sexuality—that is, how do they write about sex, what do they say, and what does their saying reveal about their understanding (or misunderstanding) of sexuality as a political issue, as a dense node in the intersection between the personal and the political?

How do sexuality and literacy interconnect in complex ways? That is, how is an understanding of sexuality a key component in being literate in contemporary Western culture and society?

How can we create pedagogical environments to invite students—safely, productively, and insightfully—to compose about sex and sexuality, particularly in ways that will help them (and us) foster a greater appreciation for the intertwining of sexuality and literacy in our culture?

I firmly believe that studying how students develop sophisticated literacy skills through critically thinking about sexuality should shed light on literacy, sexuality, and their interconnection in our society.

Granted, as a specialist in composition and writing studies, and as someone who has also built a scholarly record in sexuality studies, it is only natural that I consider my two areas of scholarly interest in light of one another. I have done so tentatively in previous projects, and this book-length study will build on that earlier work and expand it in ways that I hope will link productively the study of sexuality to the study of student literacies and, in the process, extend the social-epistemic project and further complicate composition's "social turn." Indeed, the preceding discussion in this introduction can only begin highlighting and drawing our attention to the kinds of connections between sexuality and literacy that I believe powerfully permeate public discourse. The remainder of this book will explore these connections more fully and richly. I also want to make the claim that such connections should be of crucial concern to writing and literacy instructors, which assumes, of course, that in many ways they have *not* been of much importance in the past. And they haven't been. As such, this book may be of most interest to those who have tentatively considered sex and sexuality as significant to literacy issues, but who otherwise do not know how to approach the topic of sexual literacy, as I have defined it here, in their composition classrooms. My goal in these pages is to provide such readers with powerful theoretical and pedagogical tools for exploring sexual literacy with their students.

A word on overall methodology. My approach in this book is not focused on analyzing and promoting entire courses organized around sex and sexuality as topics. While I believe such courses are useful, challenging, and productive for students (having taught them myself), my goal is more to demonstrate, through an analysis of writing exercises and essay assignments, that (1) students can write powerfully and critically about sexuality; and that (2) we can do much to help them develop a strong sense of the connections between sexuality and literacy. It is this latter dimension of literacy that we are often missing in our courses, and I conceive of this book as both a theoretical and pedagogical intervention, inviting—even insisting—that we assist our students in developing more nuanced discourses and sophisticated literacies to understand the centrality of sexuality as a construct of knowing, thinking, and being in our culture. In "Inventing the University," David Bartholomae asserts in a well-rehearsed and widely accepted argument that "writers, in order to write, must imagine for themselves the privilege of being 'insiders'— that is, of being both inside an established discourse, and of being granted a special right to speak" (2001, 516). Bartholomae is thinking of the specialized academic discourses that we variously ask students to adopt and write within as they progress through their college careers, and the development of fluency in such discourses is important, surely. But we shouldn't lose sight of the very powerful discourses that already inhabit us, such as discourses of sexuality that are so often central to our personal and cultural identifications. We are already always "inside" such discourses, and paying attention to them is an important first step in developing a critical sexual literacy that will allow us to understand them, challenge them, and critique them when necessary. A failure to pay attention to such discourses, to a sexual literacy, is a failure to prepare students for rich participation in a culture that understands sexuality as fundamental to some of our most important cultural narrations of self and other, as individuals and as various political collectives.

To promote a richer understanding of sexual literacy, then, the following chapters examine both some of the venues in which many students are currently writing about sex and sexuality and some of the ways in which we, as writing instructors, might create provocative exercises to help students—and ourselves—explore sexual literacy. To undertake such an examination, I use a variety of methods, including case studies of classroom practices, interviews with students and teachers, reviews of teaching materials, and surveys of some of the forums in which students are writing, often critically, about sexuality and literacy. While such surveys can hardly be exhaustive, they should serve as a provocative insight into how our students are using a variety of communications platforms to explore constructions of sex and sexuality in our culture. In fact, one of my primary claims, which I hope to demonstrate in these chapters, is that students are already creatively and even critically talking and writing about sex in ways that can enliven our classrooms, address their concerns and issues, and enable all of us to understand more critically the complex relationship between literacy and sexuality in our culture.

The first chapter, "Discursive Sexualities: Bridging Sexuality and Literacy Studies," sets the stage for the rest of the book by exploring recent theoretical work in queer theory, sociology, and linguistics that explores the construction of knowledge about sex and sexuality in the West. I connect work in these fields to the New Literacy Studies to demonstrate how the seemingly "personal" discourses of sex and sexuality are inextricably bound up in larger public discourses, and literacies, of culture and politics. Such a connection makes a compelling case for the importance of studying how sexuality and literacy are interpolated throughout our society and its attendant culture and politics, and this chapter moves toward articulating a theoretically capacious and pedagogical efficacious definition of *sexual literacy*. At then end of the chapter, I turn our attention to teaching and the classroom, asking how a sexual literacy might impact what we do as compositionists, as literacy specialists.

The second chapter, "Beyond Textbook Sexuality: Students Reading, Students Writing," offers a brief consideration of how our field overlooks the connection between sexuality and literacy in some of its primary pedagogical materials, namely, composition textbooks; in contrast, student writing *outside* the composition classroom—in blogs, on Web sites, through video games, and other forums—demonstrates not only a profound interest in sexuality but an emerging critical awareness of the importance of sexual literacy. Specifically, student writers are concerned with significant issues, such as sexual health, reproduction, and the possibilities and potential perils of polyamory. Key concerns continue to focus significantly around sexuality and sexual identity; students are concerned about what their sexual practices and desires say about themselves as people with complex identities and needs.

The following chapters turn our attention to student writing *in the classroom* and how many students' interest in sex and sexuality might productively be used to foster a greater awareness of the importance of sexuality in becoming literate. Each chapter offers detailed case studies of specific classroom experiences and assignments that illuminate this awareness. The third chapter, for instance, "Queer Theory for Straight Students: Sex and Identity," considers some of the uses of queer theory in designing writing assignments that prompt students to consider more fully how narratives of selfhood are often intimately constructed around issues of sex and sexuality—whether the narratives are about gay or straight identities. The fourth chapter, "Transgender Rhetorics: Sex and Gender," explores how recent theories emerging out of transgender studies can enliven our and our students' thinking about the relationships among gender, sexuality, and identity, particularly as all three are articulated, understood, and constructed in language. The fifth chapter, "Straight Talk about Marriage: Sex and Politics," expands on earlier discussions of sexuality and identity to consider the notion of "sexual citizenship," and how participation in public discourse presumes certain knowledge about (and ideological understandings of) sex and sexuality. To explore this material, the chapter offers a case study of how one instructor, a straight married man, explored with his students through reading and writing assignments the conflicted position of marriage in contemporary American society. Students' writing in this class revealed a complex engagement with issues not only of marriage, but also of monogamy, polyamory, prostitution, and reproductive rights and responsibilities.

The concluding chapter, "Susie Bright in the Comp Class: Confronting Resistances," considers theoretical and practical issues concerning possible student—and instructor—resistances to considering the interrelationship between sexuality and literacy. Resistances are inevitable; how we cope with them can shape productively how we introduce and work with difficult and "sensitive" topics. In the final chapter, I also offer suggestions for promoting a greater awareness of how literacy and sexuality are co-constructed in our culture. I maintain that we need to explore how we as writing instructors might capitalize on some of the creative discussions that students are already having about sex and sexuality—in an effort to expand our mutual understanding of how constructions of and knowledge about sexuality inform, and are informed by, what passes as "literate" in our society.

Inevitably, one book can only do so much, and, as I have worked on this project over the past few years, I have felt again and again remiss in the number of subjects that I have *not* covered. As I stated earlier in this introduction, sexual literacy should be taught alongside and in conjunction with gender, racial, religious, and class literacies. Further work along these lines needs to be done, and I can only gesture in its direction in this text. I also realize that I have focused my inquiry on *sexuality*, particularly as it intersects with issues of individual and collective identity. Of course, "sex" is a huge terrain; many dimensions of sexual literacy—such as literacies and discourses about reproductive freedom—need further consideration and exploration to enhance our collective understanding of sexual literacy. I discuss some of the possibilities in the concluding chapter. Ultimately, as I hope to demonstrate in the following pages, our students' (and our own) sense of literacy, of being *literate* in contemporary Anglo-American culture, may depend in many ways on our understanding of sex and sexuality.

SITES OF THEORY AND WRITING

1

DISCURSIVE SEXUALITIES
Bridging Sexuality and Literacy Studies

Let me begin at a very personal point—a portion of my own literacy narrative—as a way to approach thinking of literacy and sexuality together. For some readers, pairing literacy and sexuality might seem a stretch, but for me, the connection began early and felt natural.

I wasn't always a reader. In fact, I was a pretty "borderline" student in English and reading courses in grammar school throughout the 1970s. Or I *was*, until our fifth grade reading teacher read to us one chapter a day from C. S. Lewis's *The Lion, the Witch, and the Wardrobe.* I was hooked. Before that experience, reading assignments went largely unfinished, and the novels our teachers assigned—classics such as *Little Men* (for the boys) and *The Prince and the Pauper*—went unread. But Lewis's story changed that. When the teacher, an older lady named Mrs. Cermak, finished the book in class, I went home and begged my mother to take me to the bookstore, where I bought the second book in the Narnia series, *Prince Caspian,* the first book I ever read. From that moment, I become a lifelong reader, first of fantasy literature, then of its near neighbor, science fiction, and then of anything that interested me.

There's much about Lewis's book that obviously appealed to my childhood and boy sensibilities. *The Lion, the Witch, and the Wardrobe* is a rousing tale, for one thing, including not just lions and witches, but strange creatures, the threat of temptation, and a dramatic concluding battle. But more than this, I clearly remember being struck by the final chapters, which Mrs. Cermak read slowly and deliberately, asking us questions. *What does this story remind you of? Does Aslan's sacrifice seem familiar in any way?* I was attending a Catholic school at the time, and most of us were, like any other kids, enthralled by the story, our khaki- or plaid-clad bottoms squirming in our seats, anticipating Aslan's triumph—and successful answers to the teacher's questions. Indeed, it was important to Mrs. Cermak, as both a reading instructor and a Catholic educator, that we understand that Aslan's sacrifice paralleled Christ's, both heroic figures laying themselves down for others that they might be saved. It was thrilling.

Indeed, I believe it was that moment that captivated me the most—realizing, through Mrs. Cermak's guidance, how a writer could take a story, recast it, and tell it all over again in a new way. I was not a particularly religious child—my family wasn't even Catholic—so the spiritual message of sacrifice and redemption wasn't particularly profound for me. Rather, what enthralled me was Lewis's "theft," as well as his creativity. He could take something we all knew about and make it alive again. He could steal a story, even a sacred one, and make it his own.

I wanted to experience again and again that creative thievery. I would later come to understand this as an experience of intertextuality. At the time, I just thought it was cool. After devouring the remaining six books in the Narnia series, I looked to other books on adjacent shelves and found works by L. Frank Baum, Lloyd Alexander (no relation, unfortunately), and J. R. R. Tolkien. One shelf over lay Isaac Asimov, Ray Bradbury, and Arthur C. Clarke, and I began thrilling to *their* creativity, loosely based in science as it was.

As I reflect on this initial experience and my subsequent reading practices, I see in my reading choices some trends that resonate powerfully for me with aspects of my emerging sexual self. At a very simple level, these stories provided escape from pubescent pressures, both personal and peer-induced. Who hasn't wanted to escape into a much more thrilling and adventurous world when your face is breaking out into a million pimples and your voice is cracking uncontrollably? I was also a gangly and unathletic kid, more than a little shy and increasingly bookish. Moreover,I was frequently bullied, if only verbally, and, in middle school and high school, some classmates began taunting me with sexually flavored epithets, such as "fag" or "queer." Given this, the stars seemed a much better destination. Playgrounds, lunchrooms, and the PE field were, by comparison, too fraught with danger.

At another level, my reading choices operated, I believe, as more than just a mechanism for escape. They weirdly paralleled my developing bierotic sexual consciousness—and how I attempted to deal with it. I knew, from teachers, preachers, priests, and parents, that my eyes weren't supposed to be lingering over another boy's buttocks, that I shouldn't be sneaking peaks at other kids as we changed for PE, that my thoughts as I touched myself shouldn't drift to my best guy friends, or a male teacher. As I entered high school and such thoughts persisted, I read more furiously, seeking escape and solace. Perhaps I could escape the fires of hell on a rocket ship. But, looking back, I see that those stories, particularly my fascination with C. S. Lewis and L. Frank Baum, portended another connection between reading and sexuality. In both stories, about Narnia and Oz, children not only escaped into another world where they were valued and loved, but they also had *secrets*. They could not come back to this world and readily tell others of their adventures. I think many kids could—and can—relate to such a situation. But I believe I felt it all the more deeply given the emerging secret that I had to hide. I desperately didn't want others to know that I was going to hell or that I was "sick and wrong." Like Dorothy in the contemporary movie version of *The Land of Oz*, I might be sent away to a "special doctor" for telling my secret in the "real" world.

In a way, then, Lewis's wardrobe was my first closet. Fantasy and sci-fi provided escape, but their stories of strange and unbelievable adventures set in contradistinction to our all-too-real universe served as a trope for my life—an interior experience of forbidden interests and longings that I carried around with me as I moved through the sometimes terrifying and all-too-real worlds of school, church, and home.

As I grew older, my reading habits shifted and expanded, and I turned to headier works. I encountered my first real literary queer at sixteen in Frank Herbert's *Dune*. The infamous Baron Vladimir Harkonnen, who had a taste for young men, whom he slept with and then killed. I'll admit it; I was enraptured. I knew, even then, that Herbert was painting his villain as *particularly* evil by making him a murderous queen, but I loved finding someone like me, even if just a little bit, in the books that I read. Perhaps more importantly for me, the baron wasn't hiding his interests. Everyone knew. And he didn't care that they knew. Unlike the baron, I don't believe I wanted to murder anyone, but I thrilled to his audacity. And, frankly, at some level in my adolescent subconscious, his murderous impulses must have resonated with my developing anger—at having to hide so carefully, at having to watch every move I made and every word I said, so as not to give away my queerness. Eventually, at seventeen or eighteen, I began finding gay characters in books set in *this* world, and I remember huddling over a copy of Bret Easton Ellis's *Less Than Zero*, in which young adult characters made it with male and female friends, living a California life of which I could only dream. Ellis's fiction seemed as fantastic as anything I'd found in Lewis, Baum, Asimov, or Bradbury. But it was all the more comforting in that it purportedly took place in the "real" world.

Given this background, I cannot help but think of my literacy experiences as intimately connected to issues of sexuality. And while they may not be as intertwined for others as for me, I believe that literacy and sexuality are connected for all of us in socially complex and often very personal ways. Several other authors and thinkers have explored such a connection in their own far more complex literacy narratives. Audre Lorde's *Zami*, Gloria Anzaldua's *Borderlands/La frontera*, Mark Doty's *Firebird*, and David Wajnorowicz's *Close to the Knives* are all works that speak powerfully to how an individual's emergences into sexual and literate self-awareness are often tied together in complex ways. Like me, though, all of these writers articulated *queer* experiences, in addition to other experiences of "outsiderhood," such as racial, ethnic, or class "marginality." So the connections between sexuality and literacy drawn in these works may seem somewhat *necessary* given the experience of marginality.

Recent work in the field of sexuality studies, however, is beginning to underscore powerfully that sexuality and literacy are connected for *all* of us in contemporary Anglo-American culture. While authors writing from particularly queer experiences may have insights into this connection because of their "outsider" status, the insights they articulate also point to a profound intertwining between sexuality and literacy *in general*. While I cannot claim in the following pages to provide an exhaustive account of the possible impact of sexuality studies on our conception of literacy, I nonetheless want to suggest some significant ways in which insights from this emerging field of study can provoke us as compositionists to explore more nuanced and sophisticated understandings of literacy as it functions socially, culturally, politically, and personally.

More specifically, what I aim to do is bring critical work in sexuality studies, which has paid enormous attention to the *discursive* construction of sexualities and sexual identities, to bear on our understanding of literacy and what a capacious literacy studies might do. The development of queer theory and other discursive theories of sex and sexuality have promoted an understanding of the social constructedness of sexuality and, as such, they locate the "meaning" and our "understanding" of sex in the symbolic field: that is, sexuality has meaning as it circulates and is articulated through a variety of complex human communications systems. Hence, I argue, this understanding of sexuality is deeply tied to issues of literacy, of what it means to communicate, to learn how to communicate, and to find some forms of communication forbidden or foreclosed upon. A significant consequence of this connection is the further linkage of sexuality to issues of citizenship; specifically, our understanding of the "good" or "appropriate" or "normal" citizen is one who has and articulates a particular sexuality and who talks about that sexuality in certain prescribed ways. It is precisely at this juncture that the New Literacy Studies (represented by theorists such as Brian Street, James Paul Gee, and Lisa Delpit) can augment our understanding of literacy as an ideological event and practice; I use these theorists to make what I hope is a compelling case for understanding how discourses surrounding sexuality are powerful, often prescriptive, and sometimes even empowering literacy events themselves. I conclude the chapter with a pedagogical example that shows these critical insights at play in the composition classroom.

THE DISCURSIVE TURN IN SEXUALITY STUDIES

Sexuality is among the most complex of human experiences, existing in a dense matrix of the biological, anatomical, psychological, cultural, social, and political. In an effort to understand and appreciate this dense matrix, sexuality studies has emerged as a fairly new interdisciplinary field, consisting of a complex conversation among many different fields, including sociology, psychology, education, medicine, political science, the humanities, and the arts. Certainly, feminist studies, critiques, and analyses from the 1960s onward have laid the groundwork for approaching sex, sexual activity, and identities based on sexuality. But while feminist and gender studies focus on issues of gender and the construction of masculinities and femininities and their relation to power, sexuality studies focuses on the construction of identities, communities, and sociocultural norms based on sexual activity and desire, as well as perceptions of what is appropriate (and inappropriate) sexual expression or identification.[2]

One of the chief characteristics of sexuality studies is its emphasis on how conceptions of sex and sexuality change over time and in relation to sociocultural and political spaces. In *Histories of Sexuality: Antiquity to Sexual Revolution,* Stephen Garton notes, "In the second half of the twentieth century the history of sexuality has emerged as a major field of historical inquiry. Sexuality, instead of being something natural, came to be seen by historians as subject to historical change. But how sexuality was made historical, and what might be the motors of historical change, became the object of intense scholarly and theoretical dispute" (2004, 28–29). Garton's point about historical change is well taken.

Concomitant with the rise of sociology and a growing sense of historical relativity at the end of the nineteenth and the beginning of the twentieth centuries, a variety of professionals interested in sexuality began considering the impact of social change on our conceptions of sex and sexuality, and many thinkers began seriously questioning the idea of sexual desire as purely natural or biologically innate.

Indeed, a significant dimension of the debates surrounding sexuality has revolved around two opposing understandings of sexuality: is sexuality internally driven, that is, is it innate and biologically or psychologically determined, or is it socially constructed, and thus determined by social and cultural paradigms? Freud dominated Western understanding of sexuality at the beginning of the twentieth century, figuring it as a set of biologically innate drives that are shaped by internal psychic conflicts, such as the Oedipus conflict. Freud believed that such conflicts were essentially universal, occurring cross-culturally and transhistorically. More recently, though, writers such as Wilhelm Reich, Herbert Marcuse, and Norman O. Brown, early to mid-century post-Freudian thinkers, attempted to reconcile Freud and Marx and to understand sexuality as a deeply rooted part of political economy. This tension between innate and socially oriented perspectives has led some thinkers to trace the shifting historical perception of sexuality across the centuries, and this tension can readily be seen in debates between social constructionists and essentialists.

Anthropologist Gilbert Herdt, of the National Sexuality Resource Center, identifies five "great cultural paradigms of sexual ideas" spanning the modern period in the West, from the 1600s to the present. These paradigms highlight how sex and sexuality have been understood and interpreted through shifting social lenses; thus, the seemingly most personal aspects of humanity have always been filtered through complex social matrixes. First, in the early modern period, sex was understood in a largely Christian-dominated social context as sinful unless carried out in particular sanctioned contexts. As such, any sex act outside of that context—marriage—was considered sinful and subject to legal and spiritual penalty equally. Second, by the 1800s, the shift toward rational and scientific modes of thinking contributed to the emergence of a variety of medical discourses, which conceived of certain kinds of sexuality as "disease," targeting in particular the dangers of masturbation and nymphomania (i.e., female interest in sex). Third, the rise of the science of sexology in the late nineteenth century and the labeling of sexual acts were central to the development of an understanding of sex as "identity." In particular, as sexologists and other medical professionals developed extensive case studies about individuals' sexual activities and preferences, a variety of sex acts was classified and codified, leading to the creation of terms such as *heterosexual* and *homosexual,* which became markers not just of what someone did sexually but of who they were as people. Put another way, *acts* that were once condemned under Christian-influenced legal paradigms become constituent *characteristics* of individuals who did them. If one performed homoerotic acts, one then *became* a homosexual. Fourth, by the 1960s, and concomitant with the widespread feminist movement and increasing availability of birth control, sex began to be understood as "pleasure," and many theorists and writers began to advocate the pursuit of pleasure, in all of its many varied forms, as a natural expression of our humanity.

Fifth, in the contemporary world, many theorists, activists, and scholars are exploring sex as "human right." The emergence of a rights-based paradigm has most likely been influenced by the AIDS pandemic, as well as increasing concern globally for the inequitable and unjust treatment of women and children. Activists on the global stage agitate, for instance, for women's rights to be sexually self-determining and for children's rights to be free from sexual exploitation. In general, sex activists promote the right of *all* people to reliable information about sexually transmitted infections and to adequate reproductive health care and treatment. Major conferences, such as the 1974 World Health Organization Conference and the 1994 Beijing Conference on Women, as well as the rise of the Internet, have been key in spreading information about sex, sexuality, and sexual health. It is important to keep in mind that all five paradigms and frameworks still exist simultaneously. Many Christian and Islamic fundamentalists understand sex as sin, while many liberal political activists advocate for sexual rights (Herdt et al. 2006).

FOUCAULT, DISCOURSE, AND SEXUALITY

The historical approach to sex and sexuality has been greatly augmented, even provoked, by the work of Michel Foucault. Of all of the many scholarly, theoretical, and lay works produced on sex and sexuality in the last fifty years, it has been perhaps Michel Foucault's publication of the first volume of *The History of Sexuality* that has had the greatest impact on scholars and thinkers across multiple disciplines. James Faubion's introduction to *Aesthetics, Method, and Epistemology,* a collection of some of Foucault's short essays and interviews, begins with a list of the various labels applied (so far) to the notoriously enigmatic philosopher: "structuralist, idealist, neoconservative, post-structuralist, antihumanist, irrationalist, radical relativist, theorist of power, missionary of transgression, aestheticist, dying man, saint, or, if nothing else, 'postmodern'" (1998, xiii). Even the term "philosopher" doesn't quite fit since Foucault's work borrows substantially from multiple areas of scholastic inquiry and knowledge production (such as history, literature, the fine arts, medicine, psychology, sociology, criminology), transforming each of them—and philosophy—in the process. So the experience of reading, and thinking through, Foucault is never just hearing what the philosopher thought about various social or philosophical issues; it is, instead, encountering how a brilliant mind problematizes how we have thought about each of those issues.

Much of Foucault's most-cited work, including the important masterwork *Discipline and Punish*, elucidates the ways in which we are all "subjects"—that is, subject to the many social and cultural forces, from the obvious power of legal strictures to the less perceptible movements of educational belief and even "common sense." All of these forces combine to create within us a sense of who we are, a selfhood, which is culturally and socially shaped and conditioned. Foucault is famous for his insistence that there is no "outside" to power, in much the same way that Jacques Derrida, arguably Foucault's only rival to the title of most important philosopher of the century, is famous for saying there is nothing "outside" the text, meaning there is no escape from the various languages used to create our lives. Power is inescapable; it surrounds and permeates everything we do. It is not just the exercise of oppression, but it is present even as the oppressed fight back. For instance, consider Foucault's analysis of gay identity as its own "power/knowledge": early twentieth-century homosexuals fought their oppression and stigmatization as pathological, and in the process created an identity around and through their medical classification as pathological. In Foucault's view, homosexuals exercised power, the power of resistance, as they fought their oppressors; and, in turn, the identity they created through the use of resistance has come to be characterized by its own set of rules, knowledges, and powers. How many times have you spent thinking about who is and who really isn't gay? The question is made possible only by the formation of an identity, the exercise of knowledge about that identity, and the power to make critical distinctions based on what you think you know—all of which was made possible by the resistance of those pathologized by early sexologists as "homosexuals" to being labeled *as pathological.*

As such, Foucault was key in helping to develop our understanding of sexuality as socially constructed and historically situated. In his view, sex and sexuality are imbricated in dense social matrixes and often categories of knowledge, which are inevitably tied to categories of power. Since knowledges produced and disseminated about sex and sexuality become the lenses through which we construct our own sense of self, and of our own most "private" desires, Foucault's thinking has contributed substantively to a more *discursive* understanding of sexuality.[3] Foucault says, for instance, in his theoretically groundbreaking work, *The History of Sexuality,* that, particularly in the last one hundred years, "[i]t is through sex . . . that each individual has to pass in order to have access to his own intelligibility, . . . to the whole of his body, . . . to his identity" (1990, 155–56). Sexuality, then, is the knowledge complex (and complex knowledges) about sex and sexuality that informs how we understand ourselves and one another, as well as the cultural values that we share—or fail to share. Gary Dowsett, deputy director of the Australian Research Centre in Sex, Health, and Society, refers to this knowledge complex as "sexual subjectivity" to underscore how our identities are subject to shaping by the various knowledges about sex and sexuality that circulate in our cultures (Herdt et al. 2006).

For Foucault, the rise of sexology and the medicalization of sex at the end of the nineteenth century were the great turning points in how Western culture conceives of and constructs sex. Briefly, the invention of homosexuality, and then of heterosexuality, at the end of the nineteenth century occurred at a time of great social change, and that change must be factored into any account of the sexological turn in our understanding of sex and sexuality. As John D'Emilio has pointed out in his now-famous article, "Capitalism and Gay Identity" (1999), the rise of identity categories codifying sexuality occurred during a period of rapid industrialization, as people moved from rural to urban areas to find work. An additional crucial aspect of this sociocultural context is the move from religion-based to science-based ways of thinking about individuals and groups. Specifically, as the "death of God" began to be felt throughout the Western world, many turned to the sciences—such as the emerging sciences of psychology and sociology, as well as the more traditional sciences of biology and medicine—for an understanding of ourselves and our place in the world. Indeed, scientific theories of personality, including sexual orientation identities, have come in many ways to dominate our late modern sense of self.

Given this historical backdrop, Foucault challenges our assumptions about Victorian prudishness, and insists rather that the late Victorian era saw a great increase in talk about sex, resulting in increasingly complex discourses about sex and sexuality: "Rather than the uniform concern to hide sex, rather than a general prudishness of language, what distinguishes these last three centuries is the variety, the wide dispersion of devices that were invented for speaking about it, for having it be spoken about, for inducing it to speak of itself, for listening, recording, transcribing, and redistributing what is said about it: around sex, a whole network of varying, specific, and coercive transpositions into discourse. Rather than a massive censorship, beginning with the verbal properties imposed by the Age of Reason, what was involved was a regulated and polymorphous incitement to discourse" (1990, 34). That "incitement to discourse," the call to articulate and tell the story of your desires and thus your identity, has linked (in the West) a sense of one's sexuality with a sense of one's identity—so much so that the two are at times hardly distinguishable: we *are* our sexuality.

Identifying Foucault as a significant theorist in the history not just of sexuality but of rhetoric as well, Patricia Bizzell and Bruce Herzberg highlight the *discursive* dimension of this linkage in the following summary of Foucault's thinking: "Foucault's theory of discourse describes the relationship between language and knowledge; the function of the disciplines, institutions, and other discourse communities; the ways that particular statements come to have truth value; the constraints on the production of discourse about objects of knowledge; the effects of discursive practices on social action; and theses of discourse to exercise power" (1990, 1127). Put bluntly, Foucault says in *The History of Sexuality* that "[i]t is in discourse that power and knowledge are joined together" (1990, 100). In "Technologies of the Self," Foucault elucidates his view: "My objective for more than twenty-five years has been to sketch out a history of the different ways in our culture that humans develop knowledge about themselves: economics, biology, psychiatry, medicine, and penology. The main point is not to accept this knowledge at face value but to analyze these so-called sciences as very specific 'truth games' related to specific techniques that human beings use to understand themselves" (224).

In other words, in being called to identify myself, I choose labels—or more likely, have labels chosen for me—that situate me in the social matrix and hierarchy. These labels, though, are not just social roles; as they are often connected to issues of gender and sexuality—labels such as male, female, heterosexual, homosexual—they are also deep signifiers that I have taken as expressing some of the most personal elements of my being. Thus the intersection of knowledge of self with social power cuts to the very core of who we conceive ourselves to be as people. Being a man is both a deeply personal sense of self and an identity that is imbricated in broad social demands about who a man is and how a man behaves. Being a heterosexual articulates both a deeply perceived sense of self and one that is intertwined in profoundly social senses of what it means to be straight, what is appropriate to desire *as a straight person*, and what kinds of desires and intimate connections should be eschewed. Similarly for female and homosexual identifications. As such, these identities speak powerfully about power—about who you are called to be, how you are called to behave, whom you are called to be intimate with, and whom or what kind of behavior you are called to shun as unacceptable. As William B. Turner puts it, "For Foucault, the exercise of power and the production of knowledge intertwine inextricably" (2000, 52–53).

David Halperin, perhaps the foremost living Foucauldian scholar, claims Foucault as the most important intellectual progenitor of "queer theory," and he has a point, since queer critical powerhouses Eve Kosofsky Sedgwick and Judith Butler rely heavily on Foucault for theoretical underpinnings in their critique of homosexuality as an identity. Specifically, Kosofsky, Butler, and other queer theorists, drawing on Foucault's complex and subtle analyses in *The History of Sexuality*, argue for the fluidity of all sexual orientations, suggesting that "homosexual" does not signify a stable, coherent, essential, natural identity—and neither does "heterosexual," for that matter. These are only socially created labels used to organize people into groups to meet the needs of various moral, social, and even economic agendas. Mixing the labels up, or at least revealing their origin in the social and not the natural, might allow people to break out of the restrictive identities ("straight" and even "gay") through which the social matrix creates, monitors, and "disciplines" us.

Critics, theorists, and scholars in a wide variety of fields have been dramatically influenced by Foucault and this discursive turn in thinking about sexuality, and I would like to highlight briefly some of the theoretical formulations of these scholars who probe the construction of sex and sexuality *in language*. Surveying their thinking will help to elucidate how sexuality studies provides useful theoretical constructs for linking sexuality and literacy in profound ways.

In literary studies, Eve Kosofsky Sedgwick's *Epistemology of the Closet* has been a seminal text in the creation of lesbian and gay literary studies. In it, Sedgwick acknowledges her debt to Foucault's thinking: "[I]n accord with Foucault's demonstration, whose results I take to be axiomatic, that modern Western discourse has placed what it calls sexuality in a more and more distinctively privileged relation to our most prized constructs of individual identity, truth, and knowledge, it becomes truer and truer that the language of sexuality not only intersects with but transforms the other languages and relations by which we know" (1990, 3). As a literary scholar, Sedgwick is deeply invested in understanding constructions of sexuality in literary products, so her concern with language is obvious. But Sedgwick goes further and argues that the strong linkage of identity and sexuality in the modern world makes *necessary* an analysis of sexuality, particularly the division between hetero- and homosexuality, if we are to understand our culture. Specifically, she argues that

> many of the major nodes of thought and knowledge in twentieth-century Western culture as a whole are structured—indeed, fractured—by a chronic, now endemic crisis of homo/heterosexual definition, indicatively male, dating from the end of the nineteenth century. . . . an understanding of virtually any aspect of modern Western culture must be, not merely incomplete, but damaged in its central substance to the degree that it does not incorporate a critical analysis of modern homo/heterosexual definition; and . . . the appropriate place for that critical analysis to begin is from the relatively decentered perspective of modern gay and antihomophobic theory. (1990, 1)

Interestingly, some sociologists have also identified the significance of the stories we tell about sex and sexuality to our understanding of identity and its complex but inevitable relation to power. Ken Plummer, in his important work *Telling Sexual Stories*, argues that "when a strong sense of massive and rapid social change is in the air, stories take on a crucial symbolic role—uniting groups against common enemies, establishing new concerns, mapping the social order to come. Stories mark out identities; identities mark out differences; differences define 'the other'; and 'the other' helps structure the moral life of culture, group and individual" (1995, 178). Following Foucault, among others, Plummer notes that the key stories told about identity, difference, and community right now are sexual stories. And, much as Sedgwick argues, Plummer maintains that stories that "mark out identities" around sexuality are among the most important right now in defining one's sense of self, both at the individual and collective levels. Consider the significance of the division between gay and straight, for instance, as perhaps the most salient marker of identity in contemporary Anglo-American culture. More recently, in *Intimate Citizenship*, Plummer explores the concept of "public identity narratives" to understand how "ethical systems are built around notions of storytelling" (2003, 99). For Plummer, public identity narratives are often very personal and intimate narrations that we use to process and debate moral and ethical issues vis-à-vis sex, sexuality, and intimacy. One famous recent example of a public identity narrative at work might be found in former president Bill Clinton's affair with Monica Lewinsky and the various stories told about it. Why did Clinton lie about having sex with Lewinsky? The president, representing the people not only in matters of government but also as regards cultural norms, which are people's own form of "government" and discipline, faced huge pressures to tell a certain story about sexuality, his in particular. He attempted to preserve the narration of the happy monogamous heterosexual family; and when he could maintain that fiction no longer, he had to narrate his indiscretion with Lewinsky as "sin."

In a vein similar to Plummer's, and drawing on the work of famed sociologist Erving Goffman, as well as feminist theorists, John Gagnon was one of the foremost proponents of social constructivist theories of sexuality. Gagnon and William Simon's 1973 book, *Sexual Conduct*, unpacked the idea of "sexual scripts," proposing three different kinds of such scripts: the intrapsychic scripts, existing inside individuals as the stories they tell themselves about their sex and sexuality; the interpersonal, existing between individuals as they negotiate sexual ideas, insights, feelings, and experiences; and cultural scripts, existing in groups that are seeking normative understandings and values for sex and sexuality. Put another way, according to J. Escoffier in *An Interpretation of Desire*, "interpersonal scripts help individuals organize their own self-representations and those of others to initiate and engage in sexual activity, while the intrapyschic scripts organize the images and desires that elicit and sustain an individual's sexual desire. Cultural scenarios frame the interpersonal and intrapsychic scripts in the context of cultural symbols and broad social roles (such as those based on race, gender, or class)" (2004, xix).

Escoffier notes that Gagnon and Simon's theory of sexual scripting is in part indebted not only to anthropologists interested in sex and sexuality, such as Margaret Mead, but also to rhetorical theorists such as Kenneth Burke, who contributed to sociologists' understanding of "the explication of social context and symbolic action." Specifically, Burke "argued that social action was not merely causal, but also communicated meaning, [and] thus it too was a form of symbolic action" (2004, xix). In other words, sexual scripts and scripting are inevitably tied up with issues of language—and, by extension, I contend, with issues of literacy. Being literate in one's society, for instance, is at least in part being knowledge-able about what kinds of sexual scripts are acceptable and what are not acceptable; such literacy is also about knowing how to navigate interpersonal and cultural scripts (xviii-xix).

Philosophers, particularly rhetoricians such as Judith Butler, have further pushed our thinking about the relationship between language practice, sexuality, and social power. Butler has been particularly important because of her elucidation of the concept of performativity, which she developed out of the work of linguist J. L. Austin. Broadly, performativity, as elucidated in books such as *Gender Trouble* and *Bodies That Matter*, suggests that our most seemingly naturalized concepts of gender and sexuality are actually "performative" actions and identities that we are socially called to perform again and again. Far from being rooted in an innate corporeal reality, gender and sexuality exist largely in the discursive realm, as a set of labels evoking certain performances. As Butler asserts in *Excitable Speech*, "being called a name [gives one] a certain possibility for social existence" (1997b, 2) and "it is by being interpellated within the terms of language that a certain social existence of the body first becomes possible" (5). But Butler warns that this "being called a name" does not initiate performances that can be willy-nilly taken up and dropped at ease; rather, our calling into sociality and the repetition of norms of gender and sexuality, performed again and again, acts to naturalize those norms so that they come to seem "natural" and thus inescapable.

As an example, in *Excitable Speech*, Judith Butler critically examines hate speech, particularly homophobic hate speech, as a discursive practice. For Butler, language and identity are mutually imbricated—so much so that even our existence as *embodied* beings must be understood through the material effects of language and discourse on identity. Given this, the use of homophobic hate, or "injurious" speech, for example, has material affects—for both those who use hate speech and those on whom it is used—that construct identities, relationships, and even points of resistance. As Butler puts it, "[t]he utterances of hate speech are part of the continuous and uninterrupted process to which we are subjected, an on-going subjection . . . that is the very operation of interpellation, that continually repeated action of discourse by which subjects are formed in subjugation" (27).

But Butler, among other queer theorists, also maintains hopefully that speech and language are "[n]ot only defined by social context . . . [but are] also marked by [their] capacity to break with context" (1997b, 41). In this way, then, the movement of queering is more than just resistance, more than just negation; it's recognizing possibilities that the forces of "authorization" do not expect—it's potentially taking advantage of the excess signification of language to envision and articulate modes of being, ways of being in the world, that exceed the expectations (and limitations) of authorizing discourses. Or, to quote Butler again, "[t]he kind of speaking that takes place on the border of the unsayable promises to expose the vacillating boundaries of legitimacy in speech" (41), and "[i]ndeed, the efforts of performative discourse exceed and confound the authorizing contexts from which they emerge" (159).[4]

The works of Sedgwick and Butler, and to a lesser extent of Gagnon and Plummer, have all contributed to the emergence of queer theory in the academy—a theory that takes seriously the discursive turn in sexuality studies and launches a substantive critique against normative understandings of sex and sexuality that privilege certain kinds of sexual expression and identity over others. As you can see, this work is never purely "textual" in its aims; it is also deeply invested in social, cultural, and political interrogation and change.

William B. Turner, in *A Genealogy of Queer Theory*, links the rise of queer theory directly to a strong investment in deeply critiquing systems and structures that sustain and nurture prejudicial and discriminatory hierarchies and norms. He maintains that, "[r]ather than assuming identities grounded in rational, dispassionate reflection as the basis for scholarship and politics, queer theorists wish to ask how we produce such identities" (2000, 5). More specifically, he links sexuality directly to social structures that produce and maintain identity categories as a way of promulgating hierarchical structures of power relations: "Beginning with gender and sexuality, Butler, Lauretis, Sedgwick, and others have begun to wonder how we adopt our genders and sexualities, how those categories come to have the specific meanings that they do, what symbolic and institutional practices contribute to our sense of ourselves as selves, and how those practices both enable and constrain us" (8).

One of the primary ways in which queer theory proceeds is by questioning structures of meaning making in our culture. Turner argues thusly: "Queer theorists examine the meanings that attach to pairs of categories: man/woman/ heterosexual/homosexual, white/black, young/old, rich/poor. Rather than accept a naturalized ontology according to which such terms simply reflect existing distinctions in the world among persons, queer theorists insist that persons do not divide so neatly into binary categories" (34). In this way, then, by critiquing a "naturalized ontology" that rests on binarisms as its primary mode not only of social categorization but also of meaning making, Turner highlights how our conceptions of sexuality are connected to literacy. More specifically, the cultural divisions through which we know ourselves and communicate intimately about our lives and identities—man/woman, hetero/homo—tell the *story* of our lives. Learning that story, learning how to communicate our roles in that story to one another, learning how to transgress those stories and roles and thus articulate alternative life (and possibly collective) narratives of identity, community, and agency—these are all part of what queer theory seeks to examine and critique. Queer theory understands that these stories are intimately taken up with issues of gender and sexuality, with the binarisms we construct around gender and sexuality, and it attempts to reveal those binaries for what they are: attempts to foreclose upon alternative narrations of identity and community. In this way, then, our literacies, our ability to imagine and articulate ourselves, is wrapped up in our sense of sexuality and the stories that we individually and collectively tell about it. Queer theory helps us critique those stories and thus expand our own sexual literacy.

Among the most powerful critical tools that queer theory has given us is the concept of heteronormativity, or the positing of heterosexual and heteroerotic behavior as the only "normal" sexual and erotic behavior. Put in terms of literacy, the larger culture consistently narrates and disseminates a narration of heteroerotic love between one man and one woman as normative, as constituting the "normal" and desired relationship between two individuals. Efforts to secure this story of intimacy can be found throughout much of the mass media as well as in legislation across the country that codifies marriage as existing between a man and a woman. Such normative narrations play substantive roles in the "sexual scripts," to use John Gagnon's phrase, that we tell ourselves and one another and that are communicated to us throughout the larger culture. Queer theory highlights these stories and queries their naturalness and inevitableness.[5] As a quick example, we can review how one queer theorist might approach the vexed topic of marriage in contemporary society. Michael Warner's *The Trouble with Normal* offers a strident critique of making gay marriage a dominant goal for gay activists. He writes that "[m]arriage, in short, would make for good gays—the kind who would not challenge the norms of straight culture, who would not flaunt sexuality, and who would not insist on living differently from ordinary folk" (1999, 113). Warner believes, rather, that "[t]he ability to imagine and cultivate forms of the good life that do not conform to the dominant pattern would seem to be at least as fundamental as any putative 'right to marry'" (112). As such, he urges activists to move in the direction of broadly protecting sexual freedoms as opposed to ensuring that gays can be just like their straight counterparts. More provocatively, he suggests that queers have much to teach straights about sexual freedom, variety, and alternative intimacy—intimacy that exceeds the confines of traditional marriage (116). What is most salient to me as a compositionist and literacy scholar is the attention paid to issues of language and labeling and their connection to political resistance, agency, and power. Indeed, such attention to discourse is designed to interrogate the relationship between constructions of sexuality and constructions of political agency, most often captured in the concept of the "citizen"—a relationship to which we turn now.

SEXUALITY AND CITIZENSHIP

Gilbert Herdt, using the idea of sexual scripts, argues that late modern Western society consists of "two ages of sexual modernity." In the nineteenth and twentieth centuries, Herdt argues, "our scripts are organized centrally around notions of identity, erotics and pleasure." And now, in the twenty-first-century age of sexual and human rights, "our scripts are organized centrally around notions of rights, desires and health." For instance, discussions about access to birth control, termination of unwanted pregnancies, and sex education are rights-based debates (Herdt et al. 2006). Indeed, the movement toward sexual rights highlights the ways in which sex and sexuality are deeply imbricated in both social norms and larger sociopolitical issues. In many ways, though, sexuality has always been political. Labeling sexual acts as sinful and punishing sinners, imprisoning sexual deviants, pathologizing sexual acts and creating sexual identity categories—all are part of the history of sexual politics and demonstrate an ongoing Western sociopolitical concern with sex, sexuality, and the disposition of the body. Theoretical propositions about sexual rights, though, should be measured against the realities of how sex and sexuality are figured in public discourse, legal sanctions, and the lives of individuals and groups affected by norms and normative beliefs about sex/uality. An example should clarify such connections.

In the 1980s, the AIDS crisis showed us clearly that sex and sexuality are deeply politicized. The close association of AIDS with the gay community, which was adversely affected by the epidemic in its early years, was reason enough for many to ignore the disease; indeed, it took President Ronald Reagan five years to directly address the AIDS crisis. Such homophobia, coupled with a general belief that sex is a "private matter," has complicated the spread of effective prevention information about HIV and other sexually transmitted infections, and, specifically, debates about sex education continue to rage today. Conservative governments in this country have continued to favor abstinence-only or abstinence-based sex education, while research generally demonstrates that comprehensive sex education is more effective in addressing a wide range of sexual health problems, including the spread of HIV and the prevention of unwanted or unplanned pregnancies. The one thing that the AIDS crisis may have contributed positively to our culture is the need to debate these and other issues, and we live at a time when issues of sex and sexuality, if not always well understood, circulate widely in the public discourse. Recent debates, for instance, about gay marriage, the recent reconsideration of abortion rights, and new judicial precedents protecting a wider variety of sexual practices are among the many highly *public* debates being waged in the United States today.

Anthony Giddens has tracked some of the most important movements in the past century with regard to the intersection of sexuality and politics, and his frequently anthologized essay, "Intimacy as Democracy" (originally published in Giddens 1992) is worth noting in this context, particularly as it provides some theoretical backdrop for understanding the ongoing and developing politics of sexuality.

Giddens asks his central question cleverly and clearly: "Democracy is dull, sex is exciting—although perhaps a few might argue the opposite way. How do democratic norms bear upon sexual experience itself?" (2002, 451). Giddens notes in particular that sexuality and reproduction have steadily become separated in the Western world, as alternative forms of reproduction are scientifically made possible and as effective contraception prompts us to think of sexuality and sexual expression in terms beyond child bearing. As a consequence, according to Giddens, "[a]s anatomy stops being destiny, sexual identity more and more becomes a lifestyle issue" (453). But the use of the phrase "lifestyle issue" should not lead us to believe that sex is purely an aspect of *private* life now. Giddens explains that, in our Western democracies, the private and the public interact in complex ways: "There are structural conditions in the wider society which penetrate to the heart of the pure relationships; conversely, how such relationships are ordered has consequences for the wider social order. Democratization of the public domain, not only at the level of the nation-state, supplies essential conditions for the democratizing of personal relationships. But the reverse applies also. The advancement of self-autonomy in the context of pure relationships is rich with implications for democratic practice in the larger community" (451).

In Giddens's view, "democratization," or the steady move toward full equality for all people, structures relationships—both individually and collectively—so that older hierarchies—men vs. women, even straight vs. gay—are steadily challenged. As we have greater and greater "self-autonomy," we can explore relationships that problematize older norms, particularly norms surrounding the idealization of heterosexual relationship leading to reproduction.

At the same time, such moves *toward* democratization highlight *current* inequities. Indeed, Giddens's notion of "structural conditions," or the powerful social forces shaping all of our lives, underscores the intersection between some of the most seemingly "personal" aspects of intimacy and the social institutions that impinge upon and, in some cases, create or foreclose upon possibilities of intimacy. Niels Teunis and Gilbert Herdt are currently editing an anthology entitled *Sexual Inequalities*, which will be published by the University of California Press. In their introduction, Teunis and Herdt unpack the notion of sexual inequality in the contemporary Western world, and they poignantly point out that many such inequalities are products of a structural—that is, institutional, political, and cultural—unwillingness to think seriously, critically, and deeply about important sex and sexuality issues. They write:

> Sexual inequality as a form of structural violence has . . . had quite markedly worse effects in the US than other major industrialized countries. A comparison of Western European and United States epidemiological data on major areas of sexual health reveals the extent of his disconnect between research and policy in the greatly higher rates of unwanted pregnancy, higher rates of HIV, higher rates of complications due to abortion, and much higher rates of sexual violence in the US compared to Holland, France, and Germany. Americans remain largely undisturbed by the lack of equity in sexual rights and social justice. Indeed, we seem generally unmoved by the criminalization of sexual behavior, the brutal treatment of transgender people, the continued threat to lesbian rights in partner and maternal custody cases, the double stigma of being a person of color who is gay, and the humiliation of violence experienced by LGBTQ youth in high schools today. (forthcoming)

To address such inequalities and issues, Giddens calls for open debate. In "Intimacy as Democracy," he argues eloquently for informed, literate, and critical discussion:

> A forum for open debate has to be provided. Democracy means discussion, the chance for the "force of the better argument" to count as against other means of determining decisions (of which the most important are policy decisions). A democratic order provides institutional arrangements for mediation, negotiation and the reaching of compromises where necessary. The conduct of open discussion is itself a means of democratic education: participation in debate with others can lead to the emergence of a more enlightened citizenry. In some part such a consequence stems from a broadening of the individual's cognitive horizons. But it also derives from an acknowledgement of legitimate diversity—that is, pluralism—and from emotional education. A politically educated contributor to dialogue is able to channel her or his emotions in a positive way: to reason from conviction rather than engage in ill thought through polemics or emotional diatribes. (2002, 447)

In some ways, Giddens is coming close here to advocating the kind of communicative use of reason that Jurgen Habermas has proposed as necessary to debate and dialogue across diverse positions and ideological investments. Such a "reason[ing] from conviction," to use Giddens's words, would, for Habermas, be grounded in a "paradigm of mutual understanding between subjects capable of speech and action" (1995, 295–96).[6]

Queer theorists, scholars in critical sexuality studies, and even some feminists would argue that we *must* of necessity take into consideration how any "mutual understanding between subjects" is framed by norms of sexuality and sexualized norms of gender. Essentially, then, if we are to develop enlightened participation in debate we must consider the development of *sexual literacy,* and one of the few books to address the need for having an informed citizenry about sex, sexuality, and sexual issues is *The Sexual Citizen: Queer Politics and Beyond* by David Bell and Jon Binnie. In their wide-ranging survey of contemporary sexual "issues" facing Anglo-American society today, Bell and Binnie note that "the public/private divide is perhaps the most fundamental spatiality of sexual citizenship" (2000, 4). More specifically, they ask, "How can we think about intimacy without reinstating the public/private divide; without keeping intimacy's link to privacy intact? How do we think love in ways other than those hegemonically scripted by mainstream culture? What is it that we talk about when we talk about love?" (124). Picking up on Gagnon's notion of "sexual scripting," Bell and Binnie turn our attention in a very Foucauldian way to thinking about how we are called to enact, organize, and narrate our intimate, social, and even political lives around certain conceptions of citizenship that are densely tied to "appropriate" notions of sex and sexuality. They argue: "Central to our thinking . . . is the notion that *all citizenship is sexual citizenship,* in that the foundational tenets of being a citizen are all inflected by sexualities. Indeed, many of the ways in which citizenship discourses operate can be read as discourses around the 'sexing' of citizens—for example, the centering of notions of the family obviously draws on sexualized constructions of appropriate (and inappropriate) modes of living together and caring for one another" (10).

We see such discourses about "appropriate (and inappropriate) modes of "living together and caring for one another" in contemporary debates about who is allowed to be married, who is eligible for military service, and what information is permissible in public school sex education. Using the work of Diane Richardson, Bell and Binnie note that not all citizens are equal or treated equally: "citizenship is always already sexualized; we are all always already sexual citizens, but we are differently marked in terms of our sexual citizenship status, in terms of how our sexual identity fits (or doesn't fit) with the prescribed, naturalized heterosexual presumptive of the notion of citizenship itself" (2000, 27). Of course, since not everyone fits into the heteronormative ideal married life, alternative forms of sexual expression challenge the heteronormative valences of sexual citizenship. As Bell and Binnie put it, "[c]rucially, there is a naturalized, heteronormative modality of sexual citizenship implicit in mainstream political and legal formulations; and set against this, there are myriad forms of what we might label *dissident sexual citizenship*" (33).

To interrogate sexual citizenship more fully, Bell and Binnie use Jeffrey Weeks's notion of "The Sexual Citizen" (1999), in which article Weeks claims, after Foucault, that issues of sexuality have become densely tied up with issues of identity—and by extension, citizenship: "The sexual citizen exists—or, perhaps better, wants to come into being—because of the new primacy given to sexual subjectivity in the contemporary world. . . . the new personage is a harbinger of a new politics of intimacy and everyday life" (in Bell and Binnie 2000, 27). In other words, the proper citizen is the one whose life and intimacies are most closely allied with those of the reigning (hetero)normative constructions of sex, gender, and sexuality. Of course, such norms need interrogation not only for what kinds of values they assume and uphold, but also for whose lives they value and uphold at the expense of those who do *not* fit into the reigning norms. As such, Bell and Binnie, following Weeks, advocate for *reflexive sexual citizenship*. Specifically, Bell and Binnie write, "To some extent we also want to side with Weeks' notion of the reflexive sexual citizen, if that means that citizenship claims are increasingly being made by individuals and groups who choose to mobilize around their sexual identities—who see sexuality as central to their status as citizens (or non-citizens)" (33). For both Bell and Binnie, a conception of *literacy* plays a strong role in the concept of reflexive sexual citizenship, since norms are constructed and disseminated through a variety of media and meaning-making venues. As they put it, "representations [of sex and sexuality] and social power are inextricably linked, and . . . modes of representation are both informed by and themselves inform the ways in which groups are treated in real life" (2000, 70).[7]

SEXUALITY AND LANGUAGE

The "discursive turn" in sexuality studies and the emphasis on issues of representation and their connection to power have inevitably prompted some scholars to examine more specifically the close relationships between sexuality and language in the West. Deborah Cameron and Don Kulick's *Language and Sexuality*, published in 2003, is among the first books to survey broadly and summarize connections between the study of language and the study of sexuality. Clearly taking theoretical energy from a variety of scholars in sexuality studies and queer theory, Cameron and Kulick reflect on the slowly growing body of research that attempts to think critically about how language and sexuality are intertwined, and they convincingly argue that studies of sexuality must take into account language practices—and vice versa: "What we know or believe about sex is part of the baggage we bring to sex; and our knowledge does not come exclusively from firsthand experience; it is mediated by the discourse that circulates in our societies" (15–16). Even more to the point, "language produces the categories through which we organize our sexual desires, identities and practices" (19). Language also functions to discipline sexual subject positions and knowledge about sexuality within the social matrix. Analyzing how tells us much about both sexuality and language.

Beyond simply positing and exploring relationships between sexuality and language, though, Cameron and Kulick's goals are broader and more ambitious. Their aim is to "consider [new dimensions in] how linguists and other social scientists might think about, research and analyse the complex and multifaceted relationship between language and sexuality" (2003, ix). To do this, Cameron and Kulick draw on an interdisciplinary array of scholarship, describing and examining research in sociology, psychology, linguistics, women's studies, and lesbian and gay studies, and they hope their book will serve as an inaugural gesture in "map[ping] out a field of language and sexuality" (xii); as the authors say in their conclusion, "one of our main purposes in writing this book was to synthesize a diverse body of research into a coherent field that could be called 'Language and Sexuality'" (133)—a field that would stretch our understanding of the relationship between the two.

Cameron and Kulick's interest in mapping out such a field stems from their conviction that past studies in language and sexuality have been hampered and limited by too acute a focus on issues of queer identity. The authors acknowledge that good work has been undertaken in the study of language and homosexuality, and they point to studies such as Anna Livia and Kira Hall's 1997 *Queerly Phrased*, which explores speech patterns of gay men and lesbians and asks, what are the characteristics of queer speech? About such Gayspeak, Cameron and Kulick suggest that "the widely shared assumption among scholars studying Gayspeak was that the languages spoken by gay men and lesbians must have their locus in, and be reflective of, gay and lesbian identities" (2003, 92). The scholarly literature reflects, however, a fair amount of disagreement about that assumption: can gays and lesbians, in fact, be identified by the way they speak? Cameron and Kulick argue that the evidence is inconclusive at best, and they maintain that the question might even be wrongheaded, given the diversity of queer identities, practices, and possibilities—all of which suggest that drawing conclusion about language practice from a diverse and contentious identity category might be, at best, problematic.[8]

Further, the authors argue that heterosexuality, as much as queerness, needs to be studied as a sexuality in its relationship to, and construction within, language; as they forcefully put it, "heterosexuality is an important influence on people's verbal self-presentation, shaping what they say, how they say it, and also what they do not say" (2003, 11). Citing a rich body of research, the authors recap how the connection between language and *gender* has been a frequent topic of scholarly inquiry into (often unmarked) heterosexual relationships, as well as a subject for more "popular" books, such as Deborah Tannen's *You Just Don't Understand,* which analyzes miscommunication between men and women. These studies frequently examine heterosexuality as it is connected to "gender-appropriate" speech, and Cameron and Kulick contend that such studies reveal that heterosexuality is actually not "unmarked" in speech, even if it is a "normalized and naturalized" identity. Consequently, students of language and sexuality should be sensitive to the ways in which "[l]anguage-users in various contexts may be actively engaged in constructing heterosexual identities, both for themselves and for one another" (59).

As an example of such construction, the authors discuss a fascinating study by Kira Hall, who examined the language usage of telephone sex workers, or "fantasy makers" (Cameron and Kulick 2003, 59). These workers, including both men and women who are not necessarily heterosexual "in real life," present themselves, convincingly, as heterosexual in their sexual conversations on the phone. Since the interactions between people are only verbal, they provide a rich source of data for studying how one individual (who may be a straight woman, a lesbian, or even a man) can construct in language a socially "believable" identity as a heterosexual woman. Similarly, Deborah Cameron's study of conversations among straight male fraternity brothers talking to one another demonstrates how a group of men use gossip, a type of speech generally attributed to "feminine" speech, to construct and reinforce their understanding of their own and one another's masculine heterosexuality.

Beyond examining language use among those occupying queer and straight identities, Cameron and Kulick argue for pursuing a broader understanding of the relationship between sexuality and language. Their reasoning is worth quoting at length: "What we . . . want to take issue with . . . is the tendency to regard the study of language and sexuality as coextensive with the study of language and sexual identity. We are committed to the view that sexuality means something broader. All kinds of erotic desires and practices fall within the scope of the term, and to the extent that those desires and practices depend on language for their conceptualization and expression, they should also fall within the scope of an inquiry into language and sexuality" (2003, xi). More specifically, they suggest that "limiting an examination of sexuality to 'sexual identity' leaves unexamined everything that arguably makes sexuality sexuality: namely, fantasy, repression, pleasure, fear and the unconscious" (2003, 105). What might such studies look like? In the chapter "Looking Beyond Identity: Language and Sexuality," Cameron and Kulick outline possible areas of study and potential methodologies, always grounded in a sense of how the social valences of language impact our understanding of sexuality—and vice versa: "Although we may experience our sexual desires as uniquely personal and intensely private, their form is shaped by social and verbal interaction—including . . . the silences, the explicit and tacit prohibitions that are part of that interaction. It is in the social world that we learn what is desirable, which desires are appropriate for which kinds of people, and which desires are forbidden" (131).

To demonstrate this and how it might be studied, the authors provide examples from several studies, and they report that "[o]ne consistent finding of researchers who have studied intimate forms of language is that intimacy is often achieved, at least in part, through the transgression of public taboos" (2003, 115). Examples include the use of "baby talk" among adults in sexual or intimate situations, or telling children *not* to say certain words with sexual connotations or overtones; in the latter case, in particular, information about appropriate sexualities or sexual expressions is conveyed through silences and prohibitions that silence further discussion. Studying such interactions give us a broader understanding of how sexuality takes shape in and through language, over and beyond its uses in particular identity constructions.

Cameron and Kulick are also aware of the political dimensions of the work they are proposing as a unique field of study. For instance, they recount and examine studies of language use in court cases involving "homosexual panic" defenses and in the difficulty some men face in interpreting what it means when a woman says "no" to a sexual advance, as well as how women in Anglo-American culture are often socially positioned to make saying "no" difficult in such situations. The authors point out a fundamental contradiction in all of these instances: straight men seem socially permitted to understand a woman's "no" as an invitation to further attempts at seduction, while a straight man's "no" to an advance from another man is supposed to be understood as immediately and unequivocally definitive. The differing understandings of "no" in these two situations points to inequities in how women, gay men, and straight men are positioned socially and politically—inequalities linked in complex ways to our knowledges about one another and sexuality: "The real problem lies in the contradictory discourses on sexuality, gender and power which are part of our culture's background knowledge about sex, and which are therefore brought to bear on interactions about sex" (2003, 42–43).

SEXUALITY AND LITERACY

The work of scholars such as Cameron and Kulick underscores the dense and complex interconnections between language and sexuality, and it is at this point, having worked through some of the major theories in the "discursive turn" in sexuality studies, understanding the profound ways in which our notions of sex and sexuality are shaped by sociocultural and ideological narratives, that I would like to propose the "literacy turn" in our understanding of sexuality—and work toward a formal definition of "sexual literacy." Along these lines, the work of the New Literacy Studies has been particularly useful in helping me theorize a "sexual literacy."

The New Literacy Studies challenges older, cognitivist approaches to literacy acquisition that figured literacy development along (at times) somewhat universal continuums; for instance, the structures enabling literacy development were considered part of who we are, making literacy acquisition a rather "natural"—hence "neutral"—process. Instead, as Brian Street argues in "The New Literacy Studies," *interestu*

Researchers dissatisfied with the autonomous model of literacy . . . have come to view literacy practices as inextricably linked to cultural and power structures in society and to recognize the variety of cultural practices associated with reading and writing in different contexts. . . . A number of researchers in the new literacy studies have also paid greater attention to the role of literacy practices in reproducing or challenging structures of power and domination. Their recognition of the ideological character of the processes of acquisition and of the meanings and uses of different literacies led me to characterize this approach as an "ideological" model. (2001, 433–34)

We know now that students become literate at different rates and in different ways, not just because of cognitive differences, but because of both (1) inequities in schooling systems (often undergirded by economic disparities supported through class and racial divides); and (2) cultural differences that understand and value a variety of literacy practices in often vastly different ways.

To flesh out this understanding of literacy, James Paul Gee, in "Literacy, Discourse, and Linguistics," distinguishes between what he calls "primary discourses" and "secondary discourses": "After our initial socialization in our home community, each of us interacts with various non-home-based social institutions—institutions in the public sphere, beyond the family and immediate kin and peer group. . . . Each of these social institutions commands and demands one or more Discourses and we acquire these fluently to the extent that we are given access to these institutions and are allowed apprenticeships within them. Such Discourses I call *secondary Discourses*" (2001, 527). Obviously, not everyone participates in the same "non-home-based social institutions," creating situations in which different groups of people have access to and become fluent in different discourses.

Literacy, then, is the varying degrees of fluency that one has with *both primary and secondary discourses*. Secondary discourses are particularly important, for, according to Gee, such "discourses are intimately related to the distribution of social power and hierarchical structure in society. Control over certain discourses can lead to the acquisition of social goods . . . in a society. These discourses empower those groups who have the fewest conflicts with their other discourses when they use them" (2001, 539). Knowing, for instance, how to communicate successfully in the business world or in the dominant public sphere becomes crucial when applying for jobs, seeking access to benefits, or making cases within judiciary systems. At the very least, fluency with the prevailing dominant modes of discourse is often necessary to communicate sophisticated insights and critiques. As such, Gee argues that fluency with second discourses, those which most notably enable access to and negotiation with shared, social meanings, is extremely important for social (hence economic and even political) viability and success. When primary and social discourses are relatively consonant with one another, as in the case of many in the white middle classes of the United States, then individuals have an easier time moving from home-based discourses into social discourses. When a greater degree of separation exists between primary and secondary discourses, individuals, often even groups, must spend a lot of time trying to "catch up."

Lisa Delpit, in *Other People's Children: Cultural Conflict in the Classroom*, critiques Gee's work, particularly Gee's suggestion that acquiring secondary discourses is extremely difficult if your social positioning does not allow for an alignment of primary and secondary discourses. For instance, Gee suggests that "it is difficult to compete with the mastery of those admitted early to the game when one has entered it as late as high school or college" (2001, 532). Delpit maintains, though, that "[i]ndividuals *can* learn the 'superficial features' of dominant discourses, as well as their more subtle aspects. Such acquisition can provide a way both to turn the sorting system on its head and to make available one more voice for resisting and reshaping an oppressive system" (1995, 166). Delpit is particularly concerned in her work with interrogating unequal access to literacy education along racial and class lines, and other scholars have followed suit in examining how social groupings based on race, class, ethnicity, and even gender create inequitable situations *specifically by limiting people's access to literacy skills*. Lalita Ramdas, for instance, in "Women and Literacy: A Quest for Justice," explores the importance of literacy for women, so that they can name and articulate their particular experiences in male-dominated and patriarchal societies that have often dismissed health issues specific to women. Doing so allows women, particularly in the Global South, to claim access to equal treatment, not only in areas of health, but also those of law and social justice. In this way, then, literacy is one of the primary enabling tools of civic participation. Such connections between literacy, identity, community, and social power have prompted Brian Street to argue for understanding literacy not as "an individual cognitive tool or as a neutral function of institutions," but rather as an "ideological practice

[that] opens up a potentially rich field of inquiry into the nature of culture and power, and the relationship of institutions and ideologies of communication in the contemporary world" (2001, 437). Seeing how individuals are ushered into or denied access to various literacy skills and practices is one powerful way, for instance, of tracing the distribution of power in our societies.

Given this understanding of literacy, we can see how understanding sex and sexuality as not just biological or "personal" practices but as *literacy events* can offer us access to understanding the norms, values, and pressures that circle around them and that thus affect and shape our lives at fundamental levels. In particular, I maintain that literacies about sexuality straddle *both* Gee's primary and secondary discourses, as people learn about sex and sexuality both at home and in the larger public sphere through interactions at school, at work, and in common meeting grounds such as movie theaters, bars, and other public forums. As the theorists discussed in this chapter make clear, knowledge about sexuality is constantly put into discourse, where it is shared, created, challenged, and revised; Halperin, for instance, has written most eloquently about the cultural processes that shape discourses about sexuality. He argues in *One Hundred Years of Homosexuality*, much like Foucault and the queer theorists, that "[w]e must acknowledge that 'sexuality' is a cultural production no less than are table manners, health clubs, and abstract expressionism, and we must struggle to discern in what we currently regard as our most precious, unique, original, and spontaneous impulses the traces of a previously rehearsed and socially encoded ideological script" (1990, 40).

Far from being a purely "personal" or "natural" phenomenon, what we know about sex/uality comes to us through a variety of discourses surrounding us and in which we frequently participate. In the context of the New Literacy Studies, then, these "socially encoded ideological scripts" represent various discourses to which people have access through both primary and secondary domains. Certainly, ideological positions vis-à-vis sex and sexuality are passed on to children through family units, but discourses of sex and sexuality—often competing discourses about what is "normal," "natural," "right," or "fair"—comprise significant portions of our day-to-day social lives. The ideologically valenced discourses we use to discuss sexuality—ranging from sexual orientation to the meaning of marriage—form a significant secondary discourse through which intimately personal and profoundly public issues are seen, understood, debated, and critiqued. For instance, discourses surrounding sexual orientation identity are, as Foucault asserts, extremely important in self-identity and categorization. And we know that one's sexual identity as well as how one performs it are intimately tied to, in Gee's words, the "distribution of social power and hierarchical structure in society." Gays and straights have unequal access to "social power" and participate differentially in our society's "hierarchical structures," such as marriage. The discourses that enable the division of our species into "gay" and "straight" and that define (and redefine) "marriage" in ideologically exclusionary ways are discourses that stem from home life (primary discourses) into the public sphere (secondary discourses).

Sexuality, as such, is part of multiple literacy practices through which we know, communicate about, and share our worlds, private and public. Coming into fluency with such discourses, knowing how to approach, understand, and participate in them, is part and parcel of becoming what Bell and Binnie call "reflexive sexual citizenship." It is also part and parcel of the process of developing one's sexual literacy, of understanding how those discourses are formed, maintained, and potentially challenged and even subverted.

Unfortunately, access to sexual literacy is not always equal, particularly as it is frequently a locus of social control. Janice Irvine, for instance, in *Talk about Sex: The Battles over Sex Education in the United States*, traces how cultural conservatives have attempted to limit access to information about sex and sexuality as a mode of cultural and political control—specifically as an attempt to channel sexual energy away from nonmonogamous or nonmarital sexual encounters and into the production of heterosexual families. Such conservatives worked primarily through limiting sexual literacy, or talk about sex. Irvine's analysis reveals that "Sex education opponents played on long-standing fears that sex talk triggers sex. Sexual speech, these critics contend, provokes and stimulates; it transforms the so-called natural modesty of children into inflamed desires that may be outside the child's control and thus prompt sexual activity" (2002, 132).

Offering a critical reading of Phyllis Schlafly's 1984 book *Child Abuse in the Classroom*, Irvine traces how anti-sex education conservatives conflated talk about sex with sex itself: "By the mid-eighties, opponents of comprehensive sex education escalated their claims about the performativity of sexual speech. They continued to argue that sex education caused young people to engage in sex, but they also rhetorically fused speech and action to allege that speaking about sexuality in the classroom is tantamount to 'doing it.' Sex education, they charged, *is* sexual abuse" (2002, 133). In Irvine's analysis we can clearly see the conflation of sexuality and literacy along ideological lines. Control of sexual literacy is used to direct people's lives, to move them onto particular paths, to normalize certain kinds of lives and loves. As Irvine puts it, an attempt to control sexual literacy "accomplishes significant rhetorical work" in that it "shrinks the discursive space for pleasure and expands the climate of sexual fear and shame" (2002, 137).

Perhaps another way to put this might be that *sexual illiteracy* positions people in comparably disempowered positions—particularly in terms of their ability to name their own bodies, their experiences, their relationships, their connections through relationships and intimacies to the larger social order. And if we accept the key claims of the New Literacy Studies—that literacy is an ideological event, a conduit of power through access to different socially enabling discourses—then understanding literacies of sexuality is vitally important for people to understand themselves, their relations with others, and their possibilities for meaningful self-articulation and social connection. Not having a language with which to discuss sex and sexuality hampers our ability to understand the sexual norms that order so much of our lives, positioning us to adopt certain kinds of identities, intimacies, and relationships.

Indeed, Paulo Freire, in "The Adult Literacy Process as Cultural Action for Freedom," argues that keeping people *illiterate* is a significant form of social control. Thus, "teaching men to read and write is no longer an inconsequential matter . . . of memorizing an alienated word, but a difficult apprenticeship in naming the world" (2001, 620). Given the powerful ways in which we name each other and our relations through the languages of sex and sexuality—we're men, women, transsexual, gay, straight, married, partnered, sleeping around, etc., etc.—a failure to become literate in the languages of sexuality alienates us from our world, inhibiting us from naming it—and from the possibility of *renaming* it as we question received values and norms.

So, at this point I would like to risk a theoretical axiom about the connection between literacy and sexuality by asking, what does it mean to be *sexually literate* in our society? Being literate in contemporary Anglo-American society means, in large part, knowing how to talk and communicate about sex and sexuality. More specifically, it means coming into an awareness of the norms that figure sex and sexuality *in certain prescribed and culturally normative ways*. Further, given the amount of sex talk that occurs in our society—in advertisements, in the media, in public discussions of laws and norms related to sex and sexuality, and in personal negotiations of sex and sexual pleasure—a failure to be able to communicate knowingly and critically about sex and sexuality is in many ways a failure to be critically literate.

What is at stake for the field of composition studies in forwarding such a claim, in bringing to bear insights from sexuality studies on our conceptions of literacy?

As noted in the introduction, while previous work in queerness and composition has been useful for alerting instructors to the literacy needs and issues of gay and lesbian students, little work exists on the literacy needs of *all* students as related to issues of sexuality. As such, I believe we need to begin thinking collectively as a field about how to address the intersection between sexuality and literacy for all students. We need to move beyond simply including token work by representatives of "diversity" (such as gay or lesbian writers, or references to "gay marriage") and begin thinking instead about how *all students* participate in literacies that are densely inflected by issues of sexuality. Given this, my goal in this book is not to interrogate a multicultural classroom or forward claims for an "inclusive" pedagogy. Rather, I advocate for a *critical* pedagogy that takes sexuality as a key and focal interest for the development of literate citizens. *We need a strong, critical, disciplinary sense of sexual literacy as a central literacy need of our students.* Indeed, I maintain that discussion of literacy should consider issues of sexuality in much the same way that we, in composition studies at least, have grown accustomed to considering issues of race, ethnicity, and gender and their intersections with literacy and discourse. Doing so will not only considerably advance our students' understanding of sexuality as a powerful social construction in our society, but it should also serve to advance and make more sophisticated our students' understanding of *literacy* and its complex relationship to constructions of sexuality. Such sexual literacy should *complement* developing literacies about gender, race, and class, and ideally it should be developed in tandem with them. This book can only begin the process of showing how we might develop sexual literacy curricula in first-year composition courses, but I hope it will gesture in productive directions.

SEXUAL LITERACY IN(TO) THE COMPOSITION CLASSROOM

It is at just this juncture that issues of pedagogy become most relevant, for we must consider how individuals will become both comfortable and critical in discussing sex and sexuality, as well as developing the skills to critique the cultural prescribed ways of talking about—and of being literate about—sexuality. Put another way, we might ask the following question: what are the pedagogical practices whereby one might become aware of and fluent with a critical sexual literacy? An example from one of the instructors I supervised at the University of Cincinnati, where I served as director of English composition from 2004 to 2007, serves to demonstrate the challenges—and possibilities—of engaging sexual literacy in the composition classroom. Indeed, I believe the following brief case study demonstrates not only student interest in sexuality as a topic but some of the necessity—and pedagogical promise—of working with students to develop discourses and literacies about sex and sexuality.

Molly is a full-time instructor in the Department of English and Comparative Literature of the UC. Consistently evaluated as an engaging yet challenging instructor, Molly designed and taught some of the more ambitious, even provocative curricula during my tenure as WPA. She has been particularly interested in film and popular culture, and many of her courses have utilized a variety of pop culture artifacts to invite students to develop critical literacies in response to the many "popular" narratives permeating our various cultures.

One term, when I taught a special graduate course called Writing Sex, Molly decided to follow suit—after a fashion. My course allowed me access to funding to bring in a variety of guest speakers, both theorists and creative artists, for public lectures and meetings with my graduate students. In the course, which served as an introductory survey of how sex and sexuality were figured theoretically and imaginatively throughout the twentieth century, my students and I examined theoretical texts from Freud to Foucault, placing theoretical paradigms into conversation with creative texts by D. H. Lawrence, Vladimir Nabokov, Philip Roth, Erica Jong, Scott Heim, Alison Bechdel, Jeffrey Eugenides, and Mary Gaitskill, among others. Our guests, who were universally delightful, included the theorists David Halperin, David Román, and Judith Halberstam and the creative writers Heim and Gaitskill. Many instructors across the university took advantage of these luminaries' appearance on campus and assigned their works. Women's studies and English graduate students flooded the lecture halls for the speakers' public presentations.

I was somewhat surprised but also immensely gratified to note that many of our composition instructors were also taking advantage of the opportunity to assign works by Heim and Gaitskill in their first-year writing courses, and they invited (in some cases, required) their students to attend some of the speakers' public functions. Despite my interest in promoting sexual literacy, I must admit that I had not intended this turn of events, even as I sat back and enjoyed the ensuing conversations. Molly was among the instructors who decided to "play along" with the theme of my graduate course, and she designed a second-term first-year writing course around the topic of "Sex on Film." The second-term course, English 102, is an intense introduction to researched arguments, and students generally complete a long paper, arguing through a specific claim, of about eight to ten pages. Following a cultural studies model of composition instruction, most faculty examine with their students a variety of social and political issues, such as the nature of higher education in the United States, the importance of diversity in civil society, or contemporary gender issues. For several years, education was a frequently used topic, and students read and responded to essays in Russel Durst's *You Are Here*, an anthology of readings about higher education. Other instructors had used films in this course at the primary "texts," many quite successfully. But none to my knowledge had chosen to focus students' attention on how *sex* is figured in popular film. Molly made this provocative choice and designed a stimulating section of 102 for her twenty students.

When I spoke with Molly about this course after it was concluded, she revealed that the *students* had actually chosen the topic:

> [During] the first quarter [the students in English 101 who were going to take my section of 102 the following quarter] decided to choose sex as a topic of interest. I asked them what topical issue they wanted to deal with and I gave them a couple of options such as multiculturalism or technology. You know, just large issues. They insisted on "sex"—yeah, let's do it. They were very excited. I talked with some students about what films we would pick, and then we came back the next quarter and half of the class was there and half the class wasn't. The kids who were new were initially very taken aback. I said, we are going to talk about sex and deal with that. It was interesting. The two movies we dealt with were *Closer*, which has no sex scenes in it but it talks about sex continually, and *Secretary*, which had very few sex scenes in it but it deals with many kinds of sexuality.

Both films, *Closer* and *Secretary*, were relatively recent releases and had generated some critical commentary as provocative films about sex and sexuality. *Closer*, with a star-studded cast (Jude Law, Natalie Portman, and Julia Roberts) offers a complex tale of complex adult emotional, romantic, and sexual relationships. Characters attempt to relate to one another sexually, sometimes succeeding, often failing. *Secretary*, based on a short story by Mary Gaitskill, who visited campus during the time Molly taught her course, is another very mature film about a woman who begins to discover her interest in sadomasochism; differing from the original short story in overall tone, the film explores the awakening and exploration of "alternative" forms of desire. While students chose the theme of the course, Molly admitted that she herself chose the films: "I ended up choosing the two films partially because I wanted to show films that didn't have a lot of papers already written about them. [I also wanted] one which kind of showed a darker vision of sex and one that showed a more positive vision of sex, and films that dealt primarily with sex but not primarily with sexuality. I was less interested in the 'discovery' and the coming-of-age films, although *Secretary* has a lot of that in it."

I appreciate Molly's distinctions here. She wanted to teach films that had less to do with "coming-of-age" themes and more with exploring complex themes about sex and sexuality. She knew that her students had encountered a variety of coming-of-age narratives in high school; her choices suggest a desire to move considerations of sexuality into more sophisticated—and adult—dimensions. In this way, Molly was seeking to expand her students' sexual literacy.

Naturally, some students were initially a bit nervous about the course—as was Molly, by her own admission. Despite the fact that her students had chosen the course topic, some students still had some understandable hesitancy talking about sex and sexuality: "I was nervous about this course. Half of the students didn't know how to talk about sex in the movies. We had discussion that they didn't know how to talk about it with guys in the classroom or with gals in the classroom. I found that the gals were far more open to stating their opinions. I also think that some students were worried that their views were maybe a little bit more challenging to the political correctness of the time. They would write or talk to me or they would whisper to me that they could not say this or that 'out loud.'"

I believe that such hesitancy is attributable not only to residual puritanical notions in our culture but also to *a lack of sufficient vocabulary and terminology* for thinking and speaking about sex in intelligent, public ways. Such terminology exists, among academics in particular; but it is not a form of literacy that most students encounter until they are well into adulthood, if then. Molly acknowledged that this lack of sexual literacy contributed to students' initial hesitations, and she designed an ingenuous activity in response: "[I told students,] I'm not going to give you a vocab test, but every single day I'm going to put up on the board a word—a word related to sex or sexuality. I chose words such as fellatio, or heteronormative. Most days I just had that word up in the background and usually it was related to something we had recently been discussing." Such tactics helped students develop a more mature way of speaking about sex and sexuality, as well as a critical apparatus to approach the representation of sex in more sophisticated ways.

And students needed such assistance, particularly in what has traditionally been a very challenging course. By most any measure, the English 102 research and argument writing course is fairly difficult. If students are going to get "snagged" in a writing course, it's this one, and of all of the composition courses at UC it is the one that students most often repeat to achieve a passing grade (C- or higher). Students have to learn to navigate, discuss, and analyze a variety of texts, coming up with their own viewpoints, articulating those views, and supporting them while considering possible counterarguments. Given both the difficulty of the course and the course's topic, Molly made sure that her students were going to have sufficient resources to tackle a "difficult" subject and write about if effectively. She had students write from the very beginning of the course, attempting to get them used to writing about sex and sexuality: "My initial assignment was for them to come up with any initial argument that they had about sex in the movies. This was the very first week of class. I said, I want that paper in one week. The quickness of the assignment threw them back into argument and got them thinking about the subject before we started reading and looking at specific films. I wanted to get their ideas so we could start talking as a group. It also let me know where people were and allowed us to get some of the ideas out in the open."

Molly also assigned them sample texts as readings that modeled how good writers think and compose about film: "The first piece that we dealt with was an article that looked at gender in the films *When Harry Met Sally* and *Sex, Lies, and Videotape* so that they could get a baseline of how people talk about film and how people talk about gender politics. We looked at a number of movie reviews, and from that point on we dealt with those two movies." To help students further develop their ability to talk about film, Molly also assigned them a comparative essay, in which students compared the treatment of gender or sex in two different films.

Such assignments—the initial assignment assessing incoming students' views, the reading assignment, and the comparative analysis—comprised roughly the first half of the course, serving as an introduction to writing critically about the representation of sex in film. From the beginning of the course, Molly emphasized that films were subject to multiple interpretations—interpretations that could become the basis of engaging and sustained argumentative claims about what a film means. In her assignments, particularly the comparative essay, she emphasized close reading of the films under discussion, thoughtful consideration of outside sources such as reviews and articles about the films, and careful attention to how other viewers of the films might disagree with different interpretive claims about the films. In such ways, Molly sought to adhere to the composition program's overarching goals for the English 102 course—students' production of sustained, well-considered, researched arguments—while inviting students to tackle subject matter of acute interest to them.

Once Molly and her students had started to develop critical ways of talking about sex and sexuality in contemporary film, she invited them to consider their own individual writing projects, which culminated in a long, researched essay, the primary assignment of the second half of the course: "After looking as a group at the films *Closer* and *Secretary* students started to work on their own projects, which didn't have to deal with those two movies. A lot of students branched off and delved into what they were interested in. A number of people looked at homosexual portrayals in film and that led them to look at how sexuality is constructed and how it has been constructed historically. Others looked at nudity and the display of nudity in terms of gender." Students chose to tackle a variety of films, including *American Pie, Varsity Blue,* and *Brokeback Mountain.*

Students approached this longer assignment, in which they had to make an insightful claim about sex as portrayed in contemporary film and support it by a close reading of the film, through a number of invention exercises. For instance, Molly had students "debate" their position statements by creating minidialogues, in which students had to articulate their major premise and consider alternative and dissenting responses to it. Students also composed organization plans, which they reviewed with Molly and in peer review exercises.

Molly's students tackled a diversity of topics in these longer papers, and Molly noted how students' ability to talk critically—as well as maturely—about sex and sexuality progressed. Molly suggested that it helped that some students were a bit "ahead of the game" than others. For instance, she reported, "I had one openly gay student who was very open. He could talk about sexuality in film very intelligently. He was kind of the charter point." With such help, as well as a well-designed pedagogy, Molly was impressed with her students' growing sophistication. By the end of the course, she and her students were tackling complex issues, such as "the notion of what is normal sex and what is abnormal sex and trying to define those terms, as well as what are some of the legitimate terms you use, which came up right away from the film *Secretary*. We talked about that and that discussion lead to a consideration of 'consensus' in sexual relationships. That conversation took a number of discussions!"

Along these lines, Molly spoke candidly about how her course seemed to open students' minds to thinking more critically about sex and sexuality. She wanted students to learn how to tackle difficult and even controversial material in a mature, thoughtful, and critical manner. In the process of doing so, some students' views necessarily changed:

> I had lot of people in the beginning say things like, Shrek's butt shouldn't be on the screen because it puts kids in the frame of mind of sex. I'm not really sure what that means to begin with, I would tell them. We had to talk about it. What are we really saying here? Of course, some people did change how they thought about sex. But more importantly, though, the class made them realize the number of other ideas about sex that exist out there. Those are valid viewpoints as well and not necessarily ones that they agree with but that they can respect so that they could have a conversation with someone who disagrees with them. Before, students didn't want to hear it. "I don't want to hear it and sex is scary" kind of thing. "We can't talk about it." At the end people were far more able to talk about sex without hesitation, and intelligently—which was nice.

While students learned to speak and write more fluently about sex and sexuality, one wonders if their overall writing abilities improved. Interestingly, Molly suggested that students in this course actually wrote better than in her other courses, due in part, she believes, to the level of interest in the topic: "In terms of the quality of the papers, the quality of thought and the quality of discussion was wonderful. The students themselves were definitely more engaged and they talked more. They turned in more of their work and they came to class more." But more than keeping student interest and entertaining them, Molly described how the actual topic—sex and sexuality in film—helped her meet some of her own critical thinking and writing goals for her students: "I feel that with the 102 class I had struggled for a long time to figure out how to teach it. I wanted to find a way to tell my students, I want you to discover something and I want you to extend your critical thinking. I want you to do more difficult tasks. The 'sex class' seemed to keep them engaged while still not being too overwhelming for either one of us."

From my vantage point as WPA, I would have to agree with Molly's assessment. I had the opportunity to see some of the work that Molly's students wrote for her course, since some of her students submitted their essays to the universitywide English Composition Writing Context. One essay in particular, "You Show Me Yours and I'll Show You Mine: The Inequality of the Sexes in Terms of Mainstream Nude Scenes," beautifully analyzed male and female nudity in contemporary films. The author, a young woman, argued cogently that rampant female nudity devalued women's bodies while the lack of male nudity essentially maintained a sense of privilege around male genitals, figuring men and their private parts as "something special." In *American Pie*, for instance, female nudity is treated as commonplace, something for men to enjoy, while male nudity is figured as embarrassing, as something that causes anxiety. Differences in such representation speak to differential constructions in masculinity and femininity, with such differences tied to how some bodies—and senses of privacy—are valued more than others, while other bodies continue to be objectified. Such disparity, the author argues, speaks to continued sexism and inequity in our culture, and she suggests that increased male nudity in films might help the larger culture interrogate its often unacknowledged beliefs, assumptions, and values about women's bodies, men's bodies, and nudity. This essay won both the first-place prize in the English 102 category, and the "Overall Best Researched Essay" prize.

Such results suggest that Molly's carefully considered approach not only met her course goals but facilitated students' ability to think critically and write successfully. But more importantly for my argument here, such writing reveals that students were beginning to make significant connections between sexuality and literacy, understanding that the ways in which discourses of sex and sexuality move in our culture have much to do with how we perceive ourselves, the stories we tell about ourselves, and the normative narrations the society tells about itself. They were beginning to understand, in Cameron and Kulick's words, that sexuality is "mediated by the discourse that circulates in our societies" (2003, 15–16). For the author of "You Show Me Yours," the opportunity to analyze nudity in films, to begin to explore critically the kinds of popular culture images that surround her and her peers, is an opportunity to become more fluent in an important dimension of the "secondary discourse" of sexuality—the representation of and use of sexed and sexual bodies in the public sphere, such as a popular film designed for consumption by college students. What kinds of identities do subjectivities presume, or call into being? What kinds of subjectivities do they elide? By approaching such questions, the student develops a critical literacy about sexuality as a site of social power and self-knowledge. She is becoming literate about sexuality—and understanding how powerfully sexuality shapes our sense of self and other.

From Molly's perspective, students responded very well, offering high praise for the course at the end of the term: "You know, I think it was a challenge for them. Not that I think that I should make things difficult for the sake of being difficult, but I think people will rise to the challenge if we give it to them. I think they produced really good work. I would definitely teach the sex class again." But certainly, engaging sexual literacy in the composition classroom is no easy task. In my discussion with her, Molly was quite self-reflective about her approach to teaching, particularly in this case, in which she is dealing with "sensitive" topics. She suggested that an open and honest approach sets the stage effectively for having mature, increasingly sophisticated discussions:

> I think [sex is] one of those [topics] that people are very afraid to talk about. My personal way of doing it is just to confront it head-on in the beginning. In that class it was very easy because it was the very first day and I wrote "sex" on the board in bright red letters. Students knew what we were going to be discussing.
>
> I find that how one handles themselves can elevate the level of discussion instantly. If you seem to be an open person, you can bring up those issues when they come up, but you need to present yourself as willing to talk about it and I do that by being a little bit irreverent in class. Perhaps too much so at times, but I think we need to shed this idea that the classroom is not a political ground.

But moreover, Molly articulates how such openness is necessary in composition courses, where students are often first encountering mature topics and learning how to think about difficult, even provocative material in mature and intelligent ways.

> Now, I don't think we should preach politics in the class, by any means, but I think we should not be afraid to allow the exterior world within those four walls. It's not a matter of going in there and telling them, these are my politics. But if there is a major issue at the time it only makes sense to talk about it—especially in first-year composition classes because it trains students how to approach a topic critically. "Let's talk about how the language is being used by both parties. Let's talk about why we are uncomfortable with the word sex." I did it in my class. I said, okay let's talk about all of these words. Why do we have words? What's the difference between saying, for instance, "vagina" and "cunt"?

What I love about this discussion is the connection Molly makes between her course's topic—sex—and literacy.

Indeed, as a writing instructor, Molly knows that what is at stake in thinking about sex and sexuality is in no small part the development of— and the *necessity* of developing—a language with which to speak about sex and sexuality. In this sense, Molly was practicing the kind of "desocialization" that Ira Shor advocates—a demystifying of seemingly private topics so that students can understand their sociocultural and political valences (1992, 114). Doing so also serves to sensitize students *broadly* to how language is used, providing students access to talking and writing intelligently and critically about some of the most important contemporary issues they are facing. It also gives them a language to discuss the relationships among sex, sexuality, intimacy, identity, and community. As such, I think of Molly's work as clearly part of a critical pedagogical approach in composition studies—one that focuses students' attention on the power of stories to shape our sense of self and our sense of potential agency.

The pedagogical approach described above relies on a willingness to take up issues of sex and sexuality in the classroom. Of course, most any instructor, in most any discipline, will approach such material extremely cautiously, if at all. Part of the caution inevitably arises out of our collective cultural feeling that sex and sexuality are "touchy" issues, best left *out* of the public sphere and confined to the realm of the "private." As we have seen, though, in the foregoing discussion of sexuality and citizenry, sex is anything but strictly a private affair. And there is significant cause for engaging issues of sex and sexuality as pressing public concerns, issues, and subjects for debate. More importantly, if I may return to my own literacy narrative for a moment, many of us—perhaps *all* of us— grow up in a world in which our emergence into proficient language use is heavily coded with multiple aspects of gender and sexuality. We grow up learning what we might call the languages of pink and blue, the intertwining of codes and sex. And as we become literate, we learn about sex and sexuality. And, I argue, as we learn about sex and sexuality, we become more literate about our society and culture.

Still, many disciplines—and composition especially—have been very reluctant to pick up issues of sexuality and the literacy of sexuality for classroom discussion and consideration. We can see that reluctance in the *lack* of substantive engagement with sex and sexuality in a variety of first-year composition course materials. In the next chapter, we will take a closer look at what kinds of material and texts are—and are *not*—currently available to prompt students to think critically about sexuality and literacy; we will also consider, in contrast, some of the forums through which students are on their own grappling with the intertwining of sexuality and literacy. What we will find is that, while *we* as instructors may be reluctant to examine issues of sexual literacy, our *students* are not—and they are showing us some interesting ways in which to grapple with and conceptualize sexual literacy.

2

BEYOND TEXTBOOK SEXUALITY
Students Reading, Students Writing

Molly's experiences with her class are not ultimately surprising to me. Her students' enthusiasm, as well as her claim that students actually *wrote better* in her class because of the focus on sex and sexuality, corroborates much of my own experiences, as I will detail throughout this book. But more broadly, Molly's students' interest in writing and sex/uality and in exploring sexual literacies parallels trends in "extracurricular" student writing—writing that takes place *outside* the classroom, in student newspapers and in a variety of online venues. As noted in the preceding chapter, discourses about sex and sexuality permeate our society, but we also need to keep in mind that the "ecologies" in which those discourses take place are significant in constructing their ideological contents and shaping their reception. Anthropologist Dorinda Welle notes that when we talk about the "transmission" of information about sexuality, we must think about the many different ways in which information about sex and sexuality is transmitted and the many different *contexts* and *reasons* for such transmission. For instance, sex educators working with youth may be particularly invested in transmitting information about health and disease, but many young people are much more invested in transmitting information about *culture* when speaking and communicating with one another (Herdt et al. 2006). As such, understanding the dynamics of the transmission of information about sex and sexuality can contribute significantly to our understanding of how discourses of sex are not only disseminated but also constructed. Where, how, and why people talk about sex says much about both their *understanding* of sex and their *sexual literacy*. In the broadest ways, information about sex and sexuality are transmitted both "officially" and "informally." "Officially," discourses of sex are shaped in educational, governmental, and religious contexts. "Informally," such discourses are constructed in exchanges between individuals and groups in less structured settings.

Indeed, students learn a variety of literacies, not all of which are developed in school settings. Many are part of students' "underlife," the often-rich milieus in which students socialize, work, and learn from one another, as well as popular culture. Cynthia L. Selfe and Gail E. Hawisher's *Literate Lives in the Information Age* is among the most important books in our field to advocate for studying students' extracurricular literacies: "Today, the ability to write well—and to write well with computers and within digital environments—plays an enormous role in determining whether students can participate and succeed in the life of school, work, and community. Despite their growing importance, however, we really know very little about how and why people have acquired and developed, or failed to acquire and develop, the literacies of technology during the past 25 years or so" (2004, 2).

Scholars such as Selfe and Hawisher, among a growing number of others in the field of computers and composition, have done much to forward the study of young people's literacies, particularly as such are mediated through the new communications technologies.[9] In terms of literacies about sex and sexuality, such venues are a rich source of knowledge, opinion, insight, and literacy development. Without a doubt, the Internet in particular offers us a significant venue for examining a less formal exchange of information, ideas, insights, and beliefs about sex and sexuality—a venue frequently far less "regulated" and "disciplined" than more formal contexts, such as the classroom.

In the introduction and chapter 1, we examined some of the more compelling theoretical connections between sexuality and literacy, suggesting that sexuality studies offers us useful ways of thinking about their intertwining in contemporary Anglo-American culture and politics. In this chapter, I would like to move our attention to the "real world" in which discussions of sexuality take place. More specifically, I want to take a look at some of the venues in which many of our students—those most likely to take our college-level first-year composition courses—are likely to encounter, participate in, and engage discourses and literacies about sexuality. To do this, this chapter examines some student writing *outside* the composition classroom—in blogs, on Web sites, in student newspapers, and other forums—that demonstrates not only a profound interest in sexuality but an emerging critical awareness of the importance of "sexual literacy"—of developing a fluency with sexuality as an important set of "secondary discourses" through which individuals and groups understand themselves, question normalizations, and potentially find agency. Student writers are variously concerned with significant issues, such as sexual health, reproduction, sex and the media, and the possibilities and potential perils of polyamory. In contrast, I then turn attention briefly to a variety of popular and frequently used composition textbooks and readers to demonstrate how our field overlooks the connection between sexuality and literacy in some of its primary pedagogical materials. The goal of such analyses is both to demonstrate the gaps in addressing sexual literacy in our current composition practices and to highlight some of the ways in which student writers themselves are showing us how to approach such a connection. I conclude with an example of an instructor trying to help his students—and himself—bridge that gap.

STUDENTS WRITING (ABOUT) SEX

A "column" in the mock newspaper *The Onion*, which offers completely fabricated and highly satirical news items, highlights concern about young people's sexuality—and their willingness to talk, and write, about it. The article, entitled "College Sophomore Thinks She Would Make a Good Sex Columnist" (September 15, 2004; http://www.theonion.com/content/node/30713), depicts the view of "Lisbet 'Lizzie' Gilchrist, a second-year undergraduate at Penn State University, [who] told reporters that she has the makings of a good sex-advice columnist." The report continues humorously:

"Whenever I read a sex column in a magazine or newspaper, I always think, 'I could totally write this,'" said Gilchrist, a 19–year-old undeclared major. "I'm always giving advice to my friends about what kind of condoms to get, or whether you should use lube or not. I'm not afraid to discuss things other people are too embarrassed to talk about."

Although she isn't old enough to drink alcohol, Gilchrist can identify the major kinds of sex toys, knows what "frottage" is, and understands the subtleties of bringing herself to climax.

"Sex is as natural a part of life as birth or death," Gilchrist said. "People shouldn't be so weird about it. I lay it on the line. Penis, vagina—I'm not afraid to tell it like it is."

The aspiring sexpert said she would draw from her own experiences to compose solid, reliable sex-advice columns.

"I've been in some pretty crazy situations," said Gilchrist, who is currently single but has had three relationships and five sexual partners. "So many college sex columnists—like the one who writes for *The Daily Collegian*—sound like they're copying out of a human sexuality textbook. Well, I'd talk about real-life experiences. Believe me, I've had plenty of them."

While obviously poking fun at concern over late-adolescent, college-aged students' sexual activity, this satirical article rightly suggests that students do talk about sex and sexuality—and that many are eager and willing to do so. Campus newspapers are one source among many in which students discuss, debate, and share information and ideas about sex and sexuality.

Indeed, a number of venues exist in which a variety of college-aged students talk about issues of sex and sexuality. In the following survey, I can highlight only a few, and I do not at all intend this to be either a comprehensive or "scientific" analysis of the forums or their content. Rather, I hope to be *suggestive* of the extent to which many of our students are processing—and processing intelligently and in sophisticated ways—issues of sex and sexuality.

Several Web sites offer young people with Internet access the opportunity to discuss sex, ask questions about sex and sexuality, and share information and ideas. College Sex Advice, for instance, at http://www.collegesexadvice.com/, serves as a clearinghouse for information about sex and sexuality, while College Sex Talk at http://www.collegesextalk.com/ is, according to its site, "intended to be a serious forum on human sexuality for college students across the country. CollegeSexTalk™ provides students with a place to discuss what really matters to them." Other comparable sites include Scarletteen at http://www.scarletteen.com/ and Teensource at http://www.teensource.org/. Of all of these sites, Campushook at http://www.campushook.com/ has an extended sex advice site, targeting teens and college-aged kids, ages thirteen to twenty-four, and seems as though it is run by young adults. In this case, then, other college-aged or near college-aged Web writers are helping to construct a usable, meaningful, and audience-aware sexual literacy for other traditionally college-aged students.

A bit more radically, Advocates for Youth at http://www.advocatesforyouth.org actually encourages students to become actively involved in promoting literacy about sexuality:

> Feel passionate about reproductive and sexual health rights? Looking to become more engaged in student activism? Interested in organizing for comprehensive sex education and HIV prevention on your campus?
>
> *Then apply to be a Campus Organizer with Advocates for Youth's Youth Activist Network!*

Youth Activist Network Campus Organizers serve as activists, advocates, and spokespeople on issues of youth's sexual and reproductive health. Campus Organizers work with the staff of the Youth Activist Network, running one Advocates for Youth's Rights Respect Responsibility® campaigns on their campus and in their local area. Currently, the Youth Activist Network has two campaigns. The Keep it REAL Campaign focuses on securing comprehensive education in the United States that is science-based, medically accurate, and age appropriate. The Fix the GAP Campaign focuses on advocating for young people's right, worldwide, to comprehensive HIV prevention and education. You can find out more about these campaigns at http://www.advocatesforyouth.org/youth/advocacy/yan/index.htm.

One of Advocates' campaigns, for instance, is a contest for youth interested in creating artwork that is effective in promoting and demonstrating correct condom usage. Such a site and contest attempt to increase students' and young people's sexual literacy by actively engaging them in the production of educational materials about sex.

Besides such sites, generally created by older adults and nonstudents, other sites, particularly social networking sites, provide forums in which students can post profiles, share information, create social networks, and construct a variety of ironic, satiric, parodic, or ludic critiques on a diversity of subjects in a variety of ways. Prominent social networking sites include Friendster, MySpace, and Facebook. Of these, Facebook is particularly targeted to and used by college students. (As of this writing, not all U.S. universities are represented by Facebook, but the site designers' goal is to be as inclusive as possible.) According to the Facebook Web site at http://www.facebook.com,

> Facebook is a social directory that enables people to share information. Launched in February 2004, Facebook helps people better understand their world by giving them access to the information that is most relevant to them.
>
> Facebook's website has grown to over 7.5 million people and, according to comScore, ranks as the seventh-most trafficked site in the United States. People with a valid email address from a supported college, high school or company can register for Facebook and create a profile to share information, photos, and interests with their friends. (http://uc.facebook.com/profile.php?id=21414242)

Angus Loten, writing for Inc.com, notes that

Two years ago, as a junior at Harvard, Zuckerberg developed software to help fellow students trade photos and jokes, rant on any topic they pleased, or just say "hi"—creating a searchable database of personal profiles exclusively for the college set.

It caught on. Facebook, the company he co-founded and ultimately left school to run full time, is now the seventh-most trafficked U.S. website, according to comScore Media Metrix. The site connects seven million (and counting) registered users at colleges and high schools across the globe—a full 80% of the student social-networking market. (http://www.inc.com/30under30/zuckerberg.html)

The success of Facebook is undeniable, and odds are that a majority of your students use Facebook at least to some extent.

To learn a little more about Facebook, I set up a Facebook page, using my university email account, and I was surprised that some students were eager to "network" with me. As I sifted through their pages, and their friends' pages, I was surprised to find quite a bit of clever "sex talk." Much of such "sex talk" involved ribald jokes and corny put-downs using sexualized language, but I was surprised to see how students would critique one another about a variety of sexual issues through message boards, on which users can leave messages for fellow students. While some sexist and homophobic language inevitably appears on such message boards, it was also interesting to see comments that would critique posted pictures and identified interests, asking fellow students to be more considerate in their self-representation. For instance, homophobic and sexist language, when it appears, will frequently elicit disapproving comments on message boards or in spaces in which students can comment on posted pictures. Such comments serve to develop, I believe, a discourse asking all of us to be more mindful about the way in which we use sexualized language.

Scholarly treatment of such social networking sites is just beginning, and interestingly enough, many of those writing about sites such as Facebook are particularly concerned with how such sites expose students to the possibility of exploitation, sexual and otherwise. For instance, Professor William P. Banks from East Carolina University, in a posting on TechRhet, offered the following cautionary example:

One of the more recently interesting things about Facebook to me is that it now allows users to have picture galleries, and you can post pics and link those pics to others on Facebook who are in the picture. As my students noted the other day, they have no control over the pictures their friends put up of them. If they weren't linked, that would be one thing, but since they are, seemingly anonymous friends in our pictures are now linked to lots of information. My student had complained that all the pictures her friends put up of her show her drunk—so yeah, funny to her friends, but not necessarily to her. And then the students mentioned that the campus police last semester had found pictures of students in dorms with bottles and clearly smoking pot or doing other drugs; they then somehow used that as evidence against the students to remove them from the dorms, possibly suspend them from school. This last part I never heard of, so maybe that's urban legend, but I'm intrigued by how MySpace and Facebook are getting our students hyper-aware of their images and how they're posted online.

Banks turns the potential personal hazard to pedagogical use, suggesting the "teachable moment" about visual rhetoric in students' use of Facebook. Such attention to visual rhetoric has obvious connections to sexual visual literacy as well. For instance, a commentator for the online magazine *Computer World* notes one particular danger in representing yourself through Facebook in an overtly sexualized manner: "Search engines might not find your risque profile on social-networking sites like Facebook.com, but that doesn't mean it's hidden from recruiters. Chris Hughes, a spokesman for Facebook, says he's heard that recruiters with alumni e-mail addresses log in to look up job candidates who attended the same school" (http://www.computerworld.com/careertopics/careers/story/0,10801,107810,00.html?source=x10). Along such lines, others worry about the uses of social networking sites to post sexual pictures, to facilitate sexual stalking, and to promote various forms of hate speech. Facebook, fortunately, allows users to enable a variety of privacy features, and the reported incidence of criminal misuse of sites like Facebook is low.

Still, the sites *are* used to facilitate a variety of discourses about sex and sexuality. In one of the few scholarly articles on such sites, "Friendster and Publicly Articulated Social Networking," Danah Boyd wrote in 2004 that "[w]hile Friendster users are typically 20–something, educated city dwellers, their social and sexual interests are quite diverse. As such, they bring vastly different intentions and expectations to the site." Content of profiles on Friendster is determined in part by the site design: "A Friendster Profile consists of five primary elements: 1) demographic information; 2) interest and self-description prose; 3) picture(s); 4) Friend listings; 5) Testimonials. While providing both the individual's perspective of self as well as that of their Friends is beneficial, the Profile is still a coarse representation of the individual, which provides a limited and often skewed perspective." Facebook is comparable, prompting students to provide very similar information, though my sense of the sites is different than Boyd's, particularly when it comes to the representation of sex and sexuality. Facebook users, for instance, are *required* to choose either "male" or "female" as their gender and have only recently been able to select *both* "men" and "women" when declaring whom they are "interested in." Further, there is no "relationship" option for "domestic partner," so men and women in such arrangements (whether same gender or not) have to choose "married" or "it's complicated." Still, creative transgender and bisexual students, as well as those in domestic partner relationships, can find intriguing ways around such representational limitations, built into the template itself. For instance, students have wide latitude in posting pictures and making comments, so trans- and bi-erasure can be mitigated to a large extent. And students *do* post such pictures and make such comments. And inevitably, as Boyd points out, such sites are used to "hook up": "In all online dating sites, people surf for hookups as well as potential partners. While the implied theory is that friends-of-friends are the most compatible partners, hookups use the network in a different manner. Many users looking for hookups prefer to be three or four degrees away so as to not complicate personal matters. In addition to in-town hookups, Friendster users tell me that they also use the site to find hookups when traveling." I cannot help but believe that Facebook is used in comparable ways. But does Facebook help promote in any significant way students' sexual literacy?

Some students have begun writing and publishing articles about social networking sites such as Facebook. In the *Oxford Student*, for instance, the article "Sex and the Net" offers telling and often satiric commentary about the potential sexual uses—and misuses—of Facebook-type sites: "Obviously sex has its own special place in networks. As there are the socially promiscuous, so there are also the sexually promiscuous. The boy who manages to maintain a high score and the girl who lets her defences down all too easily, have the hub-like role in a sex net that the socialite fulfils in society. Rather unfairly it may seem though, a male hub gains a reputation as a stud whilst a female hub is vilified as a slag" (http://www.oxfordstudent.com/ht2006wk5/Features/sex_and_the_net).

What I appreciate about this commentary is its attention to issues of representation and sexuality, and how representations of sexuality are inevitably double-edged. They can be both scintillating and dangerous, particularly as individuals are divided into sexually stigmatized groups, studs or slags. At the same time, users who are using sites such as Facebook to "hook up" need to know information about their potential partners. How does one—a user or a site designer—create a profile that will be true to one's needs, interests, and potential deficits *without* reinforcing the use of sex to shame others—or, as the author puts it, "to ridicule one another." Considering such question is a significant aspect of developing one's sexual literacy.

Such thinking raises the issue of potential pedagogical uses of Facebook and other social networking sites in promoting sexual literacy, and some instructors are already thinking along such lines. Sydney Duncan at the University of Alabama reported that she has used Facebook pedagogically to help students interrogate gender issues and those promote their sexual literacy. In an email to me she reported: "I've been on the Facebook as a faculty member since Spring 05, when I realized all our FYC students were obsessed with it. I used it that semester in my 102 course to talk about gender, identity, and presentation of self. I had several pretty good papers using it to analyze representations of masculinity on the University of Alabama campus." Along such lines, I have used Facebook myself in class to demonstrate potential bisexual and transgender erasure in Facebook's requirement that users identify as *either* male or female. Other possibilities of using Facebook to examine, interrogate, and further sexual literacy remain enticingly open.

Besides such Web sites, which are primarily set up and run by older adults, a number of college and university newspapers, many available online, frequently present student-written articles on a wide variety of sex and sexuality issues and topics. It is in these newspapers that we find an increasing sophistication in the discussion of sex and sexuality. At first glance, sex advice seems a common and popular topic, and articles on such advice frequently include important information about safer sex practices. For instance, Ty McMahan reported in the February 14, 2006, *Daily Oklahoman*, "Student Newspaper Addition Promotes Safe Sex" (http://www.aegis.com/news/ads/2006/AD060273.html).

> As part of National Condom Week, the staff of the University of Oklahoma's student newspaper hand-placed about 10,000 condoms on Monday's edition.

Oklahoma Daily staffers worked late into the night to tape condoms on the issue, which was complemented by stories about sex education and the need for condom dispensers in OU's dormitories.

An editorial said the paper was not trying to promote sex by providing condoms. "In actuality, we are hoping to encourage students, faculty and staff to practice safer sex if they decide to have sex at all," it read.

Other typical kinds of articles include such as those by Kate Prengaman, whose "Behind Closed Doors" advocates the importance of communication in keeping a sex life open, honest, and interesting (http://flathat. wm.edu/2003–11–14/story.php?type=3&aid=17):

We all know that communication is the key to healthy relationships. Amazingly, this is one of the few thing learned in middle school health class that actually matters in real life. A healthy, happy sex life is absolutely dependent on communication. This necessary skill comes in many essential varieties, but they all fall into two main categories: talking about sex and talking during sex.

Talking about sex tends to be slightly less entertaining then talking during sex, which is obvious, since there's not actual sex involved. Even so, this is a critical part of any and every relationship. . . . Talk about your fantasies, your favorite positions, the best foreplay to get you going—the more you talk about sex openly, the better your sex will be.

Occasionally, more radical advice surfaces. In *NeoVox*, the "International Online Student Magazine" at http://www.neo-vox.org/, a recent article entitled "Pssst . . . Pass the Handcuffs" offered advice on safe and consensual sexual bondage play. NeoVox, like many such efforts and other student newspapers, has as its primary stated goal "to allow students from around the world to learn from one another through new media while developing effective means of communication and design skills." More specifically, as the site maintains, "NeoVox is a forum for world dialogue, bringing together college students from multiple international locations. Here, we show our artwork, share our poetry and short stories, comment on the political world, critique the arts, and discuss life." Sex advice is an important topic for students, and students can "learn from one another" about a variety of safer sex and pleasuring techniques in such venues.

At times, such advice comes in the form of useful warnings. For instance, Mani O'Brien at Arizona State University reports on the potential dangers of public sex in "Sex: Banging in the Bathroom" (February 2, 2006; http://www.statepress.com/issues/2006/02/07/ arts/695524,):

> While some may be appalled by the thought of getting down in a dirty public restroom, . . . it has become the equivalent of joining the "mile-high club" for the college set. Maloney's bartender Renee Miller says such encounters are common, especially on slow nights. "People get drunk and they'll drag each other into the stalls," says Miller, who has worked at Maloney's for over a year. She says usually no one attempts to stop the couples, depending on whether other people complain about it.
>
> "If it's a good customer, then whatever," she says. "But if it's loud and out of control then we'll knock on the door and ask them to come out." According to art sophomore Aubrie Oliver, public restrooms are one of many popular sites for horny college students.
>
> "I've seen people having sex in public, on more then one occasion," she says. "They do it in all sorts of places; movies, parks, public bathrooms, parking lots, the list goes on."

Such frank discussion about actual sex acts makes many people uncomfortable—and that discomfort is the subject itself of some newspaper reportage, particularly in the "adult" media. Martha Irvine recently wrote about "Sex Columnists Causing a Stir on College Campuses" (http://www.seacoastonline.com/2002news/09142002/world/24123. htm) and a report in *USA Today* by Mary Beth Marklein noted that "Sex is Casual at College Papers" (http://www.usatoday.com/life/2002– 11–14–casual-sex_x.htm).

Certainly, the very act of talking in public forums about sex in direct, explicit, and even engaging ways seems boundary-pushing for many in our culture. These students are "outing" sex as a not-so-strictly private issue, and their open discussion suggests their investment in providing information about both sexual health and safety *and sexual pleasure*. In the first decade of the twenty-first century, when abstinence-only education essentially limits many young people's access to reliable information about safer sex, contraception, and alternative sexualities in the United States, these students are resisting a seeming unwillingness to discuss sex and sexuality openly and publicly. Furthermore, their interest in talking about *pleasure* is not just licentious; I believe it signals a move in the discourse about sex and sexuality, as Gilbert Herdt puts it, from sexual identities to sexual rights (Herdt et al. 2006). In writing in these ways about sex, these students are participating in the construction and dissemination of discourses about sexuality that advocate for open exchange of information about sexual health as well as the right to enjoy actively sexual experiences, desires, and encounters. Participating in the shaping of such discourses constitutes these young writers' sexual literacy.

In some newspapers, we find articles that pick up directly on the subject of sexual literacy, and writers interrogate sex not just as a private exchange between individuals but as embedded deeply and inextricably in our conception of ourselves as social and political beings. For instance, student writers at Canada's Dalhousie University are moving in their articles and columns beyond sex advice and speaking intelligently and sophisticatedly at times about sex in its *social* dimensions. In "Sex, I Say, Isn't Just about Getting It On," Chris LaRoche, editor in chief of *The Gazette*, Dalhousie University's student newspaper, wrote on February 23, 2006, to introduce his paper's annual "sex issue":

> A good chunk of this week's issue of *The Gazette*, as you may have noticed, is dedicated to discussing, analyzing, and exploring sex.
>
> So-called "sex issues" are a campus media staple. (To pull a totally random example out of my hat, *The Gazette* has been publishing one annually for at least ten years). Normally, the format has been simple: include a bunch of first-person narratives about relationships, put in a few raunchy articles painting differences between the sexes in broad strokes (include puns), and throw something on the cover that's as *Playboy* as the print shop will allow.
>
> With any luck, this year's sex issue will be different. And while I haven't decided to kill the clich [*sic*] and forgo a sex issue altogether, *The Gazette*'s sex-mandate is certainly different this time around.
>
> Instead of focusing on sex the verb, this issue adopts a broader definition of sex—in a social context.
>
> It's a definition of sex that includes gender identity, the changing nature of relationships, and the dangers of sexual harassment.
>
> And it's a definition that readers should take seriously—because in the face of our MTV/glossy mag-laden popular culture, it is not being given the attention it needs. . . .
>
> Sexual attraction indeed has very real physical ramifications. But sex is ultimately derived from the mind, and how it combines physical and intellectual presence. Sex is a social phenomenon that follows us around as long as we interact with other human beings. How we define ourselves sexually be this through our gender, our attraction to others, how we dress, how we

think, or even how we kiss inevitably changes that interaction.

Books like *Tropic of Cancer* are important to this broader definition of sex—because it needs to be discussed more, in the open, and its adherents must not fear persecution.

In an age when homophobia is still rampant—despite Ang Lee's best efforts—women are still not treated equally, and public sexual discourses are still widely discouraged, such a dialogue should not be forgotten and buried underneath stacks of *FHM* and *Seventeen.*

Audience, after all, is everything; an audience that prefers image over content and ignorance over discussion will eventually find itself in dire straights. Confused, it might end up banning *Tropic of Cancer* all over again. And we don't want that, do we? (http://www.dalgazette.ca/html/module/display-story/story_id/917/format/print/displaystory.print)

Other student writers express concern with media literacy and its impact on sexual literacy. In *The Edinburgh Student,* "the oldest student newspaper in Britain," "staffed entirely by student volunteers," Gabrielle Koronka and Naomi de Berker exchange a debate about "Media Whoring": "As naked bodies writhe on our screens and teenage pregnancy is on the up, we ask is there too much sex in advertising? Gabrielle Koronka argues that the media go too far, while Naomi de Berker says we should embrace this ancient tradition" (http://www.studentnewspaper.org/view_article.php?article_id=20040913135211).

Perhaps some of the most sophisticated and at times unusual discussions of sexuality occur in Harvard University's controversial student journal *H Bomb* (http://www.h-bomb.org/). According to its Web site, *H Bomb*

[i]sn't quite what you expected, is it? It isn't porn, that's for sure. We did say we were making a lit and arts magazine, after all—it's just that nobody believed us. It seems that, in the popular conscience, smart is not sexy and sexy is not smart. Harvard students are obviously too busy overachieving to have or even think about sex. Likewise, a "magazine about sex" must obviously be some kind of euphemism for pages and pages of porn. If H Bomb has a philosophy (beyond a simple and naive wish to just exist), it is that somewhere beyond porn and beyond esoteric scholarly inquiry there is a happy medium where intellectual is sexy and hot is genius, where a "Harvard sex magazine" is not a mythical entity but a pleasantly tangible reality.

This first issue is full of art and probably contains a lot more text than anyone expected. And we hope that you'll find it at least a little sexy. After all, there's more to sex than pictures of naked women—even if they are Harvard women, who can be pretty damn hot. And if you feel that there isn't *enough nudity* in the magazine, we agree completely. We like naked boys and girls who are sexy and fun and in love with each other and each other's bodies and don't mind telling everybody so—just try explaining that to career-minded Harvard students.

Combining soft-core erotica with theoretically dense musings on sex and sexuality, *H Bomb* is often a bizarre mix of philosophy, personal narrative, and art. Discussions in articles range from the pragmatic ("better condoms = better sex") to the sexual profile ("sexually-liberated urban twenty-something") to philosophical discussion ("art vs. porn"). In many ways, *H Bomb* is among the richest examples of how students are engaging in complex sexual literacies to explore sex as highly personal, thickly cultural, and densely political.

Discussion of sex in college newspapers has caused some concern among faculty, administrators, parents, and even some students, leading some schools to ban issues on sex or to censor articles on sexuality. Of many possible examples of censorship, the following is fairly typical. Kavia Kumar reported in February 2006: "Avila U. Student Newspaper Removed Because of Sex Issue" (http://www.stltoday.com/blogs/news-random-play/2006/02/avila-u-student-newspaper-removed-because-of-sex-issue/print/):

> The student newspaper at WashU didn't receive any repercussions for its risque "sex issue" this week, but another student newspaper at a different Missouri university has.
>
> According to news reports, Avila University, a Catholic school in Kansas City, removed copies of its monthly student newspaper, *The Talon,* from campus because of articles about premarital sex and birth control.
>
> The cover apparently had a picture of unzipped pants. Other stories included items on one-night stands.
>
> The university issued the following statement: "The newspaper is an institution-sponsored publication. After careful consideration, the publication was removed from circulation because it was inconsistent with the values of the institution."

Competing discourses of religion and social conservatism often attempt to squelch or recast discourses of sexuality to demonize them.

While some writing in such papers may rankle conservatives and challenge social norms and boundaries, arguments in favor of publishing articles on explicitly sexual topics or sexuality maintain that open discussion is inevitably preferable to censoring. In "Students Debating the Issue of 'Sex Talk' in College Newspapers," student writer Joseph Riippi considers a controversial case in which *The Flat Hat*, the College of William and Mary's student newspaper, published an explicit article in its weekly "Behind Closed Doors" sex column, entitled "Balls: Lick 'em and Love 'em" (http://www.musicforamerica.org/node/76856). Apparently, the article was controversial enough to catch the attention of conservative thinker and author David Brooks, who has long taken an interest in the "liberalization" of American higher education, and the pundit mentioned the article in a column in the *New York Times*. Some opponents considered the article "obscene" and called for action based on obscenity laws, and some faculty wondered about the appropriateness of students offering sexual advice to others if the students are not professional experts. The article's author neatly summarizes some of the opposing views:

> Arguments against the column have always centered on the column as being too explicit, encouraging of pre-marital sex, or representing the College in a negative light. I myself became a topic of conversation when in several of my columns I used the word "fuck." My boss at a campus job said some of her co-workers felt it was extremely inappropriate for a newspaper that prospective students read as an indicator of the school in general to contain any obscenities. It might paint for the prospective students a poor picture of the College. Later the Reviews section of *The Flat Hat*, in which my column appeared, received an email that read simply, "Dear Flat Hat—Fuck you."
>
> My attitude then, and my attitude now, is that, well, college students say "fuck," they have sex, and if there is a student newspaper, it shouldn't tailor to the needs of anyone but the students. Freedom of the press, Freedom of speech, etc. However, the faculty member who authored the letter to the newspaper seemed to think otherwise. . . .
>
> I find it hard to believe that the Virginia State Legislature would revoke funding to one of its public universities because of a column in which a student gives sex advice to other students. And whether or not it does in fact violate VA's obscenity laws is unclear. As for the science, I believe it only strengthens the fact that sex is not something to be taken lightly—never does the columnist advocate sleeping around, rather she has acknowledged that sex is something meant only for those deeply in love, and she advocates waiting for marriage if you believe in waiting. And in any case, the issue at hand

is not whether or not sex is a good idea, or whether or not "fuck" is a bad word. Rather it is whether or not they should be discussed in the print of a college newspaper.

At the same time, he notes that creating silence around issues of sex and sexuality can only serve to mystify sexuality, and thus reduce what I would call students' critical engagement with sexual literacy: "I agree that a sex column, or the incidence of the word 'fuck' in a campus newspaper paints a somewhat negative light of a college for prospective students, or perhaps more correctly, for their parents. But I also believe that even if it is more negative, it is a more honest and more real picture. The College of William and Mary does not offer a journalism program, therefore *The Flat Hat* is run entirely by students, and is thus a reflection of the students' lives, not an advertisement for the college. What should it be?"

We might expand the concluding question by asking, if *The Flat Hat* is a "reflection of the students' lives," then why should it not also be a reflection of their emerging literacies about their sexuality, one of the key components of contemporary personal, social, and political identity? Moreover, such writing shows us that students are making connections between discourses of sexuality and the kinds of literacy and critical thinking practices that will empower them to be agents in their own lives and their own communities. They seem intent on developing sexual literacy as an important "secondary discourse."

TEXTBOOK SEX, OR
IS THERE ANY SEX IN THIS CLASS?

My own experience as a writing instructor and as director of a large state university composition program is that issues of sex and sexuality are not widely—or well—represented or taken up for consideration in first-year writing courses. But this was just my hunch. In an effort to find out more, some colleagues and I undertook a research project investigating a variety of composition texts, believing that, in these books, we could see what kinds of subjects and topics writing instructors are most likely—and most likely not—discussing in their courses. At the Conference on College Composition and Communication, 2006, Martha Marinara, William P. Banks, Samantha Blackmon, and I presented some of our initial research on the treatment of sexuality, particularly LGBT sexualities and identities, in first-year composition readers. To develop a sense of how typical first-year composition textbooks present and treat issues of sexuality, we contacted the four major publishers of FYC texts (Pearson-Longman, Bedford/St. Martin's, Houghton-Mifflin, and Norton) and asked about the "best sellers" these companies produce. Our initial goal was to examine the consideration of LGBT and queer content, but I also surveyed the texts to see how issues of sex and sexuality more broadly are covered. Our decision to focus first on LGBT and queer content arose from our collective experience that many readers primarily situate issues of sexuality as queer issues; that is, if we are in our society participating in discourses about sexuality, then we are most likely talking about nonheterosexual issues and people. My colleagues and I are preparing a report based on our larger survey, so I will summarize here some of our more relevant findings.

Specifically, we reported that "[o]f the 290 readers examined, only 73 texts included readings with identifiable queer content." And indeed, as we suspected, that content accounted for nearly *all* of the references to sex and sexuality, with few exceptions such as a handful of articles on sex education (one written by a student, in fact). Moreover, queer authors are rarely identified as such—an omission we find disturbing since it contributes to the ongoing erasure of LGBT identities in our culture; while race and ethnicity are deserving of marking, queerness often isn't considered as relevant—or as worthy. Our most important findings focused on how college-level composition textbooks, particularly readers, offer an increasing spate of texts on race and ethnicity, complementing diverse readings on gender, but readings on queer lives seem relegated to periodic "coming-out" narratives and debates about gay marriage. Further, we argue that

> the placement of queer readings and texts, when they appear, is illuminating, particularly for how students are invited to understand such texts, and their issues, rhetorically. For instance, in *The Bedford Reader*, queerness appears in a pair of readings inviting debate on same-sex marriage. Katha Pollitt's "What's Wrong with Gay Marriage?" and Charles Colson's "Gay 'Marriage': Societal Suicide" appear in a section designed to spark debate about this often divisive issue. Interestingly, such a strategy is not uncommon in many texts; gay marriage is positioned primarily as a subject for binaristic argument, with little room for compromise or negotiation.

As someone who has recently published a first-year writing textbook, including a set of readings, I was not especially surprised by these findings. In fact, when my coauthor, Margaret Barber, and I were debating with our editor about what kinds of readings (including screen shots from Web sites and other graphics) to include, we were told that we had selected too many that had too much to do with sex and sexuality. We managed to include one student-written essay about gays in the Boy Scouts, screen shots from a student-composed Web site about AIDS and college students (a "prevention/information" site, actually), and other short essays about gender (women's representation on the Web) and related images/visuals. But no more. We, apparently, had talked enough about sex, and we were warned that student and instructor resistances might negatively impact book sales.

If we compare the treatment of sex and sexuality in college newspapers with comparable articles in first-year composition texts, we see that students writing in newspapers about sex do so not only with greater explicitness, but also, in many ways, with greater sophistication. These student writers certainly offer at times explicit advice, but their willingness to discuss sex in its social contexts—including, for instance, issues of censorship, sex in the media, and ideological differences between erotic art and porn—reveals an awareness of what I have been calling sexual literacy, a sense of sex not just as a private act but as connected to fundamental dimensions of identity, issues of social ideology, and aspects of political reality. Further, the sheer diversity of topics covered suggests a rich engagement with sex, sexuality, and sexual literacy. In many ways, then, the treatment of sex and sexuality in composition textbooks seems impoverished by comparison. While a first-year reader might offer a relatively safe and inexplicit gay male coming-out story, an article in a college newspaper, written by a college student, might tackle in graphic ways the experience of gay bashing and the social dimensions of homophobia that enable one person to lash out viciously against another. Certainly the latter is a far richer exploration of the intersections among the sexual, the social, and the political, and it contributes more substantively to cultivating an ability to talk in informed, complex, and critical ways about sexuality—true "sexual literacy."

For whatever reasons, however, sex seems a "taboo" subject in composition textbooks—as it is in composition courses. Moreover, connections between sex/uality and literacy are never broached, except perhaps in "coming-out" narratives, in which glancing attention is paid to *naming* sex and sexuality as one becomes conscious of sexual difference. Most likely, such discussions are taboo because of our continued sociocultural conviction that sex is a "private" matter—despite the fact that discourses of sex and sexuality are everywhere. Indeed, as we saw in the previous section, while we and the textbooks we use may remain relatively silent on issues of sex and sexuality, our students are often quite voluble—and articulate—about sex. Paying attention to what they have to say—and how they say it—might inform both innovative pedagogies and a richer understanding of the connection between sexuality and literacy. At the very least, failing to acknowledge sexuality as a significant issue about which students must develop some sense of literacy is to shortchange our students tremendously.

MAKING ROOM FOR SEXUALITY IN THE COMPOSITION CLASSROOM

In a recent article in *College English,* Jay Jordan argues that "[instructors] should encourage students to write to explore their own cultural affiliations, family backgrounds, and experiences with intercultural communication—even uncomfortable ones" (2005, 182). Clearly, many students are already engaged in this kind of writing outside of our composition courses, and such students are more than willing to tackle in their writing the "uncomfortable" subjects of sex and sexuality. As a writing instructor, when I think about what students such as the writers for college newspapers are doing in their examination of their own literacy practices, I am both impressed and desirous that we, as compositionists, learn from their interests, investments, and insights.

How can we take advantage of such energy, creativity, and critical thinking in our classrooms? How can we, as Jordan suggests, create pedagogical spaces to "encourage students to write to explore their own cultural affiliations, family backgrounds, and experiences with intercultural communication"—even when such explorations are uncomfortably about the sexual?

I can see such connections being made, such bridge-building between seemingly "private" literacies and the critical domain of the composition classroom in the experiences of one composition instructor formerly under my supervision, whose story I briefly turn to now. What I most appreciated about this instructor's approach was his ability to be open to the kinds of questions—and texts—about sex and sexuality that his students wanted to explore. Unlike Molly, his intent was not to bring into the classroom texts that would provoke discussion of sexual literacy; rather, he was comfortable (at least eventually) in allowing students to make connections across and through texts to the subjects that are important to them, such as sex and sexuality.

James was a second-year graduate student who was completing his master's degree and working as a teaching assistant in our English Composition Program at the University of Cincinnati, where I served as his immediate supervisor as director of the program. James was an excellent, award-winning instructor; he had had previous teaching experience in English as a high school teacher, and he worked very well with students in our first-year required composition sequence. He had taught the entire composition sequence at UC twice, once in his first year and again in his second year of study. The sequence consisted at the time of three quarter-long courses: English 101, an introduction to argument and academic writing; English 102, an introduction to writing researched essays, with an emphasis on developing and supporting argumentative claims; and English 103, a "capstone" course in which students wrote argumentative, researched, and interpretive essays about "complex texts," primarily literary texts, though some instructors chose to use film, long nonfiction works, or even graphic novels.

In his final term as a graduate teaching assistant, James chose to be a bit adventuresome and organized his English 103 course, in consultation with me and the associate director of the program, around literary texts written by Cincinnati authors. His texts included a book of poetry by Jeffrey Harrison, *Incomplete Knowledge,* and a longish young adult novel by Curtis Sittenfeld, *Prep.* A widely praised novel, *Prep* caught my attention because of its rather frank depictions of adolescent sex and sexuality. According to the author's Web site, *Prep*

> is an insightful, achingly funny coming-of-age story as well as a brilliant dissection of class, race, and gender in a hothouse of adolescent angst and ambition. . . .
>
> Ultimately, [the main character] Lee's experiences–complicated relationships with teachers; intense friendships with other girls; an all-consuming preoccupation with a classmate who is less than a boyfriend and more than a crush; conflicts with her parents, from whom Lee feels increasingly distant, coalesce into a singular portrait of the painful and thrilling adolescence universal to us all. (http://www.curtissittenfeld.com/prep.htm)

When I visited James's class during a routine observation of our teaching assistants, James and his students were vigorously discussing whether or not the narrator of the novel is a lesbian. Given my interest in sexual literacies, I was, needless to say, intrigued, so I made arrangements to speak with James about his text choices, assignments, and overall experience in the course.

James organized his course so that students would be spending quite a bit of time talking and writing about *Prep*. The students' primary, research-oriented essay was to be about some aspect of the novel that they found engaging and wanted to explore in greater detail. Following our program's overall guidelines, James encouraged students to pick topics about which they could stake and support an argumentative claim. Topics varied widely: "Some of the students wanted to do a research essay on boarding schools and they found interesting articles that seemed counter to the book's perspective. I even approved *Seventeen* magazine as a source because of a particular article on boarding schools. Others wanted to look at *Prep* as far as clothes and fashion are concerned, and how that defines these young girls as belonging to particular groups or social and economic classes. Of course the other big issue that some students chose to write about is some of the sexual identity issues that the main character [Lee] seems to have throughout the novel."

Clearly, though, issues of sexuality were at the top of the list of students' interests in *Prep*. According to James, many students used the experience of writing about *Prep* to explore issues of sex and sexuality that were important or at least engaging to them: "A number of students have chosen that topic. They were interested in that. I felt from the discussions we had in class that the students were very hard on this main character and the choices she was making. Lee told us what she wanted but her actions were counter to her wants. The students became very frustrated with her. When we started to talk about sexuality, I think they finally got the picture that there might be a lot going on in her head, about the kind of person she wanted to be, about what kinds of intimacies she wanted to have. Maybe we need to look at it, and try to understand it, and ask critical questions."

As noted, some students debated in class, and then in their writing, about the sexual orientation of the narrator. James prodded his students to move beyond this bit of "sexual orientation detection" and probe the reasons why it is important that we "know" someone's sexual orientation. Why *must* one's sexual orientation be known, and why do we feel deceived when we believe we have someone's orientation pegged—and we are wrong? James noted how some students really grappled in their writing with trying to determine whether or not Lee is a lesbian. For James, though, one of the benefits of *Prep* as a narration about sex and sexuality is that it makes it very difficult to categorize characters, particularly Lee, the main character; Sittenfeld depicts sex and sexuality as complex, even somewhat fluid, and her interest as an author seems in promoting a rich and challenging understanding of sexual intimacy and sexual self-understanding—one that eschews pigeonholing people into fixed categories.

What is delightful about James's approach to this novel and his students' grappling with it is how they took very seriously Sittenfeld's representation of sexuality as complex. Students took what for many of them was a very common approach to thinking about sexuality—what is your sexual orientation?—and wrote with increasing complexity about how sexual orientation is multifaceted. We all have complex emotional, psychological, and intimate entanglements with a variety of people, and our richness as people is often denied or elided through reductive categories. Moreover, students had the opportunity to explore *why* sexual orientation categories are seemingly so important. While James admits that such a discussion was only at its beginning stages, he appreciated the opportunity to connect students' interest in sex and sexuality with more rigorous approaches to thinking, questioning, and critiquing.

James acknowledges that he didn't choose *Prep* in order to have students write about sex and sexuality, and that, in fact, some students seemed to need to ask permission to write about the sexual aspects of the novel. He was delighted, though, to grant such permission, and encouraged students to write about topics that they found of interest, including sex and sexuality. Still, James spoke candidly about some of the tensions he felt—and his students felt—when discussing such "sensitive" topics. One of his male students worried, for instance, if James, as a teaching assistant, would "get into trouble" for broaching topics of sex and sexuality in the classroom with his students. Such hesitation speaks powerfully, I believe, to many students' continuing sense that sex is a "taboo" subject, not fit for public discourse. But James nonetheless responded enthusiastically when I asked him if he were interested in teaching *Prep* again: "Yeah. I try to say, write what you want. It was interesting to me. I wanted them to go for it."

The challenge facing an instructor like James, however, is not only in creating a pedagogical space in which sex and sexuality can be discussed openly and maturely, but in linking such discussion to complex, powerful, and important notions of literacy and literacy development. In questioning—and in *coming to an awareness of the possibility of questioning*—sexual orientation categories, I believe that James's students were beginning to explore a powerful way in which people's lives are organized, their desires narrated, and their identities formed. Such a pedagogical approach helps students connect literacy practice to both personal and political dimensions of their lives—and as such reflects recent calls to make such connections more visible in our composition curricula. In *English Composition as a Happening*, Geoffrey Sirc nicely summarizes what he sees as the primary problematic characteristic of that vexed space, particularly the vexed space of composition in the academy: "What should be the central space for intellectual inquiry in the academy [that is, composition studies] has become identified as either a service course designed to further the goals of other academic units or a cultural-studies space in which to investigate identity politics" (2002, 24). In contrast, Sirc urges us to rethink composition in such a way that we begin "to address deep, basic humanity in this modern, over-sophisticated age" (31). It is exactly that "deep, basic humanity" that I want to annunciate in the term sexual literacy, a deeply personal exploration that doesn't just advocate for particular identities but that links the construction of those identities to important but understudied discourses. Put another way, for our students, coming into sexual literacy is coming into critical fluency with languages and discourses that link their sense of basic humanity to overarching political structures and categories. All of the student writers discussed earlier, including those in James's course, are addressing such issues, tackling them through the lens of sexuality—truly one of the more daring ways to approach complex issues and the intersection of the personal and the political.

For the next three chapters, I want to model how I have attempted to approach sexual literacy in the composition classroom and to use the concept of sexual literacy to promote greater awareness of the complex intersections between sexuality and literacy. Doing so, I believe, simply invites students to become more literate—and more *critically* literate. The approaches I describe have been informed by a strong desire to honor student literacies, to show students how to think more critically and complexly about their various literacy practices, and to help students make connections between the literacies they engage in outside the classroom and the literacies they are called to develop and practices in more formal settings, such as the academy, the workplace, or the sphere of public debate and discourse. I think that Susan Kirtley, writing in "What's Love Got to Do with It? Eros in the Writing Classroom," nicely summarizes how I feel about this work: "I find eros everyday in the writing class, in even the smallest things. Eros is the essays students write and the letters I write in response. Eros is the palpable excitement in the writing class when we share our research projects, projects designed to draw on the students' desires as well as my own. . . . We should not be afraid to address our desire and emotions, the feelings that inspire and limit us" (2003, 66). For me, addressing our "desire and emotions" is to begin the process of understanding how what we take to be among our most private thoughts and feelings are inextricably wound up in some of the most pressing public debates of our time.

In organizing my discussions in the following chapters, I have decided to focus on three key dimensions in sexuality as a "secondary discourse": sexuality and its relationship to identity, gender and *its* relationship to identity, and marriage as a sociocultural and political construction. Each dimension of sexuality is richly loaded with discourses demanding our attention, particularly if we are to develop fluent literacies about them that help us think through, understand, and potentially revise our relationships with one another and with ourselves. To presage the following chapters, then: when we think of our personal identities, we are connecting with or resisting or complexly negotiating with dense public discourses about the complicated relationship between sexuality and identity. When we think about, feel, and experience our gendered bodies, we have the opportunity to become aware of how we are called into specific gendered and sexual roles, as well as how we call others, even unconsciously, into such roles. When we think about marriage and our intimate relations with one another, we inevitably evoke difficult debates about the connection between personal happiness and public citizenship, and whose lives and relationships are honored—and whose are not. In each case—how we articulate our identities, how we annunciate and inhabit gender roles, how we describe the personal and political nature of our relationships—we are engaging in complex literacies that are inevitably wrapped up in sex and sexuality. And we are inviting students to think with us about some of the more important "secondary discourses" through which we "think" ourselves, our society, and our cultures.

SITES OF PEDAGOGY

3
QUEER THEORY FOR STRAIGHT STUDENTS
Sex and Identity

Henry Giroux has famously advocated for a "pedagogy of difference," which, in his words, "seeks to understand how difference is constructed in the intersection of the official cannon of the school and the various voices of students from subordinate groups, but also draws upon students' experience as both a narrative for agency and a referent for critique. . . . Such a pedagogy contributes to making possible a variety of human capacities which expand the range of social identities that students may become. It points to the importance of understanding in both pedagogical and political terms how subjectivities are produced within those social forms in which people move but of which they are often only partially conscious" (1992, 138).

Along such lines, some compositionists have taken advantage of the stories, essays, and articles by and about queer people included in first-year writing textbooks (see the discussion in the previous chapter) to introduce their students to some of the "various voices of students from subordinate groups." Certainly, an aim of such inclusion has been to spark discussion about how certain groups, such as queers, narrate the story of their lives, coming to terms not only with their own self-awareness but understanding that self-awareness and their articulation of it as densely intertwined with the stories the greater society tells about sex and sexuality. As such, narrations by queers, such as "coming-out" stories, offer students and teachers an opportunity to see how a member of a "subordinate group" might attempt to make meaning out of the bits and pieces of information and narrative available to him or her in a culture whose dominant narratives about sexuality are heterocentric and frequently homophobic.

Curiously, my students at the University of Cincinnati, where I taught writing from 1998 to 2007, seemed increasingly "comfortable" with talking about sexual orientation; the "edge" is "off" our discussions of these once "touchy" topics. In many ways, this is good. I don't want the majority of my students to flinch when the topic of sexuality or sexual

Complacency with gays.

orientation comes up in conversation—or when I tell them that I am queer. And certainly, bringing in queer texts for study and analysis has probably made many students more comfortable with queer topics and issues—which, again, is good. At the same time, my students' seeming comfort may actually be complacency, or an unwillingness to think more *critically* about a topic that just *seems* passé. So there are gay people. Big deal? What does that have to do with us? Gays have had a hard time in a homophobic culture and "coming out" is a big deal. Yes, that's terrible and it should change—but again, so what? We've all seen Will & Grace. What does that have to do with us?

As such, I am left with a nagging question: as queerness "leaves the margins," are we losing a bit of that sharp vision a queer critique can offer? Put another way, is the actual work of *queer theory* getting done? For instance, are students questioning the naturalized structures of heteronormativity and heterosexism? Are they interrogating naturalized narrations of sexuality, identity, and normalcy? Beyond simply *including* queer voices into the rhetorical mix, I think that queer theories and scholarship offer us a chance to *critically* examine the ways in which gender and sexuality are constructed, narrated, and deployed in the creation of identities, modes of being, and community. Such analysis— intimately connected to the stories we tell about ourselves, the narrations we use to make sense of and question our ways of being—opens up possibilities of understanding how meaning is created and narrated for *all* lives, not just gay and lesbian ones. As such, the queer theoretical critique can help to underscore the intertwining of literacy and sexuality throughout our culture. More specifically, queer theory may offer us a chance to investigate some of the powerful "secondary discourses" of sexuality through which so much emotional, intimate, and even political energy is mobilized in the construction of and identification with categories of sexual identity—"gay" and "straight" being most dominant.

What I propose to do in this chapter, then, is explore what a queer critique might mean for self-identified *heterosexual* students in first-year writing classes and for their development of a critical sexual literacy. Specifically, I analyze in some detail an in-class exercise in which I invited my students to write about an online performance of heterosexuality. In the process of thinking about this activity with my students, I believe that we had a unique opportunity to explore the constructedness of sexual orientation as an identity category and thus increase both our critical thinking about the relationship between narration and identity and our collective sense of sexual literacy. To set the stage for this exercise, I explore first the attempt by some theorists and pedagogues to link queer theory to a critical pedagogy—an attempt that undergirds the development of my own composition pedagogy described in this chapter.

QUEER THEORY AND THE QUEER CRITIQUE: NOT JUST FOR QUEERS ANYMORE

Relatively recent work in queer theory has turned critical attention to the classroom as a site in which the insights of queer studies broadly and queer theory in particular can engage all students to consider the construction of identity and the narration of sustaining and constraining norms in our culture (see in particular Ristock and Taylor 1998). A central question when working with first-year students in particular on sexuality issues is, how do you talk about sexuality in such a way that students do not automatically assume you must be talking about queerness, and thus the "other" that does not pertain to the majority of them? How can we "out" the connection between sexuality, discourse, power, and knowledge in such a way that all of our students will understand this complex of intersections? Tackling such questions, Deborah P. Britzman, in "Queer Pedagogy and Its Strange Techniques," suggests that we push beyond LGBT inclusion and enact a "queer pedagogy" that "exceed[s] such binary oppositions as the tolerant and the tolerated and the oppressed and the oppressor, yet still hold[s] onto an analysis of social difference that can account for how dynamics of subordination and subjection work at the level of the historical, the structural, the epistemological, the conceptual, the social, and the psychic" (1998, 66). I have found myself at many times committed to such a position—at least theoretically. The pedagogical challenge remains. How?

In "'Explain It to Me Like I'm a Six-Year-Old . . .' The Pedagogy of Race, Sex, and Masculinity in *Philadelphia*," Lee Easton explores such questions by critiquing a popular and award-winning film, which, as a "teaching" movie (one that aims to educate mainstream audiences about gay men and AIDS) needs both critical and political interrogation, especially as it "mobilizes discourses around love, liberty, and fraternity to contain its hegemonic constructions of Black, gay, and white bodies, and hence secure a white heterosexual viewpoint of society" (1998, 245–46). More specifically, Easton suggests that the film "functions as a gay reading of what will 'pass' in middle America," and that its "popular appeal lies in the straight, white imagination's embrace of the images of gays that the narrative constructs" (246). A very close and skillful reading of the film follows in which the author discusses how film's various representations reinforce static notions of gay identity as primarily white and middle class.

Even more interestingly, Easton critiques the representations of race in the film, placing his analysis of racial representation in and around his queer reading. As only one of many possible examples, here's how Easton reads the film's figuring of gayness, blackness, and AIDS:

> *Philadelphia* racializes AIDS as a white disease, a move that elides the fact that AIDS is a global problem which in fact strikes hard, especially in the Third World. But again, raising these issues is problematic for the white, straight imagination. Doing so would remind viewers that AIDS in Africa and else-where is primarily a heterosexual disease, diminishing sympathy that the film intends for Andy and his white family, and overtly dealing with the issue of race in a way this narrative is unprepared to do. Because the AIDS/homo-sexual/white conflation is so integral to the movie's structure, the movie must keep AIDS as a local, not global, disease in order to maintain its internal coherence. (1998, 256)

But Easton is not interested only in critiquing the film; he encour-ages using it—and critically probing it—with students to "question heteronormative representations and to contest them by encouraging students to look critically at representations for heterosexist and heter-onormative ideas" (1998, 264). To accomplish this, the author suggests having students discuss with whom they identify in the film—and why. How would they react if their friend or brother were gay? Had AIDS? If they were Andy's lawyer, how might their interactions with him be the same? Be different? In promoting such questioning, Easton presents us with a socially active pedagogy, queering the boundaries of emotional and political sympathy and identity. This is a queer pedagogy, then, that invites students to begin thinking beyond simply tolerating lesbian and gay existences and instead interrogate more fully how sexuality func-tions in all of our lives.

Indeed, along these lines, Susanne Luhmann suggests in "Queering/ Querying Pedagogy? Or, Pedagogy Is a Pretty Queer Thing" that "*queer* aims to spoil and transgress coherent (and essential) gender configura-tions and the desire for a neat arrangement of dichotomous sexual and gendered difference, central to both heterosexual and homosexual identities" (1998, 145). More radically, "If queer pedagogy . . . is foremost concerned with a radical practice of deconstructing normalcy, then it is obviously not confined to teaching *as, for,* or *about* queer subject(s)" (151). As such, the call to "work" or think queerness in the classroom should not focus solely on *introducing* our many straight students to queer lives and stories; rather, working queerness in the writing classroom should be an invitation to *all* students—gay *and straight*—to think of the "constructedness" of their lives in a heteronormative society. Along these lines, I was reminded of what Connie Monson and Jacqueline Rhodes say in "Risking Queer: Pedagogy, Performativity, and Desire in Writing Classrooms" about bringing queer theory to the comp class: "Readers seeking a panacea for homophobia, heterosexism, and other very real political ills will not likely find it in this essay; at its best, however, queer theory can offer crucial insight into the constructions of subjectivity, desire, and literacy already operative within the institutional site of the composition classroom, providing a place from which to critique and transform those constructions" (2004, 79). Monson and Rhodes make, at least theoretically, the leap that I, too, desired to make—from inclusion to critique of the "constructions of subjectivity, desire, and literacy"—constructions that are already present everywhere, including in the identities and expectations we bring into the classroom.

Monson and Rhodes are suggestive in bringing together "subjectivity, desire, and literacy" as a set of constructions that queer theory can help critique *together*. But how? My work as a *writing* teacher in this queer theoretical vein has been influenced most by the thinking of both Ken Plummer and Judith Butler, theorists we first discussed in chapter 1. To recap briefly, then: Plummer, in *Telling Sexual Stories,* examines a wide variety of gay and lesbian "coming-out" stories, which are often very self-conscious narratives designed to construct a meaningful story about one's identity: "Identities are built around sexuality; an experience becomes an essence; *and the new stories that are told and written about [sexuality] hold it all together*" (1995, 86; emphasis in the original). Critically examining such stories not only gives students a sense of the world as viewed through "other" eyes, but can also reveal how sexuality is policed in our culture, and how certain identities and values become privileged. Butler, of course, has given us the idea of identity as "performative"— not that we can take our identities on and off willy-nilly, but that, through constant repetition, certain ways of being in the world come to seem natural, essential, and even immutable. In particular, she has used this notion of "performativity" to point out how *heterosexual* identities are naturalized, often at the expense of or via the exclusion of queer lives (1997c, 135). Butler's critique, combined with Plummer's assertion of the centrality of the narrative of sexuality as central to many people's identity, prompts me to ask, what is the *story* of "straightness"? With such a question, we can see how the critical examination of identities is also inevitably a *rhetorical* examination. More specifically, we might ask, how does one *compose* oneself or become *composed* as a "straight" person? And how does the repetition of a certain story or performance of "straightness" naturalize it, making it seem inevitable, and more socially desirable than other alternatives of identification?

These are difficult questions, particularly for straight students in our writing courses, because being straight is to inhabit and be inhabited by an "unmarked" subjectivity, one whose narration is not "re-mark-able." As Calvin Thomas puts it *Straight with a Twist: Queer Theory and the Subject of Heterosexuality,* "straights have had the political luxury of not having to think about their sexuality, in much the same way as men have not had to think of themselves as being gendered and whites have not had to think of themselves as raced" (2000, 17). From a rhetorical standpoint, we could say that straights have the "narrative luxury" of not having to consider their self-narration—at least not as closely and critically as many queers have had to. For instance, straights do not generally have to "come out"—itself an act of rhetorical staging and performance, frequently one that is carefully crafted and narrated. As such, "Don't ask, don't tell" seems a particularly "straight" formulation. There's nothing to see here, keep moving along. (In other words, don't look too closely.)

With this in mind, how do we elicit from students the "story" of straightness, or prompt them to consider "straightness" as a story itself, with a wealth of narrative twists and ideological turns? I could ask students to narrate the story of how they "became" straight or how they "know" they are straight, but I have often mistrusted such narrations offered by students, primarily because I worried that students would "tell me what I wanted to hear." In contrast, I think that Calvin Thomas asks the right question: "What does reading queer theory tell the straight reader about being queer, about being straight, about being, about becoming, what one putatively is, what one (supposedly thereby) is not, the permeability of the boundaries between the two, the price of their maintenance?" (2000, 12). Yes . . . but I don't want to just unleash a bit of queer theory on my students—or unleash my students on a bit of queer theory. It's easy to write from a paradigm, and I don't want students to simply use a little queer theory to begin replicating—dare I say *naturalizing*—stories about the social construction of heterosexuality. Jonathan Ned Katz has already given us a wonderful analysis of *The Invention of Heterosexuality*, and it would be too simple, too convenient for students to apply Katz's thinking to their own lives. Just add queer theory and mix. Rather, I have wanted to disrupt, inasmuch as I can, thinking about "normative" lives, to help students excavate some of the ideological constructions and assumptions that go into the creation of the "norm." My question is comparable to the one Lauren Smith asks in "Staging the Self: Queer Theory in the Composition Classroom": "How might I move students further in the direction of disruptive or self-conscious narratives and away from naturalized representations of self and world?" (2000, 81).

DISRUPTING THE NARRATIVE OF STRAIGHTNESS, OR PERFORMING A HOAX

Inevitably, it is easier to say you're going to disrupt something than it is to actually disrupt it. But I am convinced that straightness can—and should—be "queried." But how? Calvin Thomas suggests, "there can be nothing more terrifying to what Monique Witting calls 'the straight mind' than being 'mistaken' for a 'queer'" (2000, 26). Since declarations of one's straightness seem most common when that straightness is called into question or doubt, I have theorized that we could "tease out" for examination a narration of straightness by playing with this "soft spot" in the straight subjectivity—by poking at the point where straightness must maintain itself as an identity over and against queerness. Butler suggests that the act of subverting the norm—or, in her words, "working the weakness in the norm"—is a "matter of inhabiting the practices of its rearticulation" (1993, 237). In other words, performing a narration of straightness, inhabiting its story, might work its weakness from the inside out. Just one problem. How can I, as a queer man, "inhabit" or perform straightness?

In an earlier essay, "Out of the Closet and Into the Network: Sexual Orientation and the Computerized Classroom," I argued that "networked classrooms, especially those with synchronous conferencing software, have allowed teachers to develop role-playing exercises that are pedagogically important in two specific ways. First, role-playing is the quickest way for one individual to experience another's social positioning, especially a position that the student may never have had the opportunity of

experiencing before; and second, it ensures that such experiences are
conducted in fairly safe and controllable contexts" (1997, 212). In the
remainder of that essay, I described a pedagogical experiment in which,
using Daedalus Interchange, students logged on using pseudonyms to
a synchronous chat space and participated in a discussion of what their
experiences would be like in a world in which homosexuality is the
norm and heterosexuality is the stigmatized sexual orientation. My goal
in using this exercise was to show students both how stereotypes are
deployed *and* how we come to narrate, through a variety of social forces,
stories about our identities as based on sexual orientation:

> Such "in-personation" is useful in allowing students to experience situations,
> dynamics, and difficulties that their usual daily experience may never show
> them. In terms of allowing students to gain insight into the experiences of
> marginalized or oppressed peoples, role-playing serves a valuable function,
> even as it allows the traditionally marginalized the opportunity to speak
> with new power and voice. Utilizing the pseudonym capabilities of Daedalus
> INTERCHANGE, for instance, students and teachers can write from different
> subject positions and take on identities that are not their own and experi-
> ment with different subject positions' discourses. . . . It is my contention,
> based on my classroom experience, that such stereotyping and categorization
> vis-à-vis sexual orientation can become just as obvious and that students can
> become aware of how all our sexual identities are heavily inflected by social
> and cultural forces. (1997, 212–213)

While I believe that such an exercise was very useful in demonstrating
how sexual orientation is never purely personal but also always densely
social (in construction, in our understanding, in our relations with others), I also felt that the "lessons" of the exercise could be discounted
because the primary premise—a fantasy in which homos are the norm—
was just that: a fantasy.

With that critique in mind, I searched for other pedagogical projects
to highlight how some of the dominant stories we tell about sex, sexuality, and sexual orientation circulate in contemporary Anglo-American
society, and how such stories are densely intertwined with our own self-
understanding and our coming into identity.

I took a clue from "hoax sites," such as *The Onion* online, and I pos-
tulated that I might be able to create a Web site that did my theoretical
poking for me. For instance, one of the first hoax sites I ever used in
a composition class was the Senator Kelly Mutant Watch campaign site

(www.mutantwatch.com), which is a "hoax site" serving as an advertise-ment for the film *The X-Men*. The site *seems* like a campaign site for Senator Kelly, the archconservative who wants to keep the world—and your children—safe from the "evil" mutants. (Sound familiar, anyone?) What's wonderful about this site is how cleverly—and closely—the site designers mimic both a campaign site and the rhetoric of an unthink-ing, knee-jerk conservatism, and many writers and fans have noted how the antimutant rhetoric deployed on the site is startlingly similar to that of antigay conservatives such as former conservative senator Jesse Helms. Using such sites in class offers an engaging way to examine how rhetoric is used to create, sustain, and promulgate various ideological stances, often based on misinformation, unfounded assumptions and—frequently—the demonization of "others." As such, a hoax site seemed a good vehicle to *queer* various rhetorics, to push at the soft spots in certain ideological constructions.

I wondered: could the same medium be used to push at the soft spots in heterosexuality? And what would this look like? With such questions in mind, I created a hoax site, a personal homepage, about a straightboy, Dax, who has a "secret." His site, Straightboyz4Nsync (http://www.geoci-ties.com/straightboyz4nsync), is about a college-aged male student who is trying to "come out of the closet," as it were, about his fascination with the boy band Nsync. His homepage is a "fan site," largely about his inter-est in the band, and it contains links to other Nsync fan sites and a devel-oping short story (to which you can contribute) about a straightboy's fas-cination with a boy band. Like many other fan sites, Straightboyz4Nsync also has pictures, a short bio, and even a link to a Yahoo! Group so that other straightboy fans of Nsync can communicate with one another.

My creation of such a site readily reveals my pedagogical—and per-sonal—investments, which is *not* to say that I'm a fan of Nsync. I'm not. Really. And Straightboyz4Nsync is not just a revenge fantasy—virtually giv-ing a straight guy a "shameful" secret he has to hide for fear of rejection or castigation. (Okay, maybe it's a little of that, but not much.) Rather, Straightboyz4Nsync is an attempt to provoke discussion: about the ways in which "straightness" is "performed," is narrated, is constructed and main-tained as an identity. What would happen if students were confronted with a "straightboy" with a "secret"? How would they "read" his sexuality and his self-narration? What insights about the narration of straightness might be teased out with a site in which someone marks himself as "straight"? More generally, what thoughts, insights, or even defensive reactions about straightness might the site evoke, or disrupt? By giving a self-identified "straightboy" a secret—a secret that could homophobically bring his "straightness" into question—I hoped to prompt discussion about how one's "straightness" is constructed and maintained. In other words, I hoped to ask—and provisionally answer—the question, what is the "story" of "straightness"? Moreover, what might teasing out that story tell us about the politics—and rhetoric—of heterosexuality in our culture?

I also decided to use a Web site because, as Charles Cheung points out, a personal homepage acts for some as a site of "emancipation," in which "those who want to present 'hidden' aspects of themselves—things they are cautious to reveal in 'real life' because of fear of rejection or embarrassment," can do so virtually (2000, 48). Of course, since Straightboyz4Nsync is a hoax site, its "author," Dax, could not be "liberated," but I hoped that the site would provoke discussions that might at least lead students to think more critically about some of the ways in which narrations of sexual identity take shape in our culture.

But the site taught me much, much more.

My intention in the remaining pages of this chapter is not to present you with an "experiment" that I conducted in deploying queer theory in the composition classroom. I do not have enough "data" for such an enterprise, and, frankly, I remain unsure what such an analysis would tell me. Rather, my goal here is to discuss an exercise I have used in a few classes—two first-year writing courses and one sophomore-level course focused on understanding the cultural impact of the Web—and work through some theoretical implications of that exercise for my understanding of the possible uses of queer theory in the composition classroom. As such, my enterprise here is not to present a quantifiable "study" as much as it is to explore how my students' responses to an exercise have enlarged my understanding of the potential pedagogical efficacy of queer theory in the teaching of writing.

PROTESTING A LITTLE TOO MUCH: COMMENTS FROM STUDENTS

I used my hoax site in three separate sections. Two were fairly identical courses, both third-term (on the quarter system) first-year writing courses, which serve as "capstone" courses in which students write long, argumentative research papers. My focus in this course was on issues surrounding HIV/AIDS, personally, socially, and politically. Students participated in service-learning assignments, composing pamphlets, text for Web sites, and other projects for local AIDS service organizations.

The other course I used the exercise in was a "Web Literacies" course that I designed for our communications program; this course examined the Web in its sociocultural dimensions, as a tool for individual identity performance, community building, and even political organization and activism. In all three classes, we eventually discussed issues pertaining to homosexuality and homophobia, noting, in the writing classes, the continued association of AIDS with gayness and, in the communications class, the use of the Web by many queers to experiment with identity and find community. Since all three classes met in computerized classrooms, I frequently had the opportunity to show students queer-themed homepages and sites for discussion, both face-to-face and electronically enabled. I began to think, though, that it was easy for many students to understand such sites as "other," as indicative of queer experience, and thus as having no connection to their own, avowedly straight lives. Straightboyz4Nsync was designed in part to "queery" that.

After viewing the Web site, students were asked to respond, comment, and discuss via a Blackboard discussion board.[10] I encouraged openness of discussion and response, directing students only to think about the site, its author's possible intentions and purposes, and the site's potential effects on visitors. Of course, class context is important in framing discussions, and I used this site in three separate courses: a sophomore-level Web literacies course, in which we discussed "fan communities" on the Web; a first-year writing course in argumentative writing, in which we explored issues of social movements; and a first-year capstone writing course focused on sexuality issues. Oddly enough, responses from all three sections—disparate as they were—followed very comparable lines of discussion and analysis. Moreover, I could not detect any clear "split" in opinion or response along racial or gender lines; women were just as likely as men to respond "negatively" to the site, and black students seemed just as likely to be supportive of this Nsync-loving white straightboy as other white straightboys and -girls. No one in any of the classes was openly gay, and no one had disclosed his or her queerness to me privately.

Some students responded to the site negatively because of its—admittedly—unoriginal Web design. I must admit that this actually surprised me—not because I think the site is particularly well designed, but because I was interested in students' responses to the *content* of the site, not to the site's layout. However, comments about design are revealing:

> well, disregarding the content, the site is easy to navigate and clear on what is where. As for the attractiveness of the site, it is kind of lame. Its a little boring, a little to straight forward, yet he handled the subject matter ok. overall, i dont like it, and there doesnt seem like much time and effort was put into the web design.
>
> yeah i didn't like this so much. I like i just told you thought that this site was very obnoxious
>
> but enough of my rambling, apparently the guy had about as much skill in web design as he had musical taste. . . .
>
> this website really sucked the pics were distorted and if this is supposed to be a fan club about n sync why dont they have any facts about n sync or something like it?
>
> I didn't really care for this NSYNC fan club site. They could've put a little more work into it.
>
> i think this is a really bad website. it has very limited amounts of information and pictures. disappointing, really

One could view such comments as perhaps skirting the issues raised by the site by focusing on the medium as opposed to the message. But I also want to take them at face value, particularly as they suggest that— for a few students—the medium will make or break the message. In fact, I would argue that students' attention to aspects of design over issues of content reveals the extent to which "production values" are significant for our often media-saturated and media-savvy students. And a failure to impress with aspects of "visual rhetoric" will often equate to a failure to communicate.

Many others, though, *did* respond to the site's content, perhaps because they felt they had to as part of the assignment—or perhaps because they were intrigued. Regardless of what motivated their responses, student comments about the content of Straightboyz4Nsync covered a *range* of opinions and offered *many* opportunities for further discussion.

Some students' responses could be characterized as representative of the "extreme ends" of the possible response spectrum: homophobic on one hand and supportive on the other. Only one response seemed blatantly homophobic, the student suggesting that Dax's "straightness" *should* be called into question; the "reasoning" offered, however, merely linked Dax's potential queerness less to his liking a boy band and more to his apparently questionable taste in music:

WHAT IN THE NAME OF ALL THAT IS HOLY IS THIS GUY THINKING!?!?!?!? Of course people would wonder about his straightness, this band consists of an undertalented group of pretty boy singers with monotonous songs, no song writing ability and some snazzy dance moves. FOR GOD'S SAKE PEOPLE PLAY A FREAKEN INSTRUMENT!!! A giutar, the drums, an accordian SOMETHING!!!!!

In contrast, some responses seemed very sympathetic, attempting to understand and even support the site's stated aims and goals—to provide a "safe space" online for straightboys who want to express their appreciation for a popular boy band.

Ok this looks like a site for male insync fans only. Obviously this site is necessary because it seems strange to most people that males are fans of insync too. It must mean that people may think your gay if your a male and like insync. This it what the title of the web page seems to suggest.

i think that this site is trying to get guys to admit that they like bands like Nsync and that it is ok if they do—it doesn't mean that they are gay if they do—i think it could be successful—people might think its cool-and funny—and go along with it—others might reject it—you never know—i think its cool for a guy to admit that he likes nsync—its cute

Some students, of course, felt that the Web site didn't raise any problem that they had:

well i guess it is none of my business if that kid likes those boy bands, i dont agree with him, but its his problem not mine.

When I queried this as a response, I received the following post:

i didnt mean problem in terms of acutal problem..i meant its not for me to think about and worry about; nor should it be for anyone else. but people obviously have a problem with the fact that a boy likes a boy band, no question there, esp if you have a discussion board about it. i think instead of problem, i more mean waste my time on the subject of something that is not my business

These responses seem to suggest simultaneously an understanding of Dax's dilemma and the writers' desire to distance themselves from it. On one hand, the posters understand the pressure of norms, particularly around sexuality and gender, but on the other hand, it's not their problem; if you do not occupy a subject position substantially outside the norm, then you (1) have nothing to worry about; and (2) need not become involved in discussions of those who might have something to worry about. In a way, these are exactly the students I wanted to "queery"—students whose sense of sexuality is, perhaps, so normative, so unquestioning, that it is easy for them to dismiss a sense of sexuality as in need of questioning, critique, and interrogation.

The majority of comments offered via the discussion board fall into two categories that, I think, invite and are willing to engage critical discussion of sexual orientation and its construction in our society—albeit in ways that are often surprising and in need of further interrogation. First, some students seemed to understand exactly what I had intended in posting the site for discussion, and they responded to the site critically, specifically pointing out the norms through which sexual orientation identities are maintained and the double binds in which they place men.

> I personally think ther is nothing wrong with a guy liking a boy band, however, it is just not the "norm" with society. Boy bands are seen as gay by society, so when a male likes a boy band they are seen as gay also.
>
> It [the site] might bring up the controversial "norms" of sexuality and why it is okay or not okay [for] one to stray away from these "norms"
>
> This is a typical example of what happens when somebody steps out of the "normal" boundaries: when guys like boy bands they are thought to be gay, why can't a guy just like a boy band?

Such responses served as useful "jumping-off" points for discussions of both how and why such "norms" are in place, as well as how difficult it is to "come out of the closet" as a transgressor of gender or sexuality norms. Indeed, we discussed Straightboyz4Nsync in terms of the "closet," suggesting that straight men's sense and performance of sexuality and gender are often carefully self-regulated to maintain the straight/ gay and even masculine/feminine binaries. Again, such a discussion quickly leads to consideration of why such norms need regulation and policing, as well as to an examination of whose interests they serve. In the process, students think critically about how sexuality and gender are tied to our senses of identity. In particular, the following comment directly alludes to the connection between gender identities and sexuality, particularly as they apply to men:

> guys care too much if people think their gay. That's the real issue. I went to lilith fair, most people think of that as a lesbian thing. But I don't really care what people think, it's just good music. No lifestyle comes with it.

The student's comment is quick to dismiss the issues as seemingly trivial, but oral discussion in response to this comment revolved around our culture's careful policing of the boundaries of maleness as opposed to femaleness, the implied sexism of such policing, and the use of strict concepts of masculinity and femininity as a tool to maintain a delimiting division of labor as well as a marketing ploy to create distinct categories of consumers. The discussion was wide ranging and varied, and I was impressed that some students could use the Straightboyz4Nsync site as a launching pad, as it were, for making connections between gender, sexuality, economics, and politics. More significantly, in terms of queer theory's questioning of the normalization and naturalization of certain identity formations, students questioned why certain gender categories and expectations exist. A student asking a simple question—such as "why can't a guy just like a boy band?"—seems, well, simplistic, but it can introduce good discussion about the construction of social, gender, and sexual roles.

Such conversations were delightful, but the majority of students debated a very different aspect of the site—one that led to our most "disruptive" discussions about identity and sexuality. These students addressed the supposed *intent* of the site, questioning why Dax felt the need both to create the site and, more radically, to identify himself as "straight." The discussion began with several students who, seemingly sympathetic to Dax, were concerned that Dax might be a bit homophobic:

> it kind of seems that he has something against gay men, and he seems to speak of them pretty stereotypically
>
> This guy seems a little too homophobic. When people act like that, their heterosexuality is debatable. This kid's beliefs seem highly dubious.
>
> . . . he feels the need to defend his sexuality for some reason . . . maybe a little homophobic?? or a little unsure about himself??
>
> i think that the site is fine. although i am a little confused about why he had to make the point that he is straight. it's fine if you like n'sync . . . whether you are gay or not . . .

This last question sounds so ironic to my queer ears; how many times have we, as queer people, been asked why we have to "flaunt" or sexuality or "make the point" that we are gay? More curiously, though, I was pleased that the students seemed to respond negatively to homophobia, as though it isn't "cool" to be a homophobe; like what you like—and you should be fine.

The comments, though, also point in another direction: a questioning of Dax's sexuality and self-identification. Indeed, some students seemed particularly concerned that Dax had taken the time to construct a Web site about Nsync, as though that in and of itself raised a "red flag." For instance, one female student remarked that

> men who do enjoy insync and make [an] ELABORATE website about them, are not completely normal.

Or, as another student put it,

> i think it brings up gender isues bc it is very girly to like boy bands and for this guy to cross that boundary and actually admit he is a fan, is very unusual. i will give him credit, i do think that it takes a lot of courage to admit such an obsession! that is right, obsession. he actually cares so much as to make an entire website devoted to them.

One pair of comments, from a young female poster, is particularly telling along these lines, summarizing several points already made:

> Well . . . I mean Is this more of a personal webpage Im some what confused. The fact that he likes NSYNC is fine I dont think its that big of a deal. The only thing is that he has to say StraightGuys for NSYNC and if hes straight then why does he have to announce it. The same as if he was gay he would need not to say Gayfor NSYNC it just stirs unneeded contravercy and here say, from my opnion. It has nothing to do with a preference in music hes some what sterotying but then again Tis His Own!!:)
>
> I suppose some need to announce it b/c of what others think thats what it boils down to right? I mean at some time in his life he was probably called something derogatory and now he feels the need to stand up against it. Or he has fallen into the stereotype that only gay guys would like boy bands and he feels the need to publiclly announce that he is not part of that.I dont know really b/c i dont know him so I dont want to pass judgment but thats what I got from what his site.

I appreciated this student's understanding of the "trap" of stereotyping, and we had a good discussion about how such stereotypes do not just demonize others (e.g., queers) but are used to support and maintain seemingly "normative" (e.g., straight) identities.

In many other ways, though, the concern that Dax is announcing he is "straight" is itself a problem, the gesture that calls his straightness into question: "if hes straight then why does he have to announce it." Indeed, as Calvin Thomas reminds us, straights do not generally have to "come out of the closet"; they do not have to announce their sexuality since it is *normative* to be straight. Conversely, marking one's *straight* sexuality is *not* without penalty. Some students stated directly their feeling that Dax is "protesting too much" on the site:

> I am going to have to say that the creator of the web-site is having some sexual identity crisis. I mean really, straightboyzforNsync or what ever. I don't know, I think it' a little fishy. I agree with his web site, but he needs to get real with himself.
>
> i thought the website was a little bizarre. the story was strange, the comments in every section were strange . . . i'm not a big fan. and as for the sexuality aspect, why does he feel the need to create something called "straighboyz" (dumb name anyway) but why cant he just create an n'sync website for all sorts of other people instead of limiting it to straight guys . . . seems a little questionable to me.
>
> UMMM . . . This website is WEIRD! I think this guy makes a point too many times to say that he's not gay, and that he likes the band, which to me seems like he really might be gay deep down, and is afraid to say something. I really don't think it's a big deal if a guy likes the band, I know a lot of guys who like them. ????????????

In a follow-up comment to this last posting, one student summarized many other students' general feeling:

> I don't know to me this guy isn't safe with his manhood? i think i read "I'm not gay" or " fag" in this website way to many times! If you like i n'sync great but why make a websit about it?

Interestingly, the word "fag" doesn't appear on the site, Dax never says specifically that he isn't gay, and he really doesn't mark his sexuality explicitly.

Such vociferous questioning of Dax's sexuality suggests a dynamic at play that deserves more attention. I *could* read such comments as questioning my ability to "perform" straightness! Rather, I think the comments serve as useful jumping-off points for provocative discussion. For instance, these self-identified straight kids largely seem to think that being homophobic is "not cool." And that's good. At the same time, many of these students are quick to identify even a hint of homophobia in someone else as potential *queerness*. And, contrary to what I had originally thought, it's not so much liking Nsync that is problematic;

when we examine the comments and when I reconsider classroom discussion, it becomes clear that, for the most part, liking Nsync is *not* the issue; many students seem willing to accept Dax's interest in Nsync at face value, and I had a few young male students say—out loud and proud—that they were Nsync fans. At the same time, Dax's implicit self-identification as "straight"—a rhetorical gesture to forestall questioning of his sexual identity and affix his heterosexuality—actually calls that heterosexuality into question. One of my intentions in creating the Straightboyz4Nsync site was to prompt discussion of homophobia, but it seems that Dax's concern with being read as "gay" is itself read as insecurity about his straightness—perhaps a "questionable" inability to keep his story "straight."

How can we explain this dynamic? Perhaps just bringing up the topic of gayness—or straightness—is itself grounds for questioning one's straightness. But why? Queer theory offers one possible answer. In *Straight with a Twist: Queer Theory and the Subject of Heterosexuality,* Calvin Thomas, a self-proclaimed straight man, uses Judith Butler's notion of performativity to elaborate a queer understanding of "straightness," suggesting, "The terror of being mistaken for a queer dominates the straight mind because this terror *constitutes* the straight mind." More specifically, "according to some queer theorists, heteronormativity, 'straightness as such,' is less a function of other-sexual desire than of the disavowal or abjection of that imagined same-sex desire upon which straightness never ceases to depend" (2000, 27). In other words, heterosexuality as an identity is dependent upon gayness for its social, cultural, political, and personal legibility. Or, as Jonathan Ned Katz (1995) puts it, heterosexuality is an "invention" with a traceable history, dependent on its supposed opposite—queerness—for its very meaningfulness. More radically, heterosexuality must suppress knowledge of this dependence on queerness in order to situate itself as normative; after all, what kind of "norm" would heterosexuality be if it openly acknowledged the queer for its very meaningfulness? So, for a queer theorist such as Thomas, "to profess straightness is to claim an identity within an economy that assumes that one identification can only be purchased at the expense of another" (30). In terms of the Straightboyz4Nsync site, it seems that Dax's calling attention to his straightness simultaneously raised the specter of queerness—a queerness that is supposed to remain suppressed; and such raising of the repressed other rebounds into questioning, doubt.

In light of such theorizing, students' comments seem somewhat homophobic, perhaps a slightly more advanced game of "spot the queer." But they can also be used to introduce other possibilities of discussion, leading students to think about *why* straightness is "unmarked," un-*remark*-able. Indeed, as we talked and wrote about the site, it became apparent that students were not necessarily keen to accept the queer theoretical position that straightness is dependent on an unacknowledged queerness, but I think it was revelatory for all of us to consider that straightness *may* be dependent on not calling it into question. As such, straightness—and its privileges—remain unexamined, normative: it just feels so *normal* because we don't have to think about it.

Once we, as a class, saw how straightness depends in part on a silenced queerness for its existence as an identification, it became easier to see straightness as a "performance," and to spot the ways it is "performed." One final example from the discussion board underscored for students both this performative nature of a straight identity and the silences that surround such a performance. A young male student, perhaps a bit tongue-in-cheek, expressed his own liking of Nsync:

> Yes I must admit Justin Timberlake is the man. He had the sexiest girlfriend in the world. Now he can just do as he pleases and get with supermodels. I wish I lived the lifestyle of JT. The website is ok.

It's hard not to read this posting as simultaneously authentic and sarcastic, with the sarcasm acting as a rhetorical defense mechanism. Also, note that this student does not say he is straight, but rather he performs his straightness by commenting on Justin Timberlake's "sexiest girlfriend in the world." The Web site, though, is just "ok." Again, straightness lies in its performance, not in self-identification.

The student's girlfriend, however, *can* comment about his straightness, and she offered this follow-up post:

> in regards to the site . . . someone that i know . . . really looks up to justin timberlake. he like the clothes he wears, how he sings, as well as his curly hairstyle. He watches all of his videos and likes his ex-girlfriend. he is not at all ashamed of having justin as his idol and rolemodel.

Again, we could read this as playful, but its pedagogical value should not go unremarked. For instance, I questioned the class about this discussion, asking, if the male student is not ashamed of having Justin Timberlake as his "rolemodel," then why doesn't he say so explicitly in his own posting? Again, students here have the opportunity to see not only the rhetorical binds of straightness but also the ways in which one can—and cannot—perform straightness.

A caveat is useful here. Some readers might think that I am misreading Butler's understanding and development of "performance" in her work. My intent is not to mistake "performance" for *chosen* identity representation, much like choosing a set of clothes in the morning: who will I be today? Rather, I firmly believe with Butler that performativity "consists in a reiteration of norms which precede, constrain, and exceed the performer and in that sense cannot be taken as the fabrication of the performer's 'will' or 'choice.'. . . The reduction of performativity to performance would be a mistake" (1993, 234). And I think my students and I were developing, through this exercise, a better sense of how restrictive our identity performances actually are. We see this in comments such as "it is just not the 'norm' with society. Boy bands are seen as gay by society, so when a male likes a boy band they are seen as gay also" and "This is a typical example of what happens when somebody steps out of the 'normal' boundaries: when guys like boy bands they are thought to be gay." This last comment is followed up by the obvious question: "why can't a guy just like a boy band?" Because the performativity of straight masculinity "precede[s], constrain[s], and exceed[s] the performer." Queer theory asks only that we begin acknowledging such performances as available for questioning.

REREADING STRAIGHTNESS

As I reflect on this exercise, a few critical observations come to mind. First, in many ways, the hoax site and discussion board helped me and my students turn a critical lens on "straightness," disrupting my own and my students' sense of the normal so we could question how identities are narrated, life stories constructed, and rhetorics of normalcy and the normative maintained. Specifically, we explored how "straightness" must be performed, and, as Butler would suggest, it must be performed again and again to maintain its seeming "naturalness." As such, we saw how simply labeling or identifying something as "straight" becomes problematic in that the identification itself questions the naturalness of the category, rendering opaque what once was not seen as needing clarification or identification.

This critical awareness alone, I believe, powerfully demonstrated to me the need to develop a pedagogy of *sexual literacy* with students—or a more critical way to discuss how sexuality is constructed and performed rhetorically. Indeed, students began to develop a sense of how narrations of identity depend as much on certain silences as they do on certain annunciations. In this sense, I think students developed a crucial understanding of an important dimension of being literate; that is, what is *not* articulated shapes our perception of the meaningful as much as what *is* articulated. Specifically, that which passes as the norm is often "unremarked" and hence never brought up for discussion—until, that is, the performance of the norm reveals its own constructedness. In that case, *much* discussion often ensues, and we have the opportunity to see how intense conversation around the normative is designed in many ways to bolster or reassert a normative sense, a normative shared understanding.

Second, the use of follow-up discussions was crucial in interrogating student responses and interpretations. In "Queer Pedagogy and Its Strange Techniques," Deborah P. Britzman suggests that "the beginnings of a queer pedagogy" might lie in an "ethical concern for one's own reading practices and what these have to do with the imagining of sociality as more than an effect of the dominant conceptual order" (1998, 67). Did students learn to "read" with the "ethical concern" Britzman proposes—imagining "sociality as more than an effect of the dominant conceptual order"? That is, did they become aware of how their own perceptions, predispositions, and *assumptions of what is the norm* come under scrutiny? I believe so—but only in that *steady* and *sustained* examination of our combined online and in-class discussions revealed to all of us some surprising insights into the silences and oversights that bolster our sense of the "norm."

In terms of fostering productive discussions about such normalization, I wonder if presenting students with images—and experiences—of not just "outing" but of "closeting" might accomplish the goal of talking about how discourses of fear, prejudice, and homophobia impact the lives and self-narrations of many queers, and even some straights who don't quite fit the "normative" models of masculinity (or femininity). These discourses are about refusing to speak, about maintaining silence—and we need to understand better why some people are invited to tell us their stories and why others are not. What norms condition our narrations? Such might perform considerable work toward developing useful sexual literacies. It took a lot of courage, as I have pointed out, for my straight male student to "out" himself as an Nsync fan; a closer examination of the closet he constructed to hide that fandom might be revealing. More broadly, sharing with students a bit more openly my own process of constructing the Straightboyz4Nsync site, borrowing as I did from my own very personal experience of inhabiting the closet at various points throughout my life, might have produced a more intense and rewarding discussion about sexuality, discourse, and the public construction and performance of selfhood. If I use this exercise again, I will certainly explore such issues, perhaps "outing" my own many "closeting" moves—both personally and teacherly—and risking them for some (hopefully) productive discussion.[11]

Other thoughts are worth considering as well, particularly when we reflect on the *intersection* of identities—sexuality, gender, race, and class. Of course, we were looking at a white guy grappling with his interest in other white guys. I fully recognize that other cultural situations, as they are inflected and shaped by issues of race, ethnicity, and class, might have led to very different discussions about the construction of normalcy, straightness, and sexual identity. And speaking of construction, in first sitting down to create Straightboyz4Nsync I realized that I was attempting to craft a "straight" persona, or perform a "straightboy" identity. All sorts of interesting questions began to pop up as I worked on the site. For instance, could I "pass" as a straightboy? Could I use the identity-masking features of the Web, as many people do, to create an online persona that is *not* me, and that others would accept as "legitimate"?

But maybe this question of "legitimacy" is the point: to question the seeming "naturalness" of identity, to use the widely acknowledged ability of the Web to simultaneously mask and construct online identities to question the construction of identity itself. In "On the Myth of Sexual Orientation: Field Notes from the Personal, Pedagogical, and Historical Discourses of Identity," Margot Francis suggests: "Perhaps the instability of the term *queer* can pose the production of *normalization* as the problem. In this context the interrogation of binaries themselves— normal/deviant, biological/social, straight/gay—can open up quite a different approach" (1998, 73). And I think this is exactly what the Straightboyz4Nsync site began to do: pose the production of *normalization*—particularly on the Web—as a "problem."

Indeed, I find the work of cultural materialists particularly relevant here, especially as such theorists turn our attention to how representations bolster the norms that idealize and naturalize certain kinds of sexualities and sexual practices and attempt to foreclose upon the possibility of imagining other kinds of intimacies and intimate relationships. Writing in *Cultural Politics—Queer Reading*, Alan Sinfield summarizes the cultural materialist perspective this way: "texts have political projects, and should not be allowed to circulate in the world today on the assumption that their representations of class, race, ethnicity, gender and sexuality are simply authoritative. We don't mind texts having political projects, of course; we believe that every representation, with its appeal for recognition—It is like *this*, isn't it?—is political. But we think the politics should be up for discussion, and that textual analysis should address it" (1994, 38).

Part of the project of becoming literate, then, is to understand the different ways in which the representations that surround us (in media, advertisements, etc.), and that we even create at times (of ourselves as we tell our own life stories) rest on certain assumptions—assumptions about intimate aspects of our lives, such as sex and sexuality, that have been given to us by our culture at large. Sinfield explains at length:

> The dominant ideology tends to constitute subjectivities that will find "natural" its view of the world (hence its dominance); this happens in subcultures also, but in ways that may validate dissident subjectivities. . . . "In acquiring one's conception of the world one belongs to a particular grouping which is that of all the social elements which share the same mode of thinking and acting," Antonio Gramsci observes. It is through such sharing—through interaction with others who are engaged with compatible preoccupations—that one may develop a plausible alternative subject position. To be sure, everyone is constructed by the dominant ideology through, we may say, the state apparatuses. But ideology, Althusser stresses, is lived in day-to-day interactions, and those socialize us also into subcultures of class, ethnicity, gender and sexuality, which may be in some respects oppositional; or at least negotiated (1994, 66).

From the perspective of critical sexuality studies, that "dominant ideology" is clearly heteronormative and heterosexist, suggesting—even demanding—that all of us align our intimate and personal lives along axes that value monogamous heterosexual reproductive sex and sexualities. Becoming aware of and being willing to understand critically to the narratives, stories, representations, legal codes, and ways of speaking that naturalize the heteronormative and bolster it is to become, in my view, sexually literate. It may also be life saving. For instance, as only one example among many possible, English professor Beth Loffreda's *Losing Matt Shepard* (2000) paints a complex portrait of how the town of Laramie dealt with the brutal, homophobically motivated murder of a young college student. Loffreda's work highlights the "real-world" dimensions not just of homophobia but also, I believe, of a failure of literacy, in that Shepard's murderers could articulate their discomfort with the homoerotic only through the torture and slaying of another human being.

In this sense, then, I believe the "Straightboyz" exercise contributed to students' development of sexual literacy in that, to borrow again from Brian Street, if we are to understand literacy as an "ideological practice [that] opens up a potentially rich field of inquiry into the nature of culture and power," then exploring how heterosexuality becomes "composed" as a norm is an important exercise in literacy development (2001, 437). As students read the "Straightboyz" site, they were beginning to question critically the narration of heterosexuality, of how someone comes to compose his straightness, and of how the narrative expectations for such "composure" are intimately tied to normative senses of what "straight" is—and is not. As such, this exercise was one of beginning to see the strong relationship between the stories we tell about ourselves sexually and the dominant, normalizing tropes of identity through which power circulates in our culture. Reading "Straightboyz" critically, then, offered a chance to develop greater sexual literacy, a more sophisticated way of understanding the relationship between the stories we tell about ourselves and their connection to knowledge and power, particularly as processed through sexuality.

With such thinking in mind, with what seems an ethical call to interrogate with students the discourses of sexuality and develop with them a more sophisticated sexual literacy, I must ask myself if this pedagogical exercise has a *critical* payoff in terms of it promoting shifts in attitude about queerness—and straightness, for that matter. Judith Butler argues that "there is no guarantee that exposing the naturalized status of heterosexuality will lead to its subversion" (1993, 231). Regardless of whether or not I might want to *subvert* heterosexuality (and I don't, really—most of the time), I can't help but ask if Straightboyz4Nsync is *more* than just a Webbed-up exercise in reading through a queer "lens." I hope so. How might I be able to tell? How might it lead to students *not* taking their heterosexuality—and its many privileges in our homophobic culture— for granted? Susanne Luhmann suggests that productive "learning becomes a process of risking the self, much like Foucault . . . suggests: 'the target . . . is not to discover what we are, but to refuse what we are.'" (1998, 151). When one of my straight male students started to "risk" himself by "coming out of the closet" as an Nsync fan, I could see a student willing *not* to take his heterosexuality for granted, willing to adopt a risky position, willing to identify with what many other students thought of as a suspect, *queer* performance of straightness. What such identification might lead to, I cannot tell, but I also can't help but think of this as personal progress.

I also count it as useful progress in the development of *rhetorical* skills and sensitivity. In the course, students gained greater fluency in reading representations of identity so that they were asking critical questions about the *ideological* work that such representations do. They were examining closely how some of the dominant constructs of identity are narrated and performed, as well as how such performances become naturalized to *suspend* critical thinking about them. Such is certainly part of the development of a *critical literacy*. But moreover, exercises in which students are writing collectively provide spaces in which they have the opportunity to challenge one another's thinking and renegotiate *in writing* commonly held assumptions and biases.

Along these lines, I can re-vision the foregoing exercise through the lens of Bruce McComiskey's work *Teaching Composition as a Social Process* to see how an analysis of the dissemination and reproduction of norms in our culture is a significant (if overlooked) part of any given rhetorical situation. Specifically, McComiskey connects writing-process pedagogies with political critique by emphasizing the ways in which both writing and the creation of social values are themselves processes. As such, "social-process pedagogy" is invested in having students analyze the processes through which "culture" is produced, disseminated, and consumed. McComiskey explains: "Social-process rhetorical inquiry . . . is a method of invention that usually manifests itself in composition classes as a set of heuristic questions based on the cycle of cultural production, contextual distribution, and critical consumption. While composition studies, I believe, has extensively explored the cognitive and social processes by which discourse is produced, the processes of distribution and consumption (and the entire cyclical process of production, distribution, and consumption) have been largely neglected. The integration of these rhetorical processes is the very function of social-process rhetorical inquiry" (2000, 54).

Although his language is heady, McComiskey rightly sees a connection between the cycle of production ("cultural production, contextual distribution, and critical consumption") and a writing process involving production of texts, critical examination of writerly and readerly contexts, and a developing intertextual sensitivity to how texts can be combined, recombined, revised, and read against one another and individually. In other words, the dissemination, reception, and revision of "texts" and "values" offer intriguing parallels that can be profitably examined in the composition classroom. Students participating in the "Straightboyz" exercise had just such a social-process pedagogical opportunity in that they could critically examine not only a representation of heterosexuality but see, with other students, how that representation was "consumed"—by other students. Making an analysis of that consumption *and* putting insights generated out of that analysis into discussion highlighted the full cycle of the rhetorical process through which meaning—and values and norms—are produced, disseminated, and maintained. In the process (no pun intended), placing different narrations of straightness against one another allowed for a recombination of "social texts" of identity that opened a space to critique dominant narrations and begin to think differently about the relationships among sexuality, sexual identity, discourse, and the power of norms—a good step in the right direction, I think, toward developing a capacious sexual literacy.

Inevitably, as hinted at throughout this chapter, we could touch in this exercise on only a few dimensions of such a sexual literacy—in this case, focusing specifically on sexual orientation (and specifically heterosexual) identity. Issues of sexuality are thickly embedded in issues of gender, a thick concept calling forth numerous enabling, competing, and ideologically vexing discourses. In the next chapter, I will explore more carefully what contemporary theories of sexuality, particularly transgender theories, have to teach us about the relationship of *gender* to narrations of sex and sexuality that circulate in contemporary Anglo-American culture.

4

TRANSGENDER RHETORICS
Sex and Gender

On the first day of a writing-intensive honors course called "Contemporary Masculinities," I brought in for discussion a couple of recent essays by Patrick (formerly Pat) Califia-Rice entitled "Family Values" and "Trannyfags Unzipped." In these articles, Califia-Rice discusses his transitioning from female to male, his relationship with another FtM (female-to-male) transsexual, and their decision to have a child together. As can be imagined, the essays sparked much discussion among this group of intelligent, mostly white, mostly straight college-aged students from largely middle-class backgrounds. Califia-Rice's life seemed strange to them, even as they applauded his willingness to undergo hormone treatments and suffer the taunts and harassment of those who do not understand his life.

Throughout our discussion, we kept returning to a deceptively simple set of questions: What *is* a man? Is Patrick Califia-Rice a "real" man? How can we tell? The majority of students—all but one—were willing to accept Califia-Rice as a man, despite his long history as a self-described dyke. Part of what students focused on in supporting their claim that Califia-Rice is indeed a man is Califia-Rice's own writing about his body. He writes both movingly and provocatively about transitioning from a female to a male body: "I am going through my own metamorphosis. My hips are smaller, my muscle mass is growing, and every day it seems like there's more hair on my face and body. My voice is deeper, and my sex drive has given me newfound empathy with the guys who solicit hookers for blow jobs. When I think that I can continue with this process—get chest surgery and pass as male—I feel happier than at any other point in my life. And when I think that something will stop me, I become very depressed" (2000).

Given such a description, such self-narration about a highly conscious and purposeful self-fashioning, students felt compelled to accept that Califia-Rice is indeed a man. In the process of the discussion, though, we had to puzzle over how gender comes to be defined in relation to biology, cultural norms, social roles, and even political assumptions about the organization of the species. Such questioning, often prompted by the writing of trans theorists and activists such as Califia-Rice, cuts to the core of the relationship among gender, sexuality, bodies, and politics. For instance, Leslie Feinberg, in *Transgender Warriors,* wonders, "Why is the categorization of sex a legal question at all? And why are those categories policed? Why did these laws arise in the first place?" (1996, 62). I think these are good questions that ask students—and instructors—to trace the genealogy of gender as a construct of power and knowledge in our society, of a powerful organizing and disciplining set of discourses that fundamentally shape our senses of self.

As I've considered the work of other trans theorists and writers, such as Califia-Rice and Feinberg, I have been shifting my consideration of gender and its composition not only to include trans voices but, in many ways, to ground my discussion of gender with my students in trans theories of gender. The result, as I hope to show in this chapter, is an approach to thinking about gender that is invigorating, critical, and insightful—one that opens up new vistas for students in considering the intersections between gender, the body, and the body politic. It is also an approach that I have come to think of as central to the development of sexual literacy in that it provides critical engagement with some of the fundamental ways in which we think of ourselves as *gendered* beings. Without a doubt, gender is a compelling, even controlling construct in our narration of identity to ourselves and others. An attempt to understand how our narrations of gender are formed, how they circulate socially and politically, and how they can be productively challenged when found to be too constricting should be an important component in becoming literate about the discourses of gender in which we are immersed and enmeshed.

To unpack in the following pages the usefulness of trans theories to the teaching of writing about gender, sexuality, and identity, I want to review a pedagogical experiment in which I attempted to take advantage of some "trans thinking" to spark in my students more provocative reflection on the construction, articulation, and representation of gender and sexuality. My goal in this chapter is twofold: first, to demonstrate how transgender theories can inspire pedagogical methods that complement feminist compositionist pedagogical approaches to understanding the narration of gender as a social construct; and second, to suggest how such theories might usefully *expand* and *extend*—for ourselves and for our students—our analysis of the stories we tell about gender. In general, I want to approach a deceptively simple question—*What is the story we tell about gender?*—and then discuss some of the possibilities that trans theorists bring us and our students for understanding that story in some provocative and complex ways. In approaching this question, I believe we are thickening our discussion and understanding of sexual literacy by considering critically how gender is intertwined rhetorically in narrations of self, particularly at the level of gender—which many consider a fundamental, even unquestionable dimension of identity and being. I also want to argue that trans theorists and pedagogical activities inspired by them can remind us to complement our understanding of gender performance with a sense of gender as a material and embodied reality. Such approaches may offer us our richest approaches yet to help-ing students develop a critical sexual literacy that questions the relation-ships among gender, the body, identity, and sociocultural power.

PEDAGOGIES OF POSSIBILITY: TRANS APPROACHES TO THE RHETORICS OF GENDER

In the introduction to this book, I briefly explored some feminist approaches to composition, pointing out how many such approaches have enabled and given us an entrance point into thinking more com-plexly about the narrations of gender that circulate in our society. In many ways, trans theorists, activists, and writers are also deeply invested in engendering in others a critical awareness of gender and in promot-ing a more capacious understanding about what gender means—and could mean—as a construct that is simultaneously deeply personal and profoundly political. Certainly, "transgender" can be a tricky word to define, and it is often used as a "catch-all" category for a range of those who "play with" or "transgress" gender norms, including cross-dressers, gender-fuckers, transvestites, drag kings/queens, and transsexuals.[12] But the aims of many self-identified trans activists and theorists are to create cracks in the monolithic structure of gender identity and to search for wiggle room in what William Pollack has aptly termed the "gender strait-jacket" (1998, 40–43). Trans activist and author Leslie Feinberg says in hir book *Trans Liberation* that the transgender movement is one of "mas-culine females and feminine males, cross-dressers, transsexual men and women, intersexuals born on the anatomical sweep between female and male, gender-blenders, many other sex and gender-variant people, and our significant others. All told, we expand understanding of how many ways there are to be a human being" (1998, 5; emphasis added).

How does such "expansion" take place? Leslie Feinberg argues that we need to acknowledge both the presence and material lives of those who are not born either specifically male or female *and* understand, more generally, the restrictive nature of concepts such as male/female and masculinity/femininity for *all* people. First, speaking of hir experience as a transgendered individual, Feinberg reminds us, "Millions of females and millions of males in this country do not fit the cramped compartments of gender that we have been taught are 'natural' and 'normal.' For many of us, the words *woman* or *man*, *ma'am* or *sir*, *she*, or *he*—in and of themselves—do not total up the sum of our identities or of our oppressions. Speaking for myself, my life only comes into focus when the word *transgender* is added to the equation" (1998, 7).

Acknowledging the presence of the transgendered is useful not only for understanding those who are differently gendered or whose presentation or experience of gender falls outside our "norms," but also for helping us interrogate the constructs of gender that we often take for granted as "natural" or "normal." Specifically, Feinberg notes: "Just as most of us grew up with only the concepts of *woman* and *man*, the terms *feminine* and *masculine* are the only two tools most people have to talk about the complexities of gender expression" (1998, 8). Part of the transgender project, then, is not just to alert others to the presence of differently gendered people or those who experience their gender in ways other than strictly masculine or feminine, but to examine critically how gender limits our potential sense of self: "Our struggle will also help expose some of the harmful myths about what it means to be a woman or a man that have compartmentalized and distorted your life, as well as mine. Trans liberation has meaning for you—no matter how you define or express your sex or your gender" (5). It strikes me that the exploration of "harmful myths" is a key part of a sexual literacy project, one that undertakes a close analysis of (with the ultimate aim of provoking productive resistance to) controlling and normalizing narratives and tropes of gender.

Many trans theorists have been inspired to think along such lines after considering the work of queer theorist Judith Butler, whose notion of gender performativity has been a useful, if contentious, approach to thinking critically about gender.[13] Butler argues in *Gender Trouble* for a reconsideration of feminism's critique of gender: "There is no gender identity behind the expressions of gender; . . . identity is performatively constituted by the very 'expressions' that are said to be its results'" (1990, 25). The result of such performances for Butler is the denaturalization of "gender" as a category; gender is not necessarily an essential and natural given, but rather a sociocultural construct whose repeated performances—as masculinity and femininity—have come to appear and seem natural. David Gauntlett summarizes well how many activists and writers, including some trans theorists, have appropriated Butler's notion of performativity to envision expansive possibilities for challenging the norms of gender: "Butler calls for subversive action in the present: 'gender trouble'—the mobilization, subversive confusion, and proliferation of genders—and therefore identity. Butler argues that we all put on a gender performance, whether traditional or not, anyway, and so it is not a question of whether to *do* a gender performance, but what form that performance will take. By choosing to be different about it, we might work to change gender norms and the binary understanding of masculinity and femininity" (1998).

Along such lines, Kate Bornstein, a prominent and popular trans activist and writer, argues in numerous texts, such as *My Gender Workbook* and *Gender Outlaw,* that gender identity is a construct in need of deep— and playful—questioning. Her *Workbook* offers a delicious parody of the self-help genre to encourage readers to query the conventional ways in which they think of gender. Specifically, she claims as her goal the following: "Providing the public discourse with the possibility of subjective proof that gender is neither natural nor essential, but rather the performance of self-expression within any dynamic relationship" (1998, 21).

As such, trans activists such as Bornstein often perform a pedagogical task comparable to that of many feminist compositionists: they seek an expansive notion of gender, a questioning of restrictive norms and categories, and an understanding of how gender is used as a politically and personally normalizing category. They promote, in short, greater literacy about gender. In fact, to highlight the *pedagogical* dimension of trans activism, Pat Califia (pre–sex change) concludes her powerful book *Sex Changes: The Politics of Transgenderism* with a series of provocative questions about gender—questions that I argue can challenge our students', as well as our own, sense of gender and its personal and political power: "If you could change your sex as effortlessly in reality as you can in virtual reality, and change it back again, wouldn't you like to try it at least once? Who do you think you might become? What is that person able to do that you don't think you can do now? What would you have to give up to become oppositely sexed? What would change about your politics, clothing, food preferences, sexual desires, social habits, driving style, job, body language, behavior on the street? Are you able to imagine becoming a hybrid of your male and female self, keeping the traits that you value and abandoning the ones that are harmful?" (1997, 277). Such writing has prompted me to ask students comparable questions, to help them explore and interrogate the sociocultural articulation of gender, as well as its connection to the sociopolitical matrix in our culture.

Originally, when considering using trans-related materials in my composition courses, I introduced students to several trans-themed Web sites, such as Leslie Feinberg's homepage, Transgender Warrior, at http://www.transgenderwarrior.org/. Such sites offered quite a bit of useful fodder for discussion with students, for a number of reasons. First, trans sites frequently deconstruct the male/female binary—one of the most pervasive modes of meaning making in our culture. Second, in deconstructing this binary, trans sites powerfully reveal gender as a social construction—as a narration that rhetorically, and politically, uses gender to maintain categories, roles, and knowledges that delimit and police our bodies and identities. Further, in examining the stories that trans activists tell about themselves, we witness the construction of counternarratives, alternative modes of identity construction, and a number of creative rhetorical moves that show how narratives of personal experience can be used to query a number of personal and sociopolitical issues. For instance, in telling a story about something as seemingly simple as using a public restroom, trans writers such as Feinberg reveal how "clear cut" our social expectations of gender performance are; gender-ambiguous individuals often face significant harassment, even bodily harm, if they are perceived as using the "wrong" restroom, which are almost exclusively designated "male" or "female."

In many ways, though, I found this approach—exposure to and discussion of trans-related Web sites—to be critically limited and thus pedagogically unsatisfying. It seemed easy at times for students to "dismiss" trans people as pretty much wholly "other," their concerns, insights, and critiques unrelated to those of my "traditionally" gendered students. Who cares if a few freaks have trouble using public toilets? Given such responses, I wanted a more provocative way to challenge our understanding of the composition of gender. Leslie Feinberg writes that "gender is the poetry each of us makes out of the language we are taught" (1998, 10); with such a thought in mind, I wanted to work with students to examine that language a bit more carefully, a bit more deeply. Moreover, I wanted to work with students on exploring, as trans theorists *and* feminist compositionists advocate, a sense of agency and possibility with respect to gender; or, as Feinberg puts it, "we need more language than just feminine/masculine, straight/gay, either/or. Men are not from Mars and women are not from Venus" (28).

The pedagogical questions I posed myself, then, were: How do we find such a language? How do develop a more capacious discourse of gender? And how is such related to the development of personal and politically efficacious sexual literacies?

TRANSPEDAGOGY: AN EXPERIMENT IN TRANSITIONING

To capture some of the critical "gender poetry" that Feinberg talks about, I took a clue from Califia's comments about virtual gender switching, and I designed an in-class writing exercise in which students were prompted to write from the perspective of another gender.14 In concocting this exercise, I sensed that I was in risky territory, potentially opening up not new possibilities for thinking about gender, but a much more sexist and stereotypical can of worms. But I wanted to know, and I wanted to examine with students, some possible answers to Califia's questions—as well as metacritically reflect on the process of gender/sex switching, even if only virtually, and what it might tell us about the narration and construction of gender in our society. So, to approach Califia's questions, I decided to use some creative freewriting as a way to help students think about the questions in an engaging, fun, and hopefully insightful manner. Indeed, I've found that, in composing creative works, students often write more openly, willingly, and even critically about issues that concern and interest them, and I hoped to use some of this creative and critical energy to think with them about gender.

Specifically, I adapted Will Hochman's (1998) "paired-fiction writing" exercise, in which pairs of students collaboratively construct fictional stories through a series of teacher-led prompts In the original exercise, the instructor asks a pair of students to compose, separately, the setting for a story. After a set time of freewriting (perhaps ten to fifteen minutes), the pair exchanges writing (or swaps seats at a computer terminal) and each is then instructed to write about a character for the setting that his or her partner composed. The students compose directly in their partner's draft, creating one text with two authors. After another switch, students have to concoct a dilemma or crisis for the character in the setting, and then, after one final switch, students have to resolve the conflict. My particular "twist" on paired-fiction writing involved having students in a second-quarter first-year writing course compose their stories from what they perceived to be the experiences and assumptions of someone of a different gender. I began by pairing students by gender; men worked with men, and women with women. About twenty students participated, producing ten complete narratives. All students were visibly traditionally gendered, and none identified themselves as transgendered or transsexual.

I used this particular creative writing assignment for several reasons. First, the resulting stories are almost always fascinating and generally very clever; students are surprised that they are able to enter into one another's texts with great ease, and they frequently find the challenge of posing and resolving fictional crises challenging but fun. Besides introducing students to some of the basic dimensions of narrative and storytelling, this activity often reveals for students some of the stereotypes, clichés, and familiar tropes upon which many narratives depend for their intelligibility and accessibility to a variety of audiences.

Further, I decided to use a narrative-based exercise because many feminist compositionists have argued, persuasively, that examining narrations of experience, even fictionalized experiences, can be quite revealing about gender constructs and their connections to larger sociocultural and political matrices, particularly normalizing discourses about gender and identity. In fact, analyzing experience—its contents, its narration and representation, its genealogy—has been a central pedagogical practice of many feminist-inflected approaches to composition, often prompting students to produce and analyze their own experiences through personal narratives.[15] "Reading and Writing Differences: The Problematic of Experience" by Min-Zhan Lu has been a particularly inspiring essay for both its theoretical sophistication and its lucidity in showing what a feminist analysis can bring to examining narrations of experience. Lu maintains: "The feminist dictum that the personal is political has taught us to recognize the centrality of the gendered experience in the production of knowledge" (1998, 241), and she argues that inviting students to consider carefully and critically the content of their own "gendered experience" is a crucial part in understanding the relationship between gender and "knowledge," or the creation of socially sanctioned and enforced norms. Such seems very comparable to the development of what I have been calling sexual literacy throughout this book. Indeed, for Lu, the pedagogical task at hand is to design writing prompts that will invite and encourage students to undertake this work: "We need assignments that ask students to explore the analytic possibilities of experience by locating the experience that grounds their habitual approach to differences; by sketching the complex discursive terrain out of and in which the self habitually speaks; by investigating how that terrain delimits our understanding of differences along lines of race, class, sex, and gender; and by exploring personal and social motivations for transforming one's existing self-location in the process of rereading and rewriting" (243) .

The result, Lu hopes, is that "experience should motivate us to care about another's differences and should disrupt the material conditions that have given rise to it" (1998, 239). With this theoretical backdrop, Lu then traces in her essay how she has attempted to craft such assignments by narrating her work in teaching and having students write about provocative texts by Sandra Cisneros and Gloria Anzaldua by filtering the issues raised in those texts through students' own "personal history" (247).

With such work inspiring me, I hoped to explore the following with my students:

1. I wanted to evoke some of Feinberg's gender poetry, to see the uses to which my writing students were putting their developing language skills in the construction of gender. If virtually trans-sexed, even if only for an hour, what stories would my students tell? What poetry would they make out of the language of gender they had been taught?

2. I wanted to "test" with students Butler's notion that "There is no gender identity behind the expressions of gender; . . . identity is performatively constituted by the very 'expressions' that are said to be its results." This is nearly a commonplace in gender and queer studies, but I wanted to probe with my students what such a formulation actually means. Specifically, does "performativity" capture, as a concept, the complex set of representations, identifications, projections, subjectifications, and even immiserations that "gender" encompasses?

3. I was also curious to see if anyone would or could, in Califia's words, "imagine becoming a hybrid of your male and female self." If so, if choosing to be *different* about gender, perhaps, as

David Gauntlett wrote, "we might work to change gender norms and the binary understanding of masculinity and femininity."

4. And, finally, what kinds of important literacies about gender and sex could be developed through such an exercise, through playing with the genres of autobiography to explore gender as a normative/normalizing force?

How did students respond to the exercise? They nearly unanimously found it "fun," "easy," and "great." Comments collected immediately after completing the exercise are intriguing:

> It wasn't really weird writing from another gender's point of view (F).
>
> I like writing fiction because you can go where ever you want to with the stories. There [are] no limits or anything holding you back (F).
>
> . . . the story is always moving in some new direction (M).

While I agree that the exercise was "fun," some of the most pedagogically interesting dimensions of the exercise opened up in the reflective discussion following it. As we read aloud and discussed some of the stories as a class, we began to see some dominant trends in how students composed (and composed about) gender—trends that suggest both a reliance on rather sexist stereotypes in thinking about gender and a sense that gender is much more than just a sense of role or "performance"; rather, like many trans theorists, the students' stories reveal a complex, if intuitive, sense of gender as embodied. Such insights, as I will argue below, suggest that this trans-inspired pedagogy opens up some exciting ways for thinking with students about gender and its composition. With that in mind, let's examine some of the stories to unpack some of these directions and insights.[16]

GENDER POETRY: STUDENTS WRITING, STUDENTS TRANSITIONING

Two stories, "Unsafe" and "Mr. Football," deploy some of the more simplistic yet pervasive gender stereotypes in our culture—feminine insecurity and masculine idiocy. Indeed, my earlier use of quotation marks around "women" and "men" indicates that students were clearly composing in stereotypes—often broad ones—and they were reliant upon clichés of gender and broad assumptions about masculinity and femininity in the crafting of their narratives. For instance, in "Unsafe," Sarah is a new student at Berkeley who is "terrified of large cities" and who has been told that her "beautiful looks can get me anywhere I want." She's lonely, having a hard time adjusting, and feels that she "will always feel unsafe in my home," despite the new security system installed by her landlord. In contrast, the most distinguishing feature of "Mr. Football" is that he has "a great 8–pack and well-defined muscles." He's a stereotypical jock with the requisite low IQ; in the story, he finds himself spellbound by the beauty of a jellyfish, only to be stung by it, resulting in an injury that will, fantastically, take all summer to heal. And heal he must, for "[i]f he doesn't play football he won't be able to afford school. His scholarship pays for all of his school needs." With such stereotypes, the male authors in the former story depict a young woman as frightened and helpless, and the female authors in the latter story poke fun of the muscle-bound idiocy of a "macho" man. As you can imagine, just reading and discussing these stories in class prompted quite a consideration of how stereotypes of gender persist and circulate in our culture; such stereotypes are generally tied to narrations of gender, with which these students are obviously familiar. Rehearsing them, particularly having the "other gender" acknowledge them in their stories, sparked much recognition of how trivializing, pernicious, and even damaging such gender narrations can be.

Two other stories, a bit longer and more detailed, are noteworthy for their commonality, specifically their deployment of an "innocence punished" trope—a more complex yet still stereotypical narration of female gender. In "Scarlet" and "Amanda," written each by two young men, the young women depicted are as every bit as "innocent," even naive, as Sarah in the earlier story "Unsafe." The critical difference here, though, is that Scarlet and Amanda compromise their original innocence to "fit in." They become, at least to the outside world, more than the little girls they are originally on the inside, and they are duly punished—in often horrifying ways, including prison time and misery. For instance, Scarlet has been involved in an underworld of drugs and murder, while Amanda, in order to finance her college education, becomes a drug dealer. In a way, their "performances" in these stories are a masking of their original innocence so they can enter the supposedly (and stereotypically) dangerous world of men:

> [Scarlet] is a very intimidating woman and she is afraid that if she does not step up to the challenge with this attractive man that she is very fond of, then she will be looked at differently.

Amanda came to one realization during her time in the ghetto; you only survive if you can fit into a society.

The performances of toughness, though, fail, and both suffer profound loss—perhaps as a result of their gender transgression: they hide and betray their feminine innocence. While we can certainly read these stories as instances of misogyny, even an interlocking mix of sexism and racism in the case of "Amanda," I would also suggest that these are stories about their authors' masculinity, or sense of being "male." For instance, the men in the stories (drug dealers and the like) are hardly models of success. But more tellingly, I think we can detect a bit of projection in the boys' crafting of their female characters: the main characters, for instance, fear not fitting in, not being "tough enough." As such, perhaps the young men's writing is actually a reading of the impossibility of masculinity, of achieving an identity as a "real man."

Two final stories, "The Little Dream Girl" and "Turnabout," are, I think, among the most sophisticated. Some stereotyping persists, but it's put to different and more complex uses. "The Little Dream Girl," written by two young men, depicts a rather strong, independent-minded high school female athlete, Ashley, who breaks out of the feminine mold set by Sarah in "Unsafe." She's bold, tries hard, faces failure, but never gives up. Hers is ultimately a story of success. That would be fine—if the narrative weren't also a thinly veiled reading and critique of my course. You can hear the metacritique in the narrative through its references to "impromptu writing" exercises and a writing assignment on feminism, which the students were working on at the time. In fact, the male writers target the writing of a "paper about feminism" as the source of Ashley's potential unhappiness with just settling down with a man; she'll want a career instead: "Because after she wrote a paper about feminism, she sees herself as wanting an impressive career." I think we can easily read some anxiety about feminism here, particularly in the snide tone that pops up here and there in the narrative ("All went well for the little dream girl from Edgewood, Nebraska."). But, to the writers' credit, they allow Ashley to succeed—even if she is only a "little dream girl." The other story, "Turnabout," written by two young women, is a wonderful revenge fantasy in which a selfish young man battles within himself about how to break up with his clingy girlfriend, on whom he is cheating. In a surprise twist at the end of the story, however, we find out that the clingy girlfriend has been cheating on him. The female authors read (and write) the clingy girlfriend as a *man's* mistaken deployment of a stereotype that comes back to surprise him—and us. The boy muses, "I don't want to break her heart but I don't care much for her anymore either"; but, by the end of the narrative, we discover, with the narrator, that the girlfriend "also had something to tell me . . . she slept with my best friend as well." As such, both stories parody the stereotypes they narrate, creating, I believe, some intelligent criticism along the way.

What do such stories suggest about the narration of gender among these students?

First, all of the stories deploy significant stereotypes, which shouldn't be surprising. In some ways, the writing situation—creation of "on the spot" narratives—called for stereotypes, familiar tropes, even clichés. I don't think it's a leap, though, to suggest that these gender stereotypes represent significant ways in which and through which students know, approach, and attempt to understand one another. As such, pointing out the more vicious or insidious stereotypes can be enlightening to them, and we had productive discussions about the stereotypes deployed in these stories. Indeed, many students were surprised at how consistently, even misogynistically, they performed unflattering characterizations of one another, based solely on gender.

At the same time, some students displayed a willingness to read the stereotypes critically, working the norms, as it were, to create resistant readings—and performances—of self and other. Even a story such as "Mr. Football," for all of its clichés of the dumb, muscle-bound, hyper-masculine jock, might signal some not unjust revenge, a bit of critical "reverse stereotyping." The dumb blond meets the even dumber jock—a meeting made more intriguing if you know that the two authors of "Mr. Football" are intelligent young women who just happen to be blond. In a more sophisticated vein, "Little Dream Girl" worries over the construction of a "politically correct" gender performance: the strong, independent woman. The story queries both this emerging stereotype and, in performing it a bit snidely, attempts to critique my perceived agenda in (perhaps) calling it forth, or inviting it to be performed in these narratives. As such, in writing and then examining the narratives, I was asking students to interrogate the "performativity" of gender—and we did.

I must admit, though, that the "gender poetry" that my students created in their narrations hardly seems transgendered, reifying instead some of the more insidious tropes of gender expression and even, in one instance, subtly but snidely deriding a fairly progressive gender performance. In my students' hands, initially at least, men *are* from Mars and women, Venus. But as I thought more about the exercise and my students' stories, I began to focus a bit more on the "transitioning" that I asked students to perform—a shift they undertook in writing from a differently gendered perspective. Certainly, in no way am I suggesting that my students experienced what it is like to be transsexual or that their narrations remotely approached the lived experience of transitioning—in body and psyche—as a transsexual from one gender or sex to another. Virtually assuming another gender's perspective, or what you *think* is another gender's perspective, for one hour in a classroom may be instructive about many things, but it does not a transsexual make. Still, I think that some recent work in transgenderism in general and transsexuality in particular offers interesting metaphors and theoretical standpoints to help us understand, and to help students understand, some of the complexities of the construction, articulation, and representation of gender in our culture.

How so? We know the stereotype of transsexuality: a woman or man feels trapped in the "wrong body" and thus seeks sexual-reassignment surgery to correct nature's "mistake." Recent writing about transsexuality, though, offers a much more complex understanding of the phenomenon and process, as well as useful insights into the ways in which the performance of gender is *embodied*. In "Transsexuality: The Postmodern Body and/as Technology," transsexual activist and theorist Susan Stryker argues: "The transsexual body as cyborg, as a technologization of identity, presents critical opportunities similar to those offered by the camera. Just as the camera offers a means for externalizing and examining a particular way of constructing time and space, the transsexual body—in the process of its transition from one sex to another—*renders visible the culturally specific mechanisms of achieving gendered embodiment*. It becomes paradigmatic of the gendering process, functioning . . . as 'a meaning machine for the production of ideal type'" (2000, 592; emphasis added).

I think we can see such "embodiment" in my students' "cyborg" narratives. The "culturally specific mechanisms of achieving gendered embodiment" abound in their tropes, in their "production of ideal type[s]." For instance, in moving from the opening paragraphs describing a setting to the second paragraphs inscribing a character into that setting, a distinct "gendering process" occurs. Look at "Unsafe" as an example:

In this place you can see that is very big, crowed, full of lights, and people. This place . . . is huge it is full of tall buildings, cars, it is crowed everywhere you go. There are some very dark street where nobody walks by, restaurants that nobody is willing to eat in because there nasty smells, but there are places out there that are beautiful with nice flowers around, big gardens and nice smells.

I, Sarah, am terrified of large cities. They are big and smelly, but I have to live in one because I am going to school at Berkley University. The changes that I have had to make are huge for me and they are hard to deal with every-day. My goal every day is to survive to the next day. I have lived in a little town my whole entire life and I loved it there. Everyone knew everyone and in the city nobody knows who you are. I feel so lost and lonely. The only way I can cope living in this city is by talking to my friends back at home. They tell me not to worry and that my beautiful looks can get me anywhere I want.

The first scene-setting paragraph is generic, even ambiguous, with some things good, some bad. The introduction of Sarah, a stereotypically insecure young woman, highlights the city's negativity, contrasting it to the innocence and security of a "little town." It is as though Sarah's feminine innocence is so powerful that it genders the landscape, pitting her insecurity and naiveté against the "big and smelly," dangerous (masculine?) city.

A similar, perhaps even more pronounced gendering occurs in "Scarlet":

Setting: An 80's pop dance club in Soho. Everyone is beautiful and wild hair and funky outfits are seen under the lights. The theme of this popular haven is black and white cubism. The waitresses wear white and black spandex and the drinks are never colored. The building is very dimly lit, and usually packed with pretty people in bright colors, to exhibit their individualism and self-gratification which was popular in the 80s. Many young people and one 75–year old man flock to the dance floor, bars, and few VIP rooms to live it up. In the back, there are "drug rooms" where many people experiment with white and black cocaine powder. The room usually smells of expensive perfume, cigarette smoke, and alcohol. The walls are 2 to 3 stories high, and a large projector screen shows silent movies from old science fiction B movies. The doorway has a receptionist desk and coat area filled with black and white plants, and an aquarium with black, white, and transparent fish. The only art or décor of the building is found in the comfy furniture in wild shapes and the interesting dance floor design of cubist black and white shapes.

Main Character: her name is Scarlet Weathers or that is what people know her as, she is a very mysterious woman. When she walks into the bar everyone stops and looks to her. All the guys begin to swarm her. She wears a bright red sequined dress, unlike many of the others in the club who wear black and white and insanely bright colors like yellow. She seems rich, like no other woman in the club. No one really knows her age because she is very mysterious. She always has a lit cigarette, but rarely puts it to her mouth. She is always the center of attention when she walks into a room.

Scarlet is the only splash of color in the otherwise black-and-white club, and she rather deliciously performs, in the second paragraph at least, a film noir femme fatale. Her distinctly gendered presence lends the landscape its only real color. In many ways, we're witnessing here a powerful "performance" of gender roles and stereotypes, as Butler describes in *Gender Trouble*: a reiteration of a norm, in narrative after narrative, to reify certain norms to the point of naturalness. Scarlet's clothing and demeanor, for instance, her red sequined dress and the dangling lit cigarette—these are some of the performed signifiers of her gender, culturally legible and understandable to everyone in the room as obvious, even "natural."

But some aspects of the stories, to my mind, point to more than just gender "performance." Indeed, of all the things my students could have imagined in(to) their narratives, the *body*—the *gendered* body—is something that several of them chose (consciously or not) to highlight in their construction of the "other" gender. Let's look again, for instance, at "Mr. Football" with Stryker's comments in mind. Our beach-loving jock is "very athletic in many different sports. He has a great 8–pack and well-defined muscles. He's around 6'4" and weighs around 210 (pure muscle)." Compellingly, much of the gender performance here is written *on the body*, and, moreover, this masculine-gendered body is a *sculpted* body, not a "naturally"occurring one. And in another narrative, we can see a bit more body sculpting to discipline the body in the performance of a gender. In "Turnabout," two female students have their male protagonist state, "As I come home from classes I go straight to Bally total fitness to manage, part time. It's an easy job, and it allows me to get in shape while being paid." Clearly, these female students feel that the pursuit of the "buff body" is a desired (and perhaps desirable) trait among males. To my mind, such embodiments seem slightly beyond the "performative"; they seem more "transsexual"—the literal crafting of the body to meet certain "ideal types" of gender "performance."

The male writers, too, narrated bodies that "speak" to particular assumptions about what gendered bodies are supposed to look like. In "Unsafe," the female narrator has been told by others "not to worry and that my beautiful looks can get me anywhere I want." In this case, a specific kind of female body is seen by the male students *as itself having agency*. The woman is seemingly only as strong as her physical attractiveness. We see a similar dynamic at play in "Scarlet," in which a woman's worth is measured by how well she can hold the attention of men: "She is a very intimidating woman and she is afraid that if she does not step up to the challenge with this attractive man that she is very fond of, then she will be looked at differently." The body—the specifically gendered body—holds power here, even if it is a fleeting power.

Further, the male gaze is strong in the stories written by men, and it's generally a gaze attuned to women's *bodies*. In "The Little Dream Girl," the athletic narrator practices alone—or so she thinks:

> She grabs the ball and shoots again, and makes it. As the janitor at the other end of the court sweeps up the popcorn and candy bar wrappers, he watches Ashley drain shot after shot as she practices late into the evening. Ashley will never quit, and she is still determined to win that scholarship for the state school. The next day, she is invited to attend a few liberal arts colleges and the State University. Eventually, she picks her school and works incredibly hard to make the starting team by her sophomore year and plays in the NCAA tournament her junior year. All went well for the little dream girl from Edgewood, Nebraska.

Even in this story, one that seemingly ends with an empowered woman stretching the bounds of gender norms, we encounter a male eyeing a woman's body in motion. What is he thinking? It's impossible to tell, but his presence highlights a reality: our bodies, particularly women's bodies, are under scrutiny—perhaps especially in this case, in which the young woman being constructed in this narrative is also being constructed as both a feminist and somebody stepping slightly outside her assigned gender role. She, and her gender transgressions, must be watched carefully.

Granted, these are the imagined bodies of imagined others, but the perception and composition of gender *as embodied* needs attention in our discourses about gender, as trans theorists argue. Indeed, some trans theorists have offered a substantial critique of how "performance" doesn't quite capture the interweaving of gender, identity, and the body, or a sense of the *embodied*ness of gender identity. Jay Prosser, in *Second Skins: Body Narratives of Transsexuality*, critiques "the equation 'camp=qu eer=performativity=transgender' that pervades [queer theory]" in that it "not only misrepresents reality but ignores the important 'narrative' of *becoming* a *biological* man or woman" (in Dickemann 2000, 463). Stryker, too, directly takes on Butler and performativity as explanatory tropes of the narration of gender:

> Gender in the Butlerian paradigm is strikingly cinematic—any stability of gender identity's visual image is due solely to the incessant, unvarying repetition of its chosen signs over time. . . . Signs of gender that we change relatively effortlessly like our clothes or relatively painlessly like the length of our hair have received the bulk of critical attention simply because they are more easily mobilized, their capacity for movement more readily perceived. . . . the flesh can be all too easily perceived as part of the fixed landscape against which gender performs itself, rather than as part of the performance itself. . . . Transsexuality offers a dramatic instance of the temporal instability of the flesh. It sets embodiment in motion. (2000, 593) 17

Similarly, Henry Rubin's *Self-Made Men: Identity and Embodiment among Transsexual Men*, in which Rubin carefully recounts and examines narratives of female-to-male transsexuality, notes: "The lives of transsexual men highlight the cultural significance of the body. Through FTM experience, we can see the modern relationship between sexed bodies and gendered identities. . . . We view bodies as the reflection of a gendered self" (2003, 180). Given these critiques and texts, as well as my students' own writing about gendered bodies, "performativity" seems at times too loose as a trope, too much like changing our clothes or cutting our hair, to explain how both transsexual theorists and, oddly enough, my students understand the narration of gender and its inscription both in the psyche and on the body.

AN EMBODIED SEXUAL LITERACY

What does such an approach to writing about gender and sexuality teach us and our students? What can we learn—personally, politically, and pedagogically—from experimenting with Califia-Rice's call to composing narratives of virtual gender swapping? What critical sexual literacies are developed? In "On Becoming a Woman: Pedagogies of the Self," Susan Romano remarks on some of the potential goals of feminist compositionist practice. She suggests that what may be "crucial to the production of equitable discourse is the possibility that when many women are present and differ in their self-representations, then 'women' as a category—represented variously—can be taken back from its reductive forms and rebuilt as multiple" (2003, 462). Part of the goal of my paired-fiction exercises was certainly to expand students' sense of the multiple ways that women—and men—exist as gendered beings in the world. But we also experienced, in writing and analyzing those narratives, a sense of the gendered body and how gender finds itself written on—and read from—the bodies we inhabit and through which we both derive and articulate a sense of self. Those bodies, though, are never simply personal; they are profoundly politicized bodies, called to a gendered scrutiny, sculpting, and legibility that determines which bodies are male and female, powerful and weak. Examining such interconnections among narrations, body, and gender is a crucial part of developing a critical sexual literacy.

Interestingly enough, transgender and transsexual theorists such as Prosser have argued forcefully that it is in the examination of *narrations* of gender that we come to a fuller and richer understanding of its "composition"—both personally and politically, in mind and on body. Prosser argues, for instance, that "transsexual and transgendered narratives alike produce not the revelation of the fictionality of gender categories but the sobering realization of their ongoing foundational power" (1998, 11). We might be tempted to think of gender as a set of roles, many stereotypical, that can be critiqued and cast off, like so many changes of clothing. But Prosser maintains, as my students' narratives reveal, that gender inscribes itself at the level of the flesh. Such is particularly true when considering narratives of gender transitioning: "Transsexuality reveals the extent to which embodiment forms an essential base to subjectivity; but it also reveals that embodiment is as much about feeling one inhabits material flesh as the flesh itself" (7). For Prosser, examining such narratives is the key to opening up a more expansive and thorough discussion of gender; as he maintains, "To talk of the strange and unpredictable contours of body image, and to reinsert into theory the experience of embodiment, we might begin our work through . . . autobiographical narratives" (96).

At the same time, as a pedagogue invested in the expansive possibilities of feminist compositionist practices, I must ask myself what potential for actual critical agency lies in a closer attention to the body and its composition in gender narrations. On one hand, I believe that my students may have encountered powerfully in the paired-fiction exercise how gender functions in our society to condition certain expectations and norms for how women and men are to behave—at least stereotypically. In this way, the exercise is in line with Will Banks's recent call for working with students on creating "embodied writing," or writing that takes into consideration the specific needs, desires, and beingness of particular bodies and of particular experiences of the body. As Banks suggests, such writing "offers us and our students spaces to think through all those multiple and shifting signifiers at work on us so that we come up with sharper understandings of ourselves and those around us" (2003, 38).

At the same time, though, the narrative "performances" of my students are suggestive of the double bind of gender—a double bind neatly evoked by transsexuality, which itself evokes tropes both of boundary crossing and the power of boundaries to (re)inscribe norms. For Susan Stryker, herself a transsexual theorist and activist, transsexuality "is simultaneously an elaborately articulated medico-juridical discourse imposed on particular forms of deviant subjectivity, and a radical practice that promises to explode dominant constructions of self and society" (2000, 594).

In her historical survey and analysis, *How Sex Changed: A History of Transsexuality in the United States,* Joanne Meyerowitz argues along a similar vein—that transsexuality in particular is a simultaneous reification, on one hand, of gender norms and expectations, and, on the other hand, a mobilization of gender: "Transsexuals, some argue, reinscribe the conservative stereotypes of male and female and masculine and feminine. They take the signifiers of sex and the prescriptions of gender too seriously. They are 'utterly invested' in the boundaries between female and male. Or they represent individual autonomy run amok in the late modern age. . . . some theories identity transsexuals as emblems of liberatory potential" (2002, 11–12).

Did my students experience that liberatory potential? Our discussions postexercise were revealing, thoughtful, and even critical. We could spot stereotypes "in action," noting how we craft stories for ourselves—and others—in which the most limiting and even sexist of gender norms are deployed again and again, for both "traditional" sexes and genders.

But does such recognition in a classroom exercise translate into increased sociopolitical agency? I'm less sure, as indeed are many feminist compositionists when considering their own pedagogies of critical agency.

Donna LeCourt, in her essay "Writing (without) the Body: Gender and Power in Networked Discussion Groups," describes her experiences with using electronic discussion venues to help women students foster and experiment with multiple voices and modes of expression, thus potentially "subvert[ing] and/or resist[ing] the power relationships that silence them in other realms" (1999, 171). LeCourt hopes that "[m]aking students metacognitive of their discursive positions and how those already constructed embody different relations of power would create a context in which the forms of textual resistance so productive in the electronic space could become consciously employed, and perhaps more importantly, equally possible in the classroom space" (173). The emphasis in LeCourt's position has to be placed on "perhaps" and "could," with meta-cognition *potentially* translating from a pedagogical venue to a more "real-world" one. Indeed, I believe my students and I used the paired-fiction exercise to think metacognitively about gender in some very critical ways; but did the fiction writing lead to resistances to gender norms outside the space of the exercise, or outside the classroom? I am less certain of that, particularly since those norms, as Stryker and Meyerowitz suggest, are so persistent and so powerful. Indeed, they are as persistent and as powerful as the *hetero* norms we encountered in the previous chapter, as students grappled with Dax's performance of "straightness."

As such, I am not sure that our narratives of gender swapping and transitioning were necessarily helping "liberate" participants from gender norms, even though I believe they offered us opportunities to explore useful insights and gain critical purchase through them—which is one of the primary goals of developing sexual literacy. If anything, they revealed the extent to which gender is much more than a set of roles and rhetorical tropes; there is a rhetoric of the body that needs careful consideration as well. As one of the students wrote in one of the stories, "you only survive if you can fit into a society." And a significant way in which we fit in—or do *not* fit in—has to do with how our bodies are perceived as complying to or deviating from sets of highly gendered norms. In *Transgender Warriors*, Leslie Feinberg argues pointedly that gender is more than just a process of naming, a performance of roles: "When I say I am a gender outlaw in modern society, it's not rhetoric. I have been dragged out of bars by police who claimed I broke the law when I dressed myself that evening. I've heard the rap of a cop's club on the stall door when I've used a public women's toilet. And then there's the question of my identity papers" (1996, 61).

While questions of agency remain complex, I am nonetheless convinced that this exercise in transitioning furthers my aims in helping students develop a greater critical sexual literacy. If I return to one of the organizing questions with which I introduced this book—*How do sexuality and literacy interconnect in complex ways? That is, how is an understanding of sexuality a key component in being literate in contemporary Western culture and society?*—I think it is pretty clear that developing a more complex way of reading the intertwining of gender and identity in our culture is productive of critical engagement with some of the more controlling tropes of gender in our culture. Put another way, having students write about gender, particularly to excavate the narrative tropes in which conceptions of gender and identity are embedded, fosters a sense of how discourse and normative rhetorics of gender are conduits of power, shaping our sense of what kinds of identities are "normal," appropriate, and allowed. Such also opens a space for questioning those very shaping norms, those powerful rhetorics.

But moreover, such work is about *writing*, about looking at gender through the critical work of *writing about gender*, and about understanding writing, particularly narrations of self, as not just the "recovery" of a self but the *construction* of self. Many feminist compositionists have promoted the use of autobiography or personal narratives as pedagogical tools for understanding the relationship between power and gender, as well as other sociocultural markers and signifiers. Wendy Hesford, in *Framing Identities: Autobiography and the Politics of Pedagogy*, argues forcefully for writing pedagogies that utilize autobiography and personal narrative in creative and *critical* ways. She says, "Autobiographical acts . . . do not reflect unmediated subjectivities; rather, they are acts of self-representation that are ideologically encoded with historical memories and principles of identity and truth. . . . I am less interested in autobiography as a chronological record of a life already lived or as the retrieval of an essential essence or truth . . . than I am with examining autobiographical acts as social signifying practices shaped by and enacted within particular institutional contexts and their histories" (1999, xxiii). Put another way, Hesford is interested in pedagogical uses of autobiography that do not excavate an essentialist notion of self unearthed through an expressivist exercise, but rather a social-epistemic approach to narrations of self that understands the construction, articulation, and representation of subjectivity as always already existing within and inflected by a sociopolitical and historically bounded matrix. As such, she argues "for the primacy of students' autobiographical texts in a feminist multicultural writing curriculum, and I urge writing teachers to recognize the identity negotiations and interplay of social discourses articulated through the processes of writing and reading autobiography" (56).

And some students and scholars are pushing us in that direction, exploring autobiography as a genre for linking insights into gender, literacy, discourse, and power. A recently published article in *Computers and Composition Online*, "'Boy? You Decide; Girl? You Decide': Multimodal Web Composition and a Mythography of Identity," by Brian R. Houle, Alex P. Kimball, and Heidi A. McKee (2004), is one of the pieces published in the field of composition studies that undertakes an analysis of the self-representational tactics and strategies of a self-identified trans person.Working on the piece with Alex, the trans person, Houle and McKee "focus on the ways in which Alex's use of multimedia enabled (or hindered) potentially transgressive expressions of and understandings of gendered and sexual identities." The self-narration was part of a composition course taught by Houle and McKee, in which students were encouraged to explore the Web as a space for constructing narrations of selfhood and identity. Intriguingly, Alex's project, as Houle and McKee point out, reveals how multimodal composition students can create sites that challenge normative understandings of gender, such as Alex's complex self-narration in which hir gender seems constantly at play, in motion. While the authors point out that viewers of such compositions may "insist" on reading a complex representation of gender in very binary ways, the text nonetheless shifts quickly enough to challenge such readings and reveal them as simplistic—as reiterating and reinforcing normative constructions of gender and identity.

But we must also remember that gender is never purely discursive. It is experienced as a material reality, even as such realities may be discursively enabled, and I maintain that working with students on the narration and construction of gender is perhaps better served by metaphors and tropes that capture some of that lived and *embodied* complexity of gender. Performativity has been useful as a trope in working toward a critical sexual literacy. Transgenderism and transsexuality may be even better. Indeed, to what extent do *many* of us steadily "transition," even unknowingly, from the bodies we are born with to the culturally idealized gendered bodies, images of which surround us in the media? At the very least, the paired-fiction exercise has taught me that it is crucial when considering *discourses* of gender with students to recognize the

material realities constructed, maintained, and enabled by those discourses. And, pedagogically, considering with students gender *beyond* its
rhetorical dimensions is not to leave rhetoric behind, but to think about
rhetoric in a more materially grounded way. Indeed, the body has its
own stories, demanding that we listen to them. Beginning to understand
one's identity as the complex narration of the meeting between body,
perception, norms, and culture is beginning to understand some of the
complexities of sexual literacy. Trans theorists can help us undertake
this work, this listening, this understanding.

Of course, gender identity is not the only way in which sex/uality
and our embeddedness in the social meet in complex and even contradictory ways. They also meet in larger socializing institutions, such
as marriage, which has become a hotly contested domain both of how
some people know themselves and of how some kinds of intimate relationships are legitimized—and others devalued. In the next chapter, we
will explore emerging sexual literacies and debates around the issue of
marriage in contemporary Anglo-American culture.

5

STRAIGHT TALK
ABOUT MARRIAGE
Sex and Politics

Without a doubt, one of the most contentious debates in contemporary American society has focused on the extension of marriage rights to gay and lesbian couples. Numerous news reports and several legal battles throughout the early years of the twenty-first century have turned attention to this issue, which has yet to reach the U.S. Supreme Court. Pundits and commentators ranging from Andrew Sullivan (pro) to Rush Limbaugh (anti) have volubly expressed themselves on the issue. Such public battles and debates in many ways turn our attention not only to the "status" of gay and lesbian two-partner relationships in the United States, but also to the *definition* of marriage itself. What does it mean to be married in contemporary society? Is marriage "religious" in nature? *Should* it be in a secular society? Do historical precedents for and definitions of marriage demand our attention as we attempt to define marriage for contemporary people? More broadly, what *are* the roles of religion and history in navigating contemporary questions?

More practically, businesses and universities across the country have grappled also with the extension of domestic partner benefits, since gay and lesbian employees, as well as those heterosexually identified people choosing not to be married, are otherwise denied benefits for their partners. Many businesses have invested in such benefits on a largely economic basis; they believe it is in their best interest to attract as wide a pool of talent and skilled professionals as they can, and hence they cannot afford to be biased against any one group. Denying benefits to gays and lesbians, for instance, would limit businesses from access to a diverse pool of applicants, particularly since potential employees often carefully vet what benefits a company is offering.

While such benefits allow nonmarried couples similar kinds of benefits, several states across the country have moved over the last few years to define marriage as *only between a man and a woman*, thus preventing the issuing of marriage licenses to gay and lesbian couples. The Defense of Marriage Act (DOMA), signed by President Clinton during his second term, says that individual states do not have to recognize same-sex marriage licenses granted in other states. As of this writing, only one state, Massachusetts, issues marriage licenses to same-sex couples. While many businesses move toward economic justice, it is clear that a different politics is at play in the codifying of terms such as "marriage."

At the heart of such debates is a rhetorical issue bleeding into a political issue: the *definition* of marriage and how such a definition confers status, responsibility, and privilege on some while denying it to others. In a Foucauldian sense, defining marriage is about establishing and codifying norms not only of behavior but also self-definition; in other words, those allowed to be married have their personal relationships *publicly* endorsed as normative, as "normal" and hence desirable by the public at large. Indeed, the place of marriage in society provides an interesting way to think about how institutional and structural norms and investments make themselves known and how they shape people's personal and intimate lives, as well as help to form how a person thinks about her- or himself.

In this chapter, I want to explore how the vexed concept of "marriage" is a rich topic for first-year writing courses, particularly since marriage is a prominent site in which personal investments and social norms often meet. Furthermore, as a site in which certain kinds of intimate and sexual relations are publicly acknowledged and privileged, marriage provides an interesting point of departure for examining critically with students how certain narrations of normative identity and normative *relationships* are reified in contemporary society. As such, critical analyses of marriage can form—one might argue, *should* form—a central part of students' developing sexual literacy. To unpack the pedagogical possibilities here, I want to explore first some of the rhetorical dimensions in which current debates about marriage foreground sexuality issues; then I will offer up a case study of how one professor's first-year writing course attempted to turn students' attention to such issues by focusing on contemporary debates about the definition of marriage.

RHETORICAL MARRIAGES: NUSSBAUM, BENNETT, AND THE SEXUAL CITIZEN

The sheer volume of articles, news reports, and other media texts, as well as book-length explorations of "gay marriage" published recently, suggests that marriage is a vexed category in contemporary Anglo-American culture. Obviously, I cannot survey even a majority of the material produced on the subject, but I think we can learn much about marriage and its connection to sexual literacy from the rhetorical ways in which marriage is figured in debates about gay marriage. To be sure, gay marriage is hardly the only public and political issue in which the meaning of marriage is considered, reconsidered, and debated. However, it is perhaps the most prominent issue in which we can easily see how rhetorically loaded debates about marriage have become. It is also the issue in which the rhetorics of different ideological visions of marriage have become highly salient. Furthermore, debates about gay marriage highlight the ways in which definitions of marriage, including a normative understanding of what kinds of people should be allowed to marry and what kinds of intimate relations should receive legal recognition and sanction, become understood as subject to revision. The story of marriage can change, and arguments rage over who will be authorized to tell that story. As such, understanding the rhetorical construction of marriage seems vital to developing sexual literacy. To develop a sense of the rhetorical nature of such debates, let's look quickly at statements from one prominent public intellectual in favor and one against gay marriage.

Martha Nussbaum's "A Defense of Lesbian and Gay Rights" examines a variety of issues related to the political positioning of gays and lesbians in American society, such as the right of consenting adults to engage privately in sexual behavior, gays in the military, Colorado's Amendment 2, and gay marriage. Throughout her essay, Nussbaum attempts to show how any form of discrimination against gays and lesbians is deeply problematical—on a number of levels. About the issue of legalizing *against* gay marriage, Nussbaum is succinct and to the point. She rejects attempts to classify marriage as strictly between a man and a woman on the following grounds: "To approach the issue at a deeper level, such classifications, it is argued, are ultimately an extension of a system of sex discrimination, because the ban on same-sex marriage is at its root a way of maintaining sharp binary boundaries between the sexes and enshrining the institution of the patriarchal heterosexual couple as the central recognized unit. Thus, the ban is a sex-based classification serving sexist goals" (1999, 203).

In a way, Nussbaum sees the attempt to ban gay marriage as not only a sexist move but a *rhetorically* sexist move. That is, we understand the "sharp binary boundaries between the sexes" not just as a biological "fact" (which is itself a problematical position given the large number of intesexed births), but also as a reality of how we use language to organize the species and narrate a story about what kinds of intimacies and couplings should be recognized. "Male" and "female," after all, are classifications that exist as much in language and in our systems of dichotomous meaning making as they do in human biology. Further, it is in *seeing* the categories of "male" and "female" as opposites, as constitutive of "binary boundaries," that a rhetorical move is made—a rhetorical move with substantive consequences socially, culturally, and politically.

For Nussbaum, though, addressing the issue rhetorically, and demonstrating the culturally relative ways in which intimacies (not to mention genders) are constructed and narrated in different societies, may be insufficient to move our current culture in the direction of embracing gay marriage: "Rational argument on this issue will not resolve all controversy because it is very likely that the resistance to full equality for gays has deep psychological roots. Fear of the erosion of traditional distinctions and boundaries, fear of a type of female sexuality that is unavailable to men, fear of a type of male sexuality that is receptive rather than assertive—all these probably play a role in making the current debate as ugly and irrational as it is" (1999, 185). Again, note how in this formulation rhetoric is at play: Nussbaum claims that people fear the "erosion of traditional distinctions and boundaries." Inevitably, those are boundaries at least partially constructed and largely maintained *in language*. Thus, while she does not address marriage in terms of sexual literacy, it seems clear from her discussion and positioning of marriage rights in terms of concern over shifting (binary) categories of meaning making that knowledges about marriage are indeed part of the domain of what I have been terming "sexual literacy."

On the other side of the debate, William J. Bennettt's book, *The Broken Hearth: Reversing the Moral Collapse of the American Family*, offers a chapter called "Homosexual Unions" that presents arguments against legalizing gay marriage. Bennettt's arguments are generally well organized and clearly presented, despite lapses into logical fallacies, such as this slippery slope argument: "Say what they will, there are no principled grounds on which advocates of same-sex marriage can oppose the marriage of two consenting brothers. Nor can they (persuasively) explain why we ought to deny a marriage license to three men who want to marry" (2001, 113).

Interestingly, despite Bennett's difference of view with Nussbaum, I believe that Bennett also figures the gay marriage debate in terms of sexual literacy, albeit a very different ideologically valenced understanding of sexual literacy. Like Nussbaum, he argues that marriage is figured as a binary arrangement:

> With all due respect to proponents of same-sex marriage, it is also important to say publicly what most of us still believe privately, namely, that marriage between a man and a woman is in every way to be preferred to the marriage of two men or two women. Because there is a natural complementarity between men and women—sexual, emotional, temperamental, spiritual— marriage allows for a wholeness and a completeness that cannot be won in any other way. ("For this reason," says Genesis, "a man will leave his father and mother and be united to this wife, and the two will become one flesh.") And, based as it is on the principle of complementarity, marriage is also about a great deal more than love. (2001, 133)

The quotation from Genesis, pivotally placed, is designed to offer further rhetorical support to an argument that is already deeply rhetorical. Although Bennett suggests (and argues elsewhere) that the "complementarity" between "men and women" is "natural," his use of a scriptural passage to bolster his point suggests that such "naturalness" must be figured rhetorically as well. In other words, the natural should be filtered and understood through the divine word in order to be understood. Anything less results in the fulfillment of our natural ("fallen," in the Christian cosmogony) predilection to sin. So, while different from Nussbaum's figuring of marriage in some key details, Bennett's position on marriage is curiously caught up in discursive moves that reveal ideological investments; that is, he believes that intimate lives should be arranged according to biblical dictates that inform a way of categorizing, understanding, and telling the story of a "godly" humanity.

More pressingly, though, we see Bennett's intuitive feel for sexual literacy in the following passage, in which he argues forcefully for how legal codes intersect with cultural and social norms: "The stated goal of homosexual activists is not merely tolerance; it is to force society to *accept*. It is normalization, validation, public legitimation, and finally public endorsement. That is a radically different matter. Once we were to codify it in law, we would be saying that homosexual life and heterosexual life are equal in all important respects, that there is nothing special about the union of man and woman in holy matrimony, that there is nothing normative about the role of father and mother in the raising of children" (2001, 121).

In Bennett's view (and I do not necessarily disagree with him here), the rhetoric of legal codes is tied in ways to "normalization, validation, public legitimation, and finally public endorsement." But this connection is what is problematic for Bennett, since rhetorics can naturalize and normalize that which, in his view, should be unnatural, not normal. In the process of rhetorical normalization, what is "special" is lost, and categorical confusion emerges. Thus, in highlighting a rudimentary connection between rhetorical and political work (codification and the creation of norms) and personal and intimate work (marriage and the "role of father and mother in the raising of children"), Bennett promotes a sexual literacy that asks us to read the political/personal situation carefully to see where rhetorical moves are challenging (conservative) ideological investments.

In *The Sexual Citizen*, David Bell and Jon Binnie underscore even more directly than either Nussbaum or Bennett how questions of marriage rights, as well as the basic question of the definition of marriage, is a deeply rhetorical issue—one in which rhetorics mobilize and enable a variety of political moves. They argue that "[t]here has been a noticeable turn towards love in recent writings on sexual politics, and it seems appropriate here to think through calls, such as Giddens', to work through the politics of intimacy and link that to democracy (and citizenship)" (2000, 123). Considering the politics of intimacy prompts them to question the connection between such intimacy and the narratives we personally and culturally tell about such intimacy: "How can we think about intimacy without reinstating the public/private divide; without keeping intimacy's link to privacy intact? How do we think love in ways other than those hegemonically scripted by mainstream culture? What is it that we talk about when we talk about love?" (124). These questions seem to me to point squarely in the direction of inquiring about our *sexual literacy*. In other words, when we consider how love has been "hegemonically scripted by mainstream culture"—or what "we talk about when we talk about love"—we are exploring our literacies about sex and sexuality, as well as how social scripts and stories themselves are part and parcel of social hegemonies (and resistances to them).

Along these lines, Bell and Binnie note that changing legal discourses about marriage, in their words, "*can* have far broader impacts, throwing light onto both the constructions of homosexuality and heterosexuality in law, and the limitations of such constructions" (2000, 56). More specifically, many interlocking discourses—from the legal and political to the popular and the personal—shift in conjunction with one another. As Bell and Binnie put it, "A focus exclusively on challenging the legal discourse around marriage, therefore, falls short of considering which aspects of *popular discourse* are contested or reaffirmed by such a move" (59). Indeed, analyses of television talk shows and sitcoms would most likely reveal how narrations of marriage, as both a personal and public construct, have been deeply inflected by the challenge of gay marriage to how we talk about sex and sexuality—its challenge to our *collective* sense of sexual literacy.

Given this brief survey of how the debates surrounding gay marriage are rhetorically rich, I believe that addressing marriage in the first-year classroom is not only appropriate but potentially pressing—both personally and politically—as a sexual literacy issue. Many of our students will consider marriage as an option for their lives, and many will participate legally by casting votes either in favor of gay marriage or opposed to it. Indeed, I do not think it an overstatement to say that critically understanding how marriage is constructed, formed, and organized in our society may be a crucial—and enlightening—undertaking for many of our students.

Interestingly, when we take up the issue of marriage as a discursive and rhetorical domain, as a powerful site for exploring sexual literacy, we find that students have *much* to say about it. And their concerns are not always focused on the "gay marriage" debate, though many use that debate as an important way in which to enter into serious critical discussion about marriage and its rhetorical construction in society. While I have used gay marriage as a way to demonstrate quickly that understanding marriage is fully part of the project of developing sexual literacy, it is certainly *not* the case that gay marriage is the sole or even the most salient way in which marriage can be understood as a powerfully rhetorical way in which people are categorized, organized, and understood (both by themselves and others). Students are often eager to pick up this analysis and extend it in interesting ways, and therefore I believe exploring with students the intersections between marriage and rhetoric is a powerful way to work with them on developing sexual literacy. In the following section, I want to examine how one instructor tackled the issue of marriage in a first-year composition course and uncovered a variety of ways to think with his students about marriage as a key "flash point" in considering sexual literacy.

MARRIAGE IN THE COMP CLASSROOM: A CASE STUDY

My colleague Gary Weissman organized a unit in his first-year advanced writing course at the University of Cincinnati, English 112, around the issue and definition of marriage. In English 112 students develop skills in rhetorical analysis, making and supporting argumentative claims, and using a variety of research methods to craft essays that explore complex issues. Students are eligible for the course only if they are placed into it after taking a writing placement test, required of all students matriculating to the university without prior credit for first-year writing courses. The course is for writers needing to fulfill first-year composition requirements but who would benefit from slightly more challenging coursework. As such, English 112 is a first-year composition course, albeit one in which students are expected to be writing at a fairly proficient level. In the section of English 112 that Gary taught, he had approximately twenty students whose majors varied across the curriculum. I interviewed Gary about his experience in his class and received permission from his students to read their essays and other assigned writing.

Gary's syllabus described course objectives that were aligned with those of the English composition program as a whole: "This course builds on your understanding of rhetoric and the writing process through an exploration of research writing. The course provides instruction and practice in the following areas: formulating significant research questions; locating, evaluating, and synthesizing primary, print, and electronic bibliographic sources; integrating source materials into original arguments; citing sources accurately and responsibly; conveying the results of research to audiences that can learn from those findings."

The emphasis in such a course is clearly on development of effective articulation of critical thinking skills that are cognizant—and that recognize such cognizance—of how other writers have tackled "significant research questions." In addition to fairly typical course requirements—such as calls for regular attendance, requests that work be turned in on time, encouragement to participate in class discussions, etc.—Gary required that students complete two research papers, which would be included in a "final portfolio." This portfolio comprised 70 percent of each student's grade. Additional writing assignments included two short-paper assignments, two annotated bibliographies, and two peer reviews of other student's work. I asked Gary to explain his criteria for evaluating papers: "Well, good writing [came from] people who found good sources and who basically learned something by doing it. It was made clear that doing the research would actually engage them in thinking about something that they would not have otherwise. They were actually interested in that. Some of them really managed to write and type a focused paper. There wasn't really a goal for them to come to certain conclusions, but at the same time I did not get any papers from people . . . who argued against gay marriage or even for a marriage amendment. They certainly could have done that." The instructor's goals, thus, are clearly to promote dialogue, discussion, and analysis, not to indoctrinate.

Gary's pedagogical innovation in this particular course was his decision to use nonfiction texts that deal with two contemporary social issues: *Just Marriage* (2004), which offers several essays presenting multiple perspectives on the definition of marriage in contemporary society, and *Branded Nation: The Marketing of Megachurch, College, Inc., and Museumworld* (2004), which grapples with the role of marketing in contemporary American society and democratic politics. I was particularly struck by Gary's choice of *Just Marriage*, a collection of essays edited by Mary Lyndon Shanley. The contributors examine primarily the issue of gay marriage, but the collection also includes essays that critically examine the role, function, and importance of marriage in Western society. For instance, *Just Marriage* offers selections such as Elizabeth F. Emens's "Just Monogamy?" Tamara Metz's "Why We Should Disestablish Marriage," and Brenda Crossman's "Beyond Marriage," which considers intimate relationships and arrangements that do not quite fit the "traditional" model of marriage as codified legally and socially in much of contemporary Western society. In many ways, then, the essays in the collection explore the debate between Nussbaum's and Bennett's views, but they also extend the discussion to explore a variety of possibilities beyond the polarizing pro/anti debate of gay marriage.

Shanley's introduction offers a good critical *and* historical overview of the development of laws around marriage (and divorce). In particular, she considers how views of marriage as a legal institution have changed over time. Part of this critical history of marriage inevitably considers the vexed place of divorce vis-à-vis marriage, as well as miscegenation laws, while more contemporary issues include, of course, gay marriage but also the issue of polygamy and nonmonogamy (or polyandry) in long-term relationships. Shanley argues eloquently that "[w]e need to insist . . . that marriage and family law can and must be made to

conform to the principles of justice that affirm the equality and equal
liberty of all citizens" (2004, 28). As such, *Just Marriage* presents marriage as a complex social institution with a complex social history and a
complex position in present society. Much of the concern throughout
Just Marriage revolves around definitional issues, as in how do we justly
and fairly *define* what "marriage" is, as well as what love, intimacy, and
relationships are.

In my interview with Gary, I asked him to talk about why he chose
marriage as an issue for a first-year writing course:

> [Both books] were directed at issues but in open ways. I began with the mar-
> riage one. . . . I think stuff about gay marriage was in the news and on my
> mind and then I was thinking about the history of marriage in Ohio. I was
> wondering, wouldn't it be interesting to see if students actually researched
> that and found out about laws about interracial marriages and so on. . . . Just
> Marriage to me seemed really good, and what I ended up liking about it
> was that instead of the gay marriage being presented in the book as either
> fair or unfair, it was about is marriage fair or unfair the way it is now. With
> that paper I wanted to them to actually feel by doing research that they can
> actually become more informed. I wanted to have this practical application.
> A research paper is not just about basically jumping through all these hoops
> to fulfill an assignment. Actually doing research will help them become
> more knowledgeable and [learn] that it's a good thing to research things
> that you only know a little bit about but not enough to have [a] really
> informed . . . opinion.

Gary's intention, then, in working with marriage as an issue in the book
Just Marriage was to invite students to participate in a critical dialogue
about marriage, one that would engage issues of marriage beyond simply debating whether or not gay marriage should be legalized nationally. It is instructive to compare this instructor's pedagogical desires
with the course materials and texts presented in many first-year writing
textbooks, which I briefly described in chapter 2. Many of those texts
present gay marriage as an important (or at least potentially "popular")
subject for rather binary debate: you're either for or against it; pick a
side and construct an argument. Gary's interest in developing his own
course was much more nuanced, I believe, in that he was invested in
helping students develop sexual literacy; that is, he wanted students not
just to argue about marriage but to use research and critical thinking
to explore how marriage actually works in our society, how it has been

codified and discussed, and how its definition is constantly undergoing reexamination and revision.

Along these lines, Gary's initial writing assignment about marriage asked students to become aware of their own definitions and assumptions about marriage. He assigned a short paper

> expressing your views on the institution of marriage. How do you define marriage? Who should, or shouldn't, be allowed to marry? How, legally, should marriage be defended or reformed? What has shaped your views on this issue? How much thought have you given to this issue before now? How much have you discussed, read, seen or heard about it?
>
> Take your short paper and edit it down into a 1–page condensed, unsigned version, to be shared anonymously in class. Make sure to include answers to all six questions asked above.

Gary explained his rationale in giving this assignment: "For that assignment I began by just having them write on marriage and what they thought about marriage before they read the book. I really wanted them to see for themselves the differences in how they thought about marriage before and after doing this assignment. I also wanted to give them some space for them to basically express all of their initial feelings, reactions, and unexamined thoughts just to get all of that out. I think that worked pretty well."

After this initial writing, which was the basis of a couple of days of in-class discussion, as well as postings on a class Blackboard discussion board, students composed an annotated bibliography for several of the essays in *Just Marriage*. After discussing their own views and those of the authors in *Just Marriage*, students composed "research questions" about marriage that they wanted to explore in their own research and writing. In consultation with Gary, students honed such questions to manageable topics, conducted research, and drafted, redrafted, and revised essays, which turned out to cover a variety of topics on marriage.

Indeed, the writing in the essays is in many ways quite remarkable— not in that is necessarily "better" than most first-year writing in large state universities, but in that students take very seriously how marriage is simultaneously a private *and* public issue, and one in which issues of sex, sexuality, and gender come together to create equally personal and social senses of self and community. In some particularly intriguing cases, students focus their critical attention on the rhetoric of marriage and examine how marriage is talked about and thus constructed in our society.

The initial exploratory pieces revealed a diversity of reactions, all thoughtfully articulated, if predicated on differing assumptions.[18] Several students, such as Kerri, expressed their pro-gay marriage convictions directly and succinctly:

> There are a few reforms that I would make[:] (1) no minors should be allowed to marry even with the consent of parents or guardians, and (2) same-sex marriages should be allowed in all states.

Another student, Jason, drawing on the experiences of friends to advocate for gay marriage, concluded:

> The fact that marriage is currently limited to a union between a man and a woman is absurd. This is because of the influence of religion on laws regarding this subject. However, I believe that if there is supposed to be a separation between church and state then this is an unjust way to treat marriage laws.

Other students writing in favor of gay marriage focused on definitional issues as the basis of their claims. Keno, in his essay "The State of Unions," proposes that we reconsider our understanding of fairness and equality:

> I can't tell you what it's actually like to be gay, or black, or even poor and be discriminated against. What I can tell you is that some of the most basic rules we have set up to govern ourselves here in this country speak to the equality of everyone under the law. I say that there must be no more compelling state interest [than] protecting this equality. When we rescind the rights of others, can our own be far behind?

In each case, students carefully considered possible counterarguments and supported their claims with a variety of research sources, including personal anecdotes and interviews with friends and others. Yet another student, Ben, linked the issue of gay marriage to other social issues:

> America is in economic crisis, spending more and taxing less. We are engaged in a way without a concrete end, our country's healthcare and education systems are in turmoil, and the primary worry of many citizens and elected representatives is two people loving each other. Americans need to step out of individuals' marriages and harmless personal affairs, and begin to become concerned about national issues that have both direct and indirect effects on all of their lives.

What's interesting about this particular student's view is his reference to other social issues but his simultaneous positioning of marriage as a "harmless personal affair." This tension surfaces, as we will see, in several students' essays as a point for further exploration and discussion. At this point, it is interesting to note how many students frame the gay marriage debate in ways rhetorically comparable to that of Nussbaum, whose views I described above; while the students do not necessarily link heterosexual marriage to the maintenance of sexist norms, they nonetheless focus on definitional issues and the ways in which defining marriage works toward establishing social norms and boundaries.

Other students, such as Ashley, were a bit more tentative in extending marital rights to gays and lesbians, though they couched their hesitancy in language that emphasized tolerance for gays and a desire to be non-discriminatory in other facets of life:

> I don't dislike gay people, and I do have gay friends and family members. I do not think that they should be denied housing or discriminated against in the workplace or in other similar situations that heterosexuals participate in without discrimination. I support common-law benefits. But marriage is different to me. Marriage is not only emotional and financial, but a moral decision and a promise before God. I understand that not every American is a Christian, or even from my same aspect of Christianity. But it is biblical that gay people should not marry; and, like it or not, America's government has been based on the Bible from its founding.

While Ashley's comments may seem reminiscent of those of Bill Bennett above, her position differs from his significantly in its willingness to accept democratically made decisions, even if such are not in line with her personal religious beliefs. She says,

> If the majority of these people decide that gay marriage should be allowed, it will be. I feel like that day is inevitable—it not sooner, than later. And if I'm still around when it happens, I will be content with that decision because it will be a choice made for America by the majority of Americans.

One gay student articulated a fairly nuanced position on gay marriage, focusing not just on the issue but on how we talk about the issue, and how his discourse about gay marriage as a gay man both legitimizes his interest and potentially delegitimizes his potential ethos, his potential efficacy, as a rhetor when speaking about the issue.

My views on marriage have been shaped by, obviously, my parents. They've been divorced since I was in seventh grade, and I imagine that my dad's mid-life crisis and subsequent affair is an all too-common occurrence. My views have also been shaped by the media coverage of the topic: my dislike of some views and like of others. I have tried to not react simply in spite of or simpl[y] because of one side or the other.

I've tried not to think of this issue, honestly. I know it's odd that I would actually avoid something [that] could potentially have a lot to do with me, but I guess that a lot of people would say my stance is automatic—and dismiss it. Then again it could be my annoyance with politics. Does it even matter who's right or who's wrong when neither side has the real advantage? Who has the advantage? [Whoever] has the most clout when it comes time to vote on the issue.

The comments may be mildly cynical, but I also see in them the seeds of a real rhetorical understanding, waiting to bud.

In the longer research papers specifically on gay marriage, students articulate a general sense that the United States is moving toward hon-oring gay marriages as legal commitments every bit as valid as hetero-sexual marital unions. But these essays also reveal a sensitivity to the complexities of the issue of recognizing gay marriages, and many advo-cate a slow, cautious approach. Curiously, many of the analyses focus on the discourses surrounding and constructing marriage in contemporary society and on an understanding of marriage as not just a personal, inti-mate arrangement but as intersecting other concerns and investments, such as economic interests.

For example, one student, Jason, wrote very personally about his own grappling with marriage:

Through most of my research I have found that no clear answer surfaces telling me to get hitched or not. I did find, however, that marriage offers the potential for economic growth and increased health. The trouble lies in actualizing the potentials. I think that there are enough possibilities, such as economic growth and increased health, which accompany marriage to give it the chance if the right person ever comes along.

Jason's research into and writing on the topic helped him develop a sense of marriage as connected to beneficial economic advantages and potential privileges. Along such lines, another student, Ryan, began articulating his sense of marriage as strongly tied to economic struc-tures; his analysis, in a paper entitled "Economic Advantages of Same-Sex Marriage," seems fairly sophisticated for a first-year student:

While many of the nation's top marketing firms have recognized the economic impact of the gay and lesbian market and even the Congressional Budget
Office has researched and shown the positive impact of same-sex marriage on
our economy, controversy continues to pervade our nation. . . . I hope that
same-sex marriage is recognized, because it would strengthen our nation's
reputation as a place that embraces diverse philosophies, viewpoints, equality
and lifestyles and also bolster our economy in local and global arenas.

For this student, marriage is clearly tied to economic interests in the
public sphere, and he seems well on his way to developing a literacy that
understands the place of intimate and sexual arrangements in social organization. Such comments are revealing when compared to those of Steven
Seidman, a sociologist who has written provocatively and persuasively in
favor of gay marriage; he positions his argument as follows: "Instead of
raging against marriage, a more politically effective strategy would be to
argue for enhanced state recognition and support of nonmarital arrangements (in the short term) and to make the case for uncoupling basic
healthcare and social security benefits from marriage (in the long term).
These strategies would have the effect of further diminishing the normative status of marriage while equalizing intimate choices—symbolically
and materially. Such strategies would also have the added political benefit
of avoiding opposing an institution that remains a fundamental type of
value commitment for the vast majority of Americans" (2005, 241).

Seidman has written at length, and eloquently, critiquing marriage
as a personal and political institution. Seidman believes that we should
problematize the "coupling" of marriage with certain social and material benefits, and I think it's fascinating that students such as Ryan are
approaching such positions on their own. If coming to an awareness of
sexual literacy is understanding the imbrication of social norms with
structures and systems that organize intimate relationships, then these
students are arguing their way toward greater and greater fluency in
terms of such literacy.

Other students, such as Carrie, in her essay, "Same-Sex Marriage: A
State or Federal Definition?" are more cautious in their approach and
sensitive to the ways in which we need to pay careful attention to *language* when discussing this issue:

If the Supreme Court finds that denying same-sex couples the right to marry
is unconstitutional, the states should have the right to decide the specifics.
For example, states should decide if civil unions are the best answer and if

the term "marriage" should be reserved for heterosexual couples. . . . If the Supreme Court decides that denying same-sex couples the right to marry is not unconstitutional, then the states would still be given the right to decide if marriage or civil unions or anything at all will be given to gay couples. In this case, states should still be required to recognize unions given in other states.

While this position seems, as I say, more "cautious," I still see this student grappling with sexual literacy, particularly in her worrying over the term "marriage" and both its meaning and deployment in the public sphere.

Along these lines, Alex wrote a probing essay about the ways in which gay marriage has been taken up as an issue in political cartoons. His essay, "Something Funny about Queers", offers insightful comments coupled with deft rhetorical analysis:

I started to think that maybe the difference I was seeing between cartoons for and cartoons against same-sex marriage was this: supporters of a constitutional amendment to ban same-sex marriage attack homosexuals as being morally inferior to themselves. Whereas those who support same-sex marriage use humor as more of a coping device in what they see as an unfair and absurd situation. To my dismay, I found both side of the fence attacking the other rather frantically. I had hoped that I could prove that supporters of non-discriminatory marriage were more moral than the people so stridently fixated on being expressly moral, which is to say, the opponents.

There is some nice, nuanced thinking here. Alex reveals here a strong desire for such important debates to be treated as important by all sides involved—not flippantly and not dismissively of others' concerns. Such coupling of rhetorical concerns with an examination of how an intimate arrangement—marriage—is treated in the public sphere demonstrates that Alex, among others, is well on his way to developing a strong sense of sexual literacy as I have been using the phrase in this book.

Of course, not everyone in the course decided to write specifically about *gay* marriage. Some essays took up issues collateral to gay marriage, such as Ashley's "Who Should Adopt?" which advocated gay parental adoption rights. Other essays, such as Erica's "Women's Employment and Marital Stability," considered the role of women vis-à-vis marriage. Interestingly, though, it is in essays about *other* marital issues that students begin to demonstrate an understanding and critique of marriage as complicit in the construction and maintenance of norms surrounding intimacy and association. Gary himself commented as follows about these essays: "I was really interested in the students who wrote on polygamy because the book makes its argument for polygamy in some essay. It just seemed so much easier to say [no] to that. I had one student who basically wrote about that. Again, I think the good thing about it is that it kind of made you actually question marriage. There were some essays that were more about treatment of families and what about families where there is not [an] amorous relationship but there are two people living together. Maybe, what if there is a child? It kind of breaks down all the preconceptions of marriage. That was interesting." Gary is clearly pointing to how his students, in reading and thinking through the essays in *Just Marriage*, were prompted to think about sexual literacy in the sense that they were exposed to how competing narrations of marriage circulate in the public sphere and in turn problematize static and normative notions of intimate arrangements.

Interestingly, in the public sphere, some thinkers have begun articulating, much like some of the essayists in *Just Marriage*, for a move toward thinking about marriage as *more* than just a "gay issue." For instance, in "Beyond Gay Marriage," Lisa Duggan and Richard Kim (2005) argue in *The Nation* that focusing on the issue of gay marriage blinds us to thinking more critically about the many ways in which Americans organize their intimate lives. Speaking about attempts by conservatives such as Bennett to define marriage as strictly between a man and a woman, Duggan and Kim ask the following question:

> Is this exceedingly narrow vision of kinship and household arrangements what voters endorsed this November? Not if we take their actual living patterns as an indication of their preferences. Marriage is on the decline: Marital reproductive households are no longer in the majority, and most Americans spend half their adult lives outside marriage. The average age at which people marry has steadily risen as young people live together longer; the number of cohabitating couples rose 72 percent between 1990 and 2000. More people live alone, and many live in multigenerational, nonmarital households; 41 percent of these unmarried households include children. Increasing numbers of elderly, particularly women, live in companionate nonconjugal unions (think *Golden Girls*). Household diversity is a fact of American life rooted not just in the "cultural" revolutions of feminism and gay liberation but in long-term changes in aging, housing, childcare and labor. . . . But if marriage is

the symbolic and legal anchor for households and kinship networks, and marriage is increasingly unstable, how reliable will that source of support be?

Given such facts, it should not be surprising that some of Gary's students chose to write about marriage issues "beyond" gay marriage, to explore the other rich dimensions in which marriage is currently being rhetorically problematized. Several focused on polygamy, for instance.

In "Polygamist Societies: The New Religious Cult," Kyle offers a critique of polygamy:

> One of the most enduring aspect of polygamy is the inability to escape the confines of the community. Poverty is the main factor for individuals to stay inside of the community.

And David, in "What's Wrong with Polygamy?" considers both pros and cons of living in polygamous relationships, particularly as exemplified by Mormon practices:

> Although it is hard to ignore how bigamy laws target a historic practice of the Mormon religion, the downsides to polygamy far outweigh the upsides. Polygamy's tendency to rely on government subsidies and result in adultery makes it a tainted practice that should continue to be banned. Bigamy laws do not violate religious freedoms, because polygamy is an optional practice for Mormons.

Another student, Kerri, chose to view polygamy through a largely feminist lens in her essay, "Women and Polygamy," and she ultimately arrived at a view that refuses to dismiss polygamy completely:

> Now just as in monogamous marriage, polygamy has both positive and negative aspects. There are some aspects of plural marriage that women involved find to be very beneficial.
>
> In conclusion, it is impossible to group polygamy as a completely good institution or a completely bad institution. . . . Still, it is hard to ignore the negatives of this institution. . . . Young teens are being forced into marriage with close relatives and beaten when insubordinate, but at the same time there are women who need polygamy as an option to help their life situation.

What is fascinating to me about such a position, as underdeveloped as it is at this stage, is the willingness it reveals to consider alternative intimate relationships as legitimate. Even the arguments against polygamy suggest that these students are willing to think about and even support an expanded understanding of marriage—provided that marriage is still a marriage between two people. Still, I appreciate and applaud the willingness of the students who wrote against polygamy to view the issue from several sides, including a variety of pro-polyandry positions. They are open to considering alternative views and argue them out in their essays.

Along these lines, Ben's essay, "Can Polygamy Be Fair?" wonderfully "outs" the rhetorical issue in considering alternatives beyond traditional marriage. He pinpoints the definitional issues at stake in such debates early in his essay:

> Historically, polygamy—the union of multiple partners—has not been a just and equal practice. Indeed, some instances may be compared to servitude or even slavery. Primarily, polygamy has been a device for men to control and oppress women. Today, as Americans begin to reconsider and redefine marriage and other kinds of sexual and romantic relationships, it is difficult to avoid reconsidering polygamy as well. We must ask the question, "Can polygamy exist as a just and egalitarian institution in the world today?"

As we "reconsider and redefine marriage," Ben believes we should sift through a variety of positions in the debate. More specifically, his question—"Can polygamy exist as a just and egalitarian institution in the world today?"—signals his understanding that shifting sociocultural and historical contexts prompt us to reconsider how we have defined intimate relationships in the past. As such, he clearly articulates an understanding of how intimate, even sexual, relationships must be understood in their historical moments, as conditioned by their appearance at certain times, in certain places. I believe such an awareness reveals a fairly high level of sexual literacy. Ben then explores what polyamory means and actually advocates "giving it a chance." At the same time, he acknowledges that polyamory is not (and would not be) unproblematic in contemporary Anglo-American society. He reviews articles that point to ongoing gender inequalities in our society, and he suggests that relationships between men and women are difficult enough that adding additional partners might complicate personal gender politics even further:

> It seems that the gender roles in relationships are symptoms of a larger cultural climate, and to make relationships and unions more just and egalitarian, we need to identify and reevaluate inequalities in all areas of our culture.

Again, Ben nicely connects the personal ("gender roles in relationships) with the political ("symptoms of a larger cultural climate"). Admittedly, there are inarticulate moments here, but this is a student groping for a language with which to articulate a complex position on a complex topic. I believe that providing students a space in which to write about such issues, even if they do not do so with complete success, teaches them much more about the connection between thinking and writing than giving them "safe" topics on which to compose their essays.

CONSIDERING MARRIAGE RHETORICALLY: A CRITICAL SEXUAL LITERACY

What I find particularly stimulating about Gary's course and his students' writing is the attention throughout to rhetorical issues, to how we culturally, socially, and politically talk about and thus construct (and reconstruct) marriage. I believe such a course thus works toward helping students (and perhaps instructors as well) develop a critical sexual literacy. I asked Gary if he felt the course was successful—and why:

> I think people were generally really interested in the topic. I think that it went well. I think that, with the book—it was a really thin book with lots of essays coming from very different directions. They were somewhat historical and some political and so on. I think that worked pretty well. Also, because marriage issues were in the news, students saw that it was relevant. Also, what I found really interesting is pretty much the class unanimously agreed that gay marriage is going to be legal in their lifetime. Clearly the majority of the class was for gay marriage, even the people who [did not think] that it was going to happen. That was interesting.

Gary contextualizes his interest in tackling marriage in first-year composition within an understanding of his own development as a writing teacher. Specifically, he describes wanting to help students address important sociopolitical issues without provoking students into feeling that they are being trained to be politically correct. Gary says, "[It is important] to have the class address issues that are of social and political importance in a way that . . . doesn't make students feel like they are going to PC mill. That's something that I've been thinking about a lot."

For Gary, part of the process of working with controversial material, of turning students' attention to analyze critically what many would consider a "private" issue, such as marriage, worked well because he placed it in a broad context by *not focusing* specifically on gay and lesbian marriage issues. Of course, such issues *were* discussed, and several students chose to write about them, but the focus of the unit was primarily on *defining marriage* and contemporary debates about the definition of marriage. "Instead of saying, let's take this incredibly controversial thing that some people see as threatening, and instead taking the thing that people perceive as normal and no matter how they stand on it and getting them to realize that it's socially constructed and historically variable and so on is a really good move. Disrupting their sense of what's normal."

Gary's pedagogical stance—"disrupting their sense of what's normal"—reminds me of the stance of the queer pedagogues I discussed in the third chapter. Those pedagogues seemed less interested in promoting a particular sense of gay or lesbian identity or interests and more interested in critically and rhetorically examining the structures through which *all* of us organize and understand our relationships, our intimacies, and our lives.

Indeed, sexuality is an important field of power in our culture, and I believe that consideration of such an important dimension of that field of power—the construction of normative marriage relations—is in line with recent calls in composition studies to engage pressing social issues and connect them to considerations of discourse, literacy, and power. In the noteworthy collection of essays from numerous nationally recognized compositionists, *Composition Studies in the New Millennium: Rereading the Past, Rewriting the Future*, Kurt Spellmeyer lambastes composition's lingering "legacy of literary studies and cultural studies," which he identities as "marginal fields where scholars write largely for each other." Instead, in a post-9/11 world, he believes that composition should turn its attention to helping students "address complex issues synthetically." Spellmeyer concludes his chapter, "Education for Irrelevance?" with striking assertions about how composition classes might consider subjects such as terrorism or the various crises in the Middle East. He says, "No single department I know of could provide the comprehensive picture that people need to see the event with some clarity, and it strikes me that the same applies to genetic technology, the environmental crisis, globalization—all of which now pose for us potentially life-and-death questions." While maintaining that "no single department" could provide such a picture, Spellmeyer argues that "writing courses offer the one place in [the] entire curriculum where issues like these might be addressed in the synthetic way they require."

Configuring composition courses as sites to do this work would place them "at the center of the undergraduate experience" (2003, 86). The last set of essays in the collection extends such an argument, with pieces by Keith Gilyard, Harriet Malinowitz, and Richard E. Miller suggesting, variously, that composition courses are sites in which students can productively engage a variety of significant sociopolitical issues, such as social inequity, the corporatization of education, and injustices of an unthinking globalization. For each of these writers and pedagogues, the complex political issues raised are *literacy* issues, tied as they are to discourses and rhetorics of power. Learning to navigate such discourses is part of becoming politically and civically literate. Miller, for instance, argues that we must teach our students "how to propose viable solutions to the insoluble problems of the twenty-first century"; more pressingly, he asks, "if we do not prepare [our students] to play an active role in making a more hospitable future, who will?" (2003, 254).

As I have argued in this and previous chapters, issues pertaining to sex and sexuality remain among the "insoluble problems" of the beginning of the twenty-first century, linked as they are to complex social, cultural, and political issues. In terms of marriage, we must not forget that when inequities are maintained through the insistence that some domains are "personal" or "private" this often elides how very *not* personal and private such institutions are. At the very least, such elision helps to maintain inequities. As such, if we are to have a "more hospitable future" for all, we must consider actively issues of sex and sexuality and their intersection with a variety of sociocultural and political discourses and rhetorics, as a proper subject of composition.

While Gary's students began, I believe, to understand issues of marriage (and not just *gay* marriage) as part of our individual and collective sexual literacies, inevitably there are blind spots in their formulations and arguments. For instance, students articulated little to no cognizance of marital issues as shifting *globally*. Other countries, including Spain, the Netherlands, Belgium, and Canada, have legalized gay marriage, but students remained relatively ethnocentric in their focus on the United States. Further, they did not pay much attention to the history and "constructedness" of marriage across time and cultures. Attention to marriage in both its global and historical contexts might have helped complexify students' arguments, and point out more forcefully linkages between discourses about marriages and other cultural, social, and political literacies. For example, discourses about marriage in the Islamic countries of the Middle East are more likely to reveal complex intersections among legal, religious, and personal discourses that describe personal and public life. When approaching the rich, complex, and complicated kinds of issues that Spellmeyer urges us to use with students, we must keep in mind that such lapses are inevitable. One course can only do so much, and we cannot expect student writers to account for all dimensions of difficult social and political issues, particularly *sexual* ones, for which they are still developing sophisticated literacies and discourses.

In terms of other difficulties or "trouble" spots, a couple of students expressed resistance to dealing with gay issues, and I cannot help but wonder if some students chose *not* to write about gay marriage and instead explored other marital issues as a way of *avoiding* queerness. Gary describes one student who grappled with how to negotiate his antigay marriage views with the writing assignment:

> Gary: I just remember one student was more clearly agitated because he was more conservative and he wasn't sure what to write on. I think I talked to him about writing on divorce. It was about protecting marriage, and whether or not it was actually already being threatened from the inside by divorce rates and so on. He was the only student I remember feeling put out by this. I remember another student that really struggled with trying to find something to write on. I think she ended up writing on psychological studies of couples. One person wrote on the question, should I get married? I thought that was very funny. It was a really funny thing.
>
> Jonathan: Was that a successful paper?
>
> Gary: I believe it was. I remember saying to him, and he wrote a lot about whether marriage is an institution he wanted to be part of. It was like, do I want to be a swingin' bachelor the rest of my days or married? I remember pointing out to him that even if gay marriage is made acceptable, that perhaps there were many gay and lesbian people who wouldn't want to get married because of how they regarded the institution and stuff. It worked. It worked well.

Gary himself seems to have realized that his course design, with a fairly open-ended approach to marriage as a broad issue, might have allowed some students the opportunity to avoid tackling challenging aspects of marriage. He says, "For some students, it allows them to avoid anything that was really threatening to their way of thinking and they could focus on something more that was just kind of relevant to issues of marriage, I guess. But most of them actually ended up thinking up pretty interesting questions. [And t]hey got to write about what they wanted to write about and then have their research question and why they wanted to write on it."

For Gary, that openness—creating a space in which students could tackle issues they felt were important—created the opportunity for some to address rather challenging issues, even as it may have allowed a few others to dodge more critical inquiry into sexual literacy and its relationship to marriage. For me, perhaps what is most exciting about such a course is that it gives students permission to examine thoughtfully and critically one of the primary narrative imperatives facing many of our students—the expectation that they will "grow up" to marry and form families that will further the story of the nuclear family in our culture. While such a storyline will be fulfilling for many students, it is worth examining, and a critical pedagogy grappling with sexual literacy cannot help but take up the narratives of marriage circulating in our culture.

SITES OF RESISTANCE

6

SUSIE BRIGHT IN THE COMP CLASS
Confronting Resistances

Susie Bright is a sex writer—a very good one, in my opinion. She has a wonderful ability to be both pragmatic and philosophical, writing candidly about the mechanics of particular sexual positions *and* why it is important to talk openly about sex and sexuality. As such, her writing in books such as *The Sexual State of the Union* is never just erotic, though much of her writing is. Rather, it's about sexual *politics*, about the silences that keep us from talking openly about sex and the many reasons why such silences damage our ability to be intimate with one another—and to understand how such silences create damaging norms about sex and gender that limit our sense of possibility, of creativity, of growth. Suggesting that our country suffers from "erotic poverty," Bright writes:

> Sexual perceptions, those false premises, are formed by ignorance, pure and desperate. It's not only the troubling things we don't understand today, but also the superstitions of years past that cling to all the dark places where people don't get information, don't get examples, don't get an opportunity to try out anything different. I'm not talking about a cave, I'm talking about everything and everyone—from entire states in this country where you can't get simple information about sexuality, to a Los Angeles radio station manager who handed me a piece of paper that said, "Please do not use the word clitoris." That's the legacy of censorship and elitism: we are erased below the waist, in the interest of the so-called public welfare—an interest so narrowly defined that it rules out just about everyone who doesn't own their own cable company or have a chair on the FCC. (1997, 17)

Bright's writing, as in this example, is often polemical. But it's neither simplistic nor naive. And in many ways, Bright's work is all about sexual literacy—about understanding how to talk about sex and sexuality in ways that are open, honest, and critical. Her work is about understanding that the ways in which we talk about sex have much to say about who we are, individually and collectively.

I once told a colleague that I was seriously considering organizing a section of first-year composition around Bright's *The Sexual State of the Union*. This colleague, herself a lesbian, flipped out. She thought I had really lost my mind. I have to admit that I began to wonder, have I gone too far? Am I incorporating *too much* sex and sexuality into my composition courses? Am I *stretching* the connection between literacy and sexuality—perhaps to the breaking point?

Perhaps I've gotten carried away. Maybe a recap is in order.

Throughout this book, I have argued for creating pedagogical spaces in which writing instructors can approach the topic of sexuality in their writing courses as a *literacy issue*—a realization that becoming increasingly aware of how "talk" about sexuality is tied to some of the most fundamental ways in which we "talk" about ourselves, our lives, our communities, our nation, and our world. Put bluntly, I have maintained that sexuality plays a significant role in how literacy is defined, understood, and articulated in contemporary Anglo-American culture. As a queer man, I am already well aware of how important such literacy is. My life has taught me that it is imperative that I "read" given situations, assess their potential threat to me in a homophobic culture, and perform identities that either keep me safe from harm or use my queerness to challenge norms of behavior, identity, and intimacy. Sometimes I have to navigate carefully between those positions, and I think that many queer people do this on a daily basis. It is part of how we are "literate" in society. So maybe my interest in Susie Bright arises out of the very frankness with which she understands and wants to talk about sexuality. She resists urges, injunctions, and demands that she be quiet about sex. She has "read" our collective cultural situation, and she wants to talk about sex and sexuality—to educate, to provoke, to excite, to question the forces that keep something so powerful "in the closet." As someone who has at times had to be silent about sexuality, I can't help but want to hear more.

But I also recognize that not all of my students will share my enthusiasm—and that they may resist the acquisition of such knowledges, such literacies, about sex and sexuality.

Indeed, I am sure that some readers are thinking it unusual that I have not covered issues of potential student resistance more substantively and earlier in this text. While I have touched on periodic resistances in the exercises and assignments I have described in preceding chapters, I have largely relegated a more thorough consideration of such resistances to this final chapter for the simple reason that *significant resistance has been uncommon in my experience of working with students on issues of sexual literacy.* Let me be clear. I do not believe that I am a gifted teacher or particularly adept at teaching and learning with students about sexual literacies. But I *do* believe that my willingness to be open and upfront with students about sex—that is, my willingness to speak respectfully but frankly about such a taboo topic—helped to create environments in which students felt comfortable to explore sexual literacy. I believe that Gary, whose course I described in chapter 5, did much the same.

In the remainder of this chapter, however, I want to consider a set of resistances—both at the disciplinary level and in actual student-centered classroom situations—that composition instructors interested in exploring sexual literacy might encounter. Inevitably, we as instructors must also face *our own* resistances when thinking, writing, teaching, and talking about sex. To my mind, exploring such resistances, at every level, is a key part of developing sexual literacy.

THE STORY SO FAR: A RECAP OF THE PEDAGOGY OF SEXUAL LITERACY

As we saw in the first chapter, some teacher-scholars invested in queer theory and queer critiques have attempted to flesh out what such a pedagogy might look like, most notably the educational theorist William F. Pinar, editor of *Queer Theory in Education.* Among the most notable essays in Pinar's collection is "Queering/Querying Pedagogy? Or, Pedagogy Is a Pretty Queer Thing" by Susanne Luhmann, who argues provocatively for "a queer pedagogy [that] exceeds the incorporation of queer content into curricula and the worry over finding teaching strategies that make this content more palatable to students" (1998, 141). Luhmann poses her goals as a series of questions interrogating what we take to be "normal": "How do normalcy and abnormalcy become assigned subject positions? How can they be subverted? How can the very notion of a unified human subject be parodied and, jointly with other discourses, radically deconstructed into a fluid, permanently shifting, and unintelligible subjectivity?" (146).

Luhmann characterizes such questioning as "one of pedagogic curiosity, from what (and how) the author writes or the teacher teaches, to what the student understands, or what the reader reads" (1998, 148). It is just such curiosity—about ourselves, about our society, about how the stories of sexuality become enmeshed and intertwined with the stories of who we are, both individually and collectively—that I have wanted to explore with students. This pedagogy of promoting sexual literacy must necessarily, as I have shown, take into consideration students' own knowledges and reflections on sex, sexuality, and literacy. As Luhmann herself argues, "[s]uch an approach, rather than assuming the student as ignorant or lacking knowledge, inquires into, for example, how textual positions are being taken up by the reading or learning subject" (149). I could not agree more, and I believe that the exercises I have described in this book have pulled on—and challenged—students' interests and insights about sexual literacy.

While a pedagogy of sexual literacy should rely initially on students' knowledge and interests, we must necessarily keep in mind that approaching sex and sexuality in the classroom seems at times a "risky business." Part of the sense of danger or risk comes inevitably from a continued sense of sex and sexuality as "taboo" subjects, best left to the realm of the private. But more broadly, questioning the stories we tell about ourselves, either individually or collectively, involves an inherent amount of risk. Put another way, "pedagogic curiosity" often runs counter to the sense with which many students (and some teachers) come into the classroom: the sense that Freire captures in the "banking model" of education, or the sense that instructors have knowledge to impart to students—*not* the sense that students and instructors *together* will explore difficult terrain, learning about it as they proceed. So, when it comes to thinking about sex and sexuality and their complex intertwining with literacy, with the very way in which we represent ourselves to ourselves and to one another, then the going is bound to be rough. We *are* dealing with highly personal material, even as we are asking students to consider the most personal aspects of ourselves as also densely and deeply public and political.

Approaching the nexus of the personal/political is tricky business, and I have relied on the thinking of others in our field to help me approach it—and to understand *why* it is crucial that we do so. In the introduction to this book I referenced Ira Shor's concept of "desocialization," which he defines as "questioning the social behaviors and experiences in school and daily life that make us into the people we are. Such desocialization involves critically examining learned behavior, received values, familiar language, habitual perceptions, existing knowledge and power relations, and traditional discourse in class and out" (1992, 114). For Shor, it is imperative that we question such received wisdom because it often contains within it values and ideologies that deeply shape not only our conception of ourselves and others but also our sense of what is possible. Critiquing how values come to be held and passed on from person to person allows us to understand their history—and to sense how they might change. For example, if we are socialized to understand sex as a purely personal matter, then we are blind to how ideologies and beliefs about sex, sexuality, and gender shape our sense of self, our sense of the normal, and our sense of future growth and possibility. As we desocialize sex and sexuality as purely personal aspects of existence, we begin to see how sexuality is tied to a number of norms that control and curtail our behavior. Indeed, some students question why I talk about issues of gender or sexuality—as though these things, sexuality in particular, really should not be talked about in public. I believe, however, that it is imperative to create pedagogical spaces to desocialize their hesitancies around sexuality issues—because so much social control is exerted through sexual orientation identities, restriction of information about sexuality, and our socially constructed views of sexuality.

Inevitably, though, resistances occur. Students do not always want to think about sexual literacy, and I am certain that some instructors reading this book have balked at the ideas that I have presented here. Let's look briefly at some of those resistances and why it is necessary, I believe, to confront them and push through to an exploration of sexual literacy, as risky as it may feel at times.

DISCIPLINARY RESISTANCES

Clearly, one of the major resistances that anyone interested in exploring sexual literacy will face, from either students or other instructors, is a strong sense of sex and sexuality as "personal" issues, as aspects of life unfit for consideration in the public space of the classroom. Since this is such a potentially pervasive resistance, I call it a disciplinary resistance, one with which our field as a whole must grapple. I hope that my arguments throughout this book about the very public and even political nature of sex and sexuality have addressed the fallacy of thinking of sex and sexuality as purely personal. Of course, sex and sexuality are also personal issues, so they need to be treated carefully and respectfully. (More on that in a bit.) What interests me about hesitancies around sexuality in the classroom is a more general unwillingness among many in our field to consider the personal in the composition classroom.

In terms of sexuality itself, Gary Dowsett of the Australian Research Centre in Sex, Health, and Society notes that when we think about young people's sexuality we tend to think of it in terms of *problems*—as in, young people are having unwanted pregnancies, are exposing themselves to sexually transmitted infections, or are victims of date rape and other forms of sexual coercion. Rarely do we think about young people's sexuality in more positive terms, much less the right of young people to explore and engage in sexual pleasures (Herdt et al. 2006). As such, cultural sexual literacy in the United States does not have much of a discourse of pleasure with which to approach sex and sexuality more positively. Given this, discussions of young people's sexuality might seem too loaded or heavy-handed or more properly the subject of private moral and ethical discussion—not public consideration in a first-year composition course.

In some ways, the personal has always been a vexed subject in composition, at least since the work of Peter Elbow and the advent of expressivism. As compositionists, we worry about how much we are asking students to disclose about themselves when composing personal narratives or when they are supporting claims with personal experiences. Will they reveal "too much" and be sorry later? Will *we* be sorry if they reveal personal information in the classroom, particularly if it's of a sensitive nature? In many ways, we are right to worry about this, in the sense that we should always tread carefully when considering other people's lives, histories, and stories. But treading carefully doesn't mean foreclosing such discussion or disallowing it because it's risky. After all, what writing, except the most rote reporting, *is not* personal to some extent?

Some compositionists have argued persuasively for a more careful and candid (re)consideration of the personal in writing. In Deborah Holdstein and David Bleich's edited collection, *Personal Effects: The Social Character of Scholarly Writing*, the editors note that "[o]ne of the reasons for the exclusion of the first person in scholarly writing is the idea that because scholarship is for everyone, narcissism is unwelcome" (2001, 19). At the same time, as Holdstein and Bleich point out, a variety of feminist and post-structuralist critiques have demonstrated that knowledge construction (and dissemination) is often grounded in the personal situations and contexts of those intimately involved in its construction. Such grounding arises from the conviction that all knowledge arises from personal investments made by knowing subjects, who are themselves products of particular times, places, and historical circumstances. As knowledge producers, we have personal stakes in the knowledge we pursue and help construct. Knowing why we are personally invested in particular knowledges helps us understand better how knowledge is constructed. But more significantly, acknowledging our personal investment in knowledge construction helps us understand and clarify our values and our *ideological* investments. Or, as Holdstein and Bleich put it, "we also want to feel the authority that may come from an elaborated and developed style of personal candor, and we want to propose understanding that is more helpful because more clearly anchored in human experience" (7).

Candace Spigelman, writing in *Personally Speaking: Experience as Evidence in Academic Discourse,* believes that we should help our students develop such a consciousness as they think, analyze, explore, and write. She argues that "[w]hile composition teachers have expressed extraordinary support for public-directed writing instruction, its attendant texts seem distant from personal discourse. Nevertheless, I suggest that experiential evidence has a place in public writing, and in the work that surrounds the teaching of these discourses" (2004, 131). More specifically, Spigelman believes that "in addition to its appeals to emotion and identification, personal experience can make logical appeals, which can be evaluated as evidence in academic writing" (107). Of course, there *are* limits to how logical the personal can actually be, but Spigelman's point is a compelling one: much of what we take to be purely logical or rational often hides personal and ideological investments. Linking personal interest to logical argument grounds our claims firmly in the realm of human experience. For instance, if I want to argue for an end to discrimination based on sexual orientation, I can present *both* logical arguments *and* my personal experiences, demonstrating the logical ill effects of discrimination in my actual life. Along these lines, Spigelman argues that we should be teaching hybrid and experimental forms and genres; she says, "*[i]t seems to me that there is a greater advantage to blending discourses: using personal writing in and as academic argument*" (14; emphasis in the original).

Beyond an unwillingness to explore the personal in the composition classroom, others continue to be uncomfortable with the move toward inclusive curricula or multicultural education in general. Such instructors may believe, as does Maxine Hairston, whose essay "Diversity, Ideology, and the Teaching of Writing" I cited in the introduction, that our courses should be invested in teaching "skills" as opposed to "ideology." Along these lines, supporters of David Horowitz's "Academic Bill of Rights" want to "protect" students from undue political influences and return classroom instruction to the unbiased pursuit of knowledge (http://insidehighered.com/news/2006/02/17/ariz). While I believe that our classrooms *should* be free of indoctrination, I also firmly believe that a significant difference exists between indoctrination and *critical examination*. Our pedagogies must be curious. We should invite students to examine their lives, the stories they tell about them, the larger cultural narratives that organize and construct meaning, and the political tales that allocate and maneuver common resources. Suggesting that certain kinds of experiences should not be discussed publicly, such as sex and sexuality, is to foreclose on the fullest understanding we might have of the human experience, both individually and collectively.

Granted, sexuality is a volatile field, rife with contradictions—but it is volatile because sexuality is also a *field of power*. Debates and discourses about sex and sexuality, and the "moral panics" they sometimes seem to incite, are often about things *other* than sexuality. They are also points of *contested* power, points where issues of power and social control are in the process of being contested and sorted out. For instance, an unwillingness to talk frankly and comprehensively about sex and sexuality in the public school system represents not just a squeamishness about sexuality or a belief that sex is a purely personal, family matter; it is also about controlling young people's lives, limiting their choices, channeling their energies into pursuits that the larger body politic deems necessary. Sexuality is a powerful connector, a powerful creative force. If young people's sexual interests and energies are directed *away* from a capacious and experimental exploration of personal intimacies and *toward* long-term career and family planning, then traditional corporate and capitalist interests are well served. As such, educating students—and becoming educated *with* them—about how the stories and narratives of sexuality move in our culture and do a variety of "power work" is essential in developing critical literacy.

Perhaps even more pressingly, the intersections among sex, sexuality, and religion are in dire need of critical attention and examination. The great social theorists of the modern period, including Freud and Marx, believed that religion would eventually diminish in importance socially and personally. However, the last few decades have seen the emergence of strong movements of religious fundamentalism, including Christian and Islamic fundamentalism, which generally oppose many sexual rights and freedoms and do not understand sex as pleasure or recreation. The rise of fundamentalism is a complex phenomenon, related no doubt to contemporary shifts in power. For instance, the demise of the Soviet Union, which attempted to squelch religious fundamentalism in areas it controlled and influenced, has allowed old animosities and conflicts to resurface with a vengeance. As fundamentalists abroad and in our own country (whether Islamic or Christian) oppose sexual freedom, it is important for all of us to ask, why? (Herdt, et al, 2006).

Let me forward a few questions based on contemporary examples that speak powerfully to the intersections among sexual orientation and religion. As sexual expression is curtailed, whose interests are served? As male youth engaging in homosexual acts in Iran are hanged publicly, who benefits? As some Christians in the United States picket funerals of gay youth, whose view of the world is challenged, whose validated, whose delimited, whose sanctioned? As Western societies generally debate the role of marriage and consider a variety of arguments, including religious ones, about the "proper" sanctioning of marriage, whose stories about intimacy and family are forwarded, whose denied, whose impoverished, whose enriched? These are just a few of the contemporary issues in which religious belief and sexual expression and relationship are clashing in significant ways. As we work toward understanding the contested stories circulating now about religion and sexuality, we should seriously consider inviting our students to participate in our deliberations, our debates. Doing so will both enhance their ability to participate as literate citizens and serve to educate them about the world they are inheriting from us.

Another significant resistance that I have encountered as I have talked about sexual literacy with a variety of colleagues and compositionists comes in the form of a question: Does this really work? Do students actually *write better* because of all of your effort in inviting them to think about sexual literacy? I call such questions "resistant questions" because they betray hesitancy by asking for "proof," for validation that my means (developing sexual literacy) are justified in the ends (better student writers), despite the benefits I have claimed throughout for exploring sexual literacy in and of itself. Don't get me wrong: I'm not dismissing the need of composition pedagogies to improve student writing and critical thinking skills. Far from it. In fact, my experiences detailed in the previous chapters, as well as the experiences of Molly (in chapter 1), James (in chapter 2), and Gary (in chapter 5) strongly suggest that attention to sexual literacy improves student writing on a number of fronts.

In a very basic way, inviting students to work with us on sexual literacy takes advantage of a topic—sexuality—that is of increasing importance to many young people. As compositionists, we know how difficult it can be to find topics, or even to assist students in finding topics, in which they can be invested. The pedagogical work throughout this book attests to the high level of investment that many students writers have when talking and writing about sex and sexuality. But more than increased investment, I believe that addressing not just sex, but *sexual literacy*, enhances students' ability to think critically. In my work with students in interrogating narrations of gender or examining representations of straight sexuality, students had to consider carefully how one positions oneself *rhetorically* as a gendered and sexually oriented subject. Such subject positions presuppose certain assumptions, so examining narrations of them closely is an acute exercise in reading for hidden, even contradictory assumptions, particularly when, as in the case of a narration of a "straightboy" who likes a "boy band," the narration is complex and nuanced. Moreover, learning to ask critical questions about things often taken for granted, such as gender and sexual orientation, attunes students to the work of critical inquiry. I believe that Gary's students in particular learned much about questioning large-scale cultural assumptions, narrations, and ideological investments in concepts such as marriage and monogamy.

In terms of more specific writing skills, I believe that students who write about sex and sexuality do so often with much careful consideration. Like us, they understand that sex/uality is a "difficult subject" and must be handled with rhetorical sensitivity. Sex/uality itself, just as a topic, raises students' attention as a subject requiring deft handling lest readers and interlocutors misunderstand one's intent and goals. I have seen students pay much more careful attention to their word choice when talking and writing about sex and sexuality than at nearly any other time or with regard to nearly any other subject. Of course, there are inevitable exceptions, but I would argue that most students are more attuned to language use when writing about sex/uality.

I have also seen significant attention paid to issues of audience in essays written on sex and sexuality. In some of my earlier work, most notably the penultimate chapter of *Digital Youth: Emerging Literacies on the World Wide Web* (2005), I describe my experiences working with first-year writing students on the development of the YOUth & AIDS Web

Project, which spanned several years during my tenure at the University of Cincinnati. During that time, students wrote extensively about sex, sexuality, sex education, sexual health, and the political battles over HIV and AIDS. One of the last phases of that work involved launching a sub-site of the main site, called "Voices of Youth," in which student writers were invited to speak candidly with fellow students about sexual health. Certainly, the pedagogical context—an invitation for students to write to one another about the "touchy subject" of sexual health—may have attuned students' attention to the importance of audience. But the actual writing (currently housed at http://homepages.uc.edu/~alexanj/voices_of_youth.htm) speaks volumes about how students will work with language to reach one another with important information—and important literacies. Students wrote about topics such as "AIDS and Youth Denial," "Myths about Condoms," and "Negotiating Healthy Relationships." In each, student writers carefully crafted information for easy access, explained difficult or confusing concepts, and wrote in what they called an "accessible" manner. Interweaving facts with narrative examples, students created pieces that are models, I believe, of persuasive writing, urging their classmates and readers of their work to think carefully about their lives, their bodies, and their intimacies.

What I most appreciated about this work was not only students' rhetorical savvy in addressing their chosen audiences, but also their increasing awareness that sexuality and literacy are deeply intertwined. As the titles above suggest, students wanted to address literacy issues— How can we become more informed about important topics? How can we debunk myths and false information? How can we negotiate our desires? The clarity of the writing in "Myths about Condoms," for instance, makes immediate and compelling claims about the importance of sexual literacy:

> Most of us have probably already been told by somebody that if you are going to have sex you should use a condom. This is true. Proper use of condoms is an important precaution that you should take to protect yourself from contracting HIV, and although this site is dedicated to the prevention of HIV/AIDS there are various other sexually transmitted diseases, along with unwanted pregnancies, that you will also protect yourself from by using a condom.
>
> Unfortunately there is a lot of misinformation out there about sex in general.

> When a subject remains taboo as sex does it creates an environment in which rumors become widely believed. Most of us have probably heard something that sounded exaggerated or just plain wrong. The problem is that when these rumors are about sex, young people might not know how to find out if they are true or false. Further, when we were younger, we may have been afraid to ask a parent, or any adult, questions about sex and we may have been left believing things that are not at all true.

What I frankly love about the writing here is its insistence that sexuality is not just an intimacy issue, but also a literacy issue. As discussed throughout this book, sex and sexuality are constructed not just through biological and scientific facts, but often through ideologically valenced beliefs and presuppositions. Understanding how stories, rumors, and often (mis)information about sex and sexuality circulate increases students' ability to understand the sociopolitical dimensions of literacy at a very fundamental—at a bodily and intensely intimate—level. Put another way, how we talk about ourselves in such basic dimensions—about our bodies, our intimacies, our identities—is vitally important. We can be misinformed, to our peril and detriment. But talking in informed ways—talking literately about sexuality—constructs healthier sexualities, healthier people. Doing so also allows one to be more critical, to be able to analyze and sift valid and useful information from rumor. In the process, one has the opportunity to see the ideological values or blind spots that support rumor and misinformation, usually in the name of making sex/uality do other ideological work. When sex is taboo, as this author suggests, ignorance about sex and sexuality keeps people afraid, sometimes unwilling to ask for information. People are kept illiterate about some of the most powerful emotions, experiences, and intimacies that they are capable of having. In many ways, such writing powerfully suggests that a failure to be sexually literate is a failure to be literate about informed living.

Given both sex and sexuality's pervasiveness in our culture and their contested position vis-à-vis other social issues (such as education, marriage, family life, reproduction, and religion), it is important that students be invited to examine sex and sexuality critically. Our discipline must put aside its squeamishness. If anything, I hope the preceding chapters have served as an argument *for developing discourses through which we can discuss with one another more positive and nurturing ways to discuss sexuality.* Such is part and parcel of developing individual, group, and disciplinary sexual literacy.

MORE PERSONAL RESISTANCES

In *Disciplining Sexuality: Foucault, Life Histories, and Education,* Sue Middleton succinctly notes the ways in which power circulates, even somewhat sexually, in classroom situations: "Through Foucauldian lenses, power indeed shows up as 'capillary,' as it flows through all parts of the school's 'corporate body.' All individuals channel power: Students and teachers police each others' outward appearance, deportment, and behavior, although it is the teacher who officially has power over the students" (1998, 21). Given this multivalent channeling and policing of power, it is not surprising that students at times will use their own power to resist what we as instructors are trying to do. Such resistance may be particularly apparent when we approach taboo subjects such as sex and sexuality.

Be that as it may, few guides to teaching writing substantively address how to think critically with students about ideological conflicts when they arise in the classroom, and I have seen precious few trainings, for either graduate teaching assistants or new faculty (or "old" faculty, for that matter) in teaching "sensitive" subjects such as sexual literacy. In terms of the available literature, Brock Dethier's *The Composition Instructor's Survival Guide* (1999) lists and briefly discusses "common problems" such as the "quiet class," the "painful conference," and the "difficult student." Comparably, *Conflicts and Crises in the Composition Classroom—And What Instructors Can Do about Them,* edited by Dawn M. Skorczewski and Matthew Parfitt (2003), has a similar focus on "practical" resistances such as grade disputes, and also contains a section on handling topics of "race," though much of the discussion is focused on issues of language difference. *Writing Relationships: What Really Happens in the Composition Class* by Lad Tobin (1993) explores very well the kinds of conflicts that can arise when students and teachers work intensely on writing together, and Tobin comes closest to understanding, I think, such experiences as truly intimate, needing careful attention to students' lives and interests. Along such lines, Suzanne Diamond notes in her essay "When Underlife Takes Over: An Insight on Student Resistance and Classroom Dynamics" (2003) that we should be attentive to students' "underlife," a sociological term used by Robert Brooke to identify disruptive behavior in classrooms—behavior that signals potential student resistances to the material being taught in particular or to the process of schooling in general. However, the topics of sex and sexuality are never mentioned, and the focus in these guides is primarily on dealing with challenges to authority rather than ideological conflicts or resistances to the material that is being grappled with in the classroom.

Increasingly, though, I believe we will see more guides to working with resistances to *topics and course content*. For instance, some online resources about talking with students about terrorism and the terrorist attacks of 9/11/2001 are easily available on the Web—signaling a growing need among instructors to be able to discuss touchy subjects as they arise nationally. Along these lines, one compositionist, Bill Wolff, describes in his essay "Reading the Rhetoric of Web Pages: Rethinking the Goals of Student Research in the Computer Classroom" (2003) how he designed a course that focused on critically analyzing how information about war, such as the various conflicts in Kosovo and the war in Iraq, is represented, constructed, and disseminated in the mass media, particularly the Web. Wolff's aim is "to develop a truly dialogic pedagogical practice that fosters critical thinking and writing." More specifically, he wants to "bridge the chasm between the traditional goals of a university liberal arts education, urgent contemporary issues, and a lack of critical thought about technology . . . by advocating the use of Web sites—both 'reliable' and 'unreliable'—which can then enable students to think more critically about issues of relevance to contemporary society." Wolff's decision to focus on the representation of war is timely—and potentially risky. But, as his goals make clear, his purpose is not to promote a particular view of war but to invite students to think rhetorically about how war is represented, which should prompt them to think more critically about the ways in which wars are supported, sustained, and legitimized. Comparable to my interest in sexual literacy, Wolff's work with war might be called "war literacy."

Other pressing issues have provoked some important discussion. A recent book from some colleagues in our field, the collection *Social Change in Diverse Teaching Contexts: Touchy Subjects and Routine Practices*, edited by Nancy G. Barron, Nancy M. Grimm, and Sibylle Gruber, focuses on handling race and racial issues in the classroom. The editors frame their project's goals in this way:

> This collection of essays opens a window on the "inside job" that committed teachers must undertake to be effective literacy educators in a racially divided

nation. This inside job includes the deeply reflective intellectual and emotional work whereby courageous teachers engage honestly with the tensions between their social roles as teachers in a nation that holds to myths of color-blindness and meritocracy, and their individual identities as people with complicated personal histories and theoretical commitments. When unspoken racial tensions undermine classroom dynamics, teachers need a high degree of social knowledge, skill, and tact to address them effectively. (2006, 10)

For Barron, Grimm, and Gruber, teachers must be willing to risk difficult discussion in working with students on developing "racial literacy," or a better sense of how the stories we individually and culturally tell about race (our various race "myths") are tied to material differences in how people are treated and to their experience (or not) of economic justice. Clearly, then, when it comes to issues of war and race, some compositionists are working hard to think critically about how such topics might be profitably encountered in the composition classroom. More significantly, as these two examples show, war and race are not simply "topics" but intertwined with literacy issues in complex ways—in much the same ways, I believe, that sex/uality and literacy are densely interconnected.

However, when it comes to thinking critically with students specifically about sex and sexuality and confronting potential student resistances, next to nothing exists in English studies literature. As such, there is little to help us as instructors sift through potential student resistances. One exception comes from one of our colleagues in literature and literary studies, a slender book called *Teaching Literature* by Elaine Showalter, which includes a brief but useful chapter called "Teaching Dangerous Subjects." Showalter at once praises English instructors, particularly literature instructors, for willingness to approach difficult material and cautions us all against doing so without some sense of caution: "the awareness literature teachers bring to representations of race, dialect, and ethnicity does not usually extend to the many other difficult subjects literature presents, and sometimes romanticizes, such as suicide, abortion, pornography and sexually graphic language, drug addiction, and alcoholism. Because we have become accustomed to treating the material as fictional or textual, teachers can overlook the sensitivity of content." A failure to consider "sensitivity of content" might very well lead to some students feeling alienated or even hostile. Such is particularly the case for students who might not want to discuss sexually loaded topics. For Showalter, honesty is the best policy in diffusing potential resistance:

"One important principle is candor and clear labeling—telling students in advance that they may be offended or upset; contextualizing the topic with some sociological or historical background; being prepared for some students to be shocked or upset no matter what you do, and allowing opportunities for them to respond" (2003, 126). Showalter is even more explicit in her advice about dealing with sexually sensitive material. She advises: "I believe that the professor's behavior and tone are crucial in shaping students' attitudes towards sexual language. If we are embarrassed, they will be embarrassed. If we are salacious, they will leer. Nonetheless, especially for women professors, sexual language and material can be problematic. I try to demystify and legitimize sexually explicit language in the classroom by using it in lecture, when reading passages from the text, without fuss or emphasis" (129).

I believe Showalter is generally correct, and my experience has demonstrated that if I approach a "sensitive" topic, such as AIDS or sex education, with respect and as though it is perfectly normal to talk about such topics, then students are likely to follow suit. As mentioned above, in a previous book, *Digital Youth*, I recount my experiences with multiple sections of first-year writing courses primarily focused on exploring HIV and AIDS as personal, social, cultural, and political issues. Students were nearly unanimously engaged with the project—not because I am a particularly good instructor, but because we committed as a class to think and write about the subject respectfully—and to respect one another's views and positions.

At times, though, some students will resist participating, if only because they are uncomfortable talking about sex and sexuality. And this is totally understandable—and *should be openly acknowledged as understandable*. Pamela L. Caughie eloquently addresses the risky nature of talking about sensitive subjects such as sexual diversity in her book *Passing and Pedagogy: The Dynamics of Responsibility*. She notes that "[w]hat makes learning about diversity so risky, as Spivak, hooks, and others have pointed out, is the imperative it brings to unlearn our own forms of privilege. . . . In unlearning forms of privilege, in responding to the challenge of their own ignorance, students, it is generally assumed, must be willing to take the risk of uncertainty and to suspend their desire for mastery. Asking them not to pass as authorities, we ask them to take the ultimate risk of not passing at all" (1999, 61). At such moments of risk, avoidance is easy. In "Conflict and Kitsch: The Politics of Politeness in the Writing Class, (2003), Wendy Ryden notes that classroom discussions that might involve conflict or ideological dissent can sometimes sidestep such dissent through the often unspoken operation of an "etiquette" that disavows the possibility of conflict. In other words, many students (and perhaps some instructors) automatically move in the direction of ignoring potential conflict as a way to "keep the peace."

In the face of such silences, I have found Dawn M. Skorczewski's advice in *Teaching One Moment at a Time: Disruption and Repair in the Classroom* to be particularly helpful. She argues for the use of a "freeze frame" technique, which she describes at length:

> To begin to think about what is happening (from the perspective of teaching) in a discussion that is moving along, I consider its opposite: the interpersonal dynamics of moments of disruption, moments when the discussion is not working. I also introduce a pedagogical tool, "the freeze frame," that I have found useful to my understanding of the classroom discussion. The freeze frame refers to a process through which we examine student-teacher interactions in a classroom by stopping the action to talk about what is happening at any given moment. The freeze frame is a break from the action, in which the facilitator halts the action of the discussion to draw our attention to what we are feeling in the room, what we are creating with the rest of the class, and how we are expanding ourselves as thinkers and writers. The majority of freeze frames are initiated because of the discussion leader's perception that something is not happening in the room that should be happening or because of her or his confusion about how to proceed. They also, more infrequently, occur at moments when the discussion is going well and the leader does not know why or how this happened. (2005, 40)

The "freeze frame" is particularly useful for discussion of sex, sexuality, and sexual literacy because it allows students to express their discomfort about talking (or writing) about sexuality. In the process of discussing such discomfort, they are taking their first steps toward desocialization around sex and sexuality—and toward sexual literacy, or being able to talk intelligently and critically about sex/uality.

But silence is not the only form of resistance. While some students might choose to remain silent about sex or sexuality topics, others might openly oppose consideration of the topics at all. Other work in the field of composition studies, while not focused on thinking about resistances to sexual literacy curricula or discussions, confronts student resistances that are potentially more active than passive silences or lack of participation. I am thinking here specifically of the work of Jim Berlin. Berlin's work with students in inviting them to think critically about the languages of advertising, of work, and of education met with some resistance, particularly as he and other pedagogues turned students' attention to unexamined assumptions and values. Indeed, he notes that "the most remarkable effect of the course has been the intensity of resistance students have offered their teachers, a stiff unwillingness to problematize the ideological codes inscribed in their attitudes and behavior" (1991, 52). His response? "We do insist . . . that students take into consideration the oppositional point of view continually forwarded by the teacher, by a number of the essays read, and by other students. . . . The result, we hope, will be to encourage a more open and tolerant society, one in which the full possibilities of democracy might be openly explored" (53–54).

Berlin's "insistence" that students "take into consideration the oppositional point of view" may serve a rhetorical purpose, but I wonder if students are left feeling coerced. Put another way, as we invite students to engage in the process of "desocialization," to borrow Shor's term, do students feel bullied into doing so? I would hope not, and I cannot support any kind of instruction that bullies students. But I am certainly well aware that inviting students to think critically and write substantively about difficult material can *seem* bullying, if some students are particularly invested in *not* considering sensitive material. I have been fortunate in my nearly two decades of instructional experience (in places as diverse as Louisiana, Colorado, and Ohio) not to have had a student flatly refuse to participate in my courses dealing with sexual literacy issues. But with some students increasingly invested in promoting religious fundamentalism, I dare say that such active resistances are certainly possible. And they may be squelching instructional opportunities to consider stories of sex and sexuality from a variety of perspectives in certain parts of our country (much less of the world).

Some compositionists are clear about the importance of addressing conflicts, particularly ideological conflicts, as they arise. Ryden suggests, though, that when conflict arises, as it inevitably does when dealing with sensitive topics or material, it should not be avoided: "I'm not sure that crisis should or even can be manufactured, but when it occurs we might need to resist the urge to contain it too handily through an evisceration of its emotional component. An expanded understanding of rhetoric might lead us to a praxis that would recognize and do justice to the primacy of emotion in intellectual exchange" (2003, 91). Susan C. Jarratt's

"Feminism and Composition: The Case for Conflict" even more directly and succinctly proposes that we *must* be willing to risk some amount of conflict if we are to teach well: "Even when teachers announce the desire to create a particular climate, they can't neutralize by fiat the social positions already occupied by their students. . . . Differences of gender, race, and class among students and teachers provide situations in which conflict does arise, and we need more than the ideal of the harmonious, nurturing composition class in our repertory of teaching practices to deal with those problems" (1991, 113). Indeed, as noted in the introduction, Gerald Graff has famously argued in his book *Beyond the Culture Wars* that we actively "teach the conflicts" as part of our higher education curricula: doing so, he maintains, may serve to "revitalize" American education by showing students democratic debate in action.

But the question obviously is, *how?* How do we allow conflict to occur and resistant thinking to find voice while still maintaining a productive learning experience for all students?

One of the most important books to confront this issue in composition studies is *Collision Course* by Russel Durst. In this book, Durst acknowledges the "strong tendency now in composition studies to focus discussion almost exclusively on ideological matters such as students' political beliefs; race, gender, and class inequalities; the oppressiveness of our institutions; and how we might effect change." While he applauds this trend, recognizing that issues of "curriculum ha[ve] always been political," he also advocates for what he calls "reflective instrumentalism," or paying attention to and honoring the goals that students themselves bring into the classroom. Put another way, Durst believes that we should both embrace a critical literacy that "focus[es] on the political . . . [as] a critical part of students' intellectual and moral development" *and* acknowledges students' interest in getting good jobs, finding satisfying careers, and achieving financial security. He explains his position thus: "In my view, we can best teach critical literacy in first-year composition not by denying or trying to undermine students' careerism. Rather, I believe we can best teach critical literacy by accepting the pragmatic nature of most students' approach to the first-year writing course, by taking students' goals into consideration when designing curriculum, and then by attempting to build a reflective, intellectual, politically aware dimension into this instrumentalist orientation" (1999, 5–6). I find myself in general agreement with Durst, and I think that students' interests and investments should be acknowledged and honored, even as we enact critical pedagogies that ask them, à la Berlin's work, to question the assumptions, values, and ideologies upon which their investments build.

If anything, I want to *augment* Durst's approach by suggesting that sex and sexuality are among the great unspoken interests and investments that students have—unspoken and unacknowledged in our composition classrooms. Durst asks the right questions: "Who are our students? What do they want? And what should be beach them?" (1999, 170). For Durst, the answer to the last question should of necessity follow, at least in part, on answers to the first two questions. Durst locates career at the top of the list of student interests. I don't disagree in general, but I also believe strongly that attention to other important aspects of our experience—sex/uality and religion being two of the most significant— is crucial. Indeed, as I have shown in chapter 3 and throughout this book, students have *much* to say about sex and sexuality. Paying attention to what they say and designing courses with them that help them address sex and sexuality issues in an intelligent and sophisticated manner serve not only to develop their (and our) sexual literacy but also to honor a significant personal interest that many students have. Doing so openly and respectfully, at the beginning of the term, can deflate much student resistance, particularly if we involve students in the design of our courses. As Durst puts it, "I would suggest that setting up composition curricula that ignore or dismiss student instrumentalism has serious negative consequences in our courses, often leading to student alienation, hostility, disengagement, avoidance behavior, and unproductive conflict" (1999, 177).

David Wallace and Helen Rothschild Ewald's *Mutuality in the Rhetoric and Composition Classroom* provides wonderful advice for how to set up composition courses that actively involve students in curricular issues. As they put it, "[m]utuality is invoked in that knowledge is not a prepackaged commodity to be delivered by the teacher but is an 'outcome' constituted in the classroom through the dialogic interaction among teachers and students alike" (2000, 4). Specifically, Wallace and Ewald argue for the following when "valuing students' interpretive agency in writing classes":

- contributing to students' agency in defining tasks and topics, and thus tapping students' prior theories about writing as part of the ongoing meaning making in the class

- requiring both teachers and students to embrace subjectivity as represented in their own sets of prior theory and as reflected in the diversity of passing theories that may emerge during, and as a result of, classroom interaction

- making it necessary to recognize ideological stances within one's own subjectivity that, if unacknowledged, may not only inhibit participants coming to a shared passing theory but also may affect the agency that students are able to assume as writers within a given classroom situation. (102)

Wallace and Ewald are invested in creating pedagogical spaces that simultaneously value students' interests *and* seek to challenge them and their assumed values and ideological stances in productive ways. I believe that such an approach is crucial not only in diffusing potential resistances but also in creating learning spaces that can address sexual literacy in a larger cultural climate that still constructs sex and sexuality as essentially private or taboo.

Perhaps one of the most important assumptions we can examine with students, particularly at the beginning of any term, is the assumption that a classroom is a value-free or neutral space. Let me be clear: inasmuch as possible, our classrooms should be relatively "safe spaces," and I believe that Wallace, Ewald, and Durst offer great ideas for helping to produce such "safe spaces." But Durst is right: they are never neutral. Honesty about that is essential.

I think that the primary reason that I object to neutrality is that some of us do not have the luxury of neutrality. For example, I cannot always pass as anything other than a queer man in my classes. And many students inevitably read my gay self as inevitably liberal. Okay, not a catastrophe—hardly. Such a reading often allows me to have rich discussions with students about how stereotypes function rhetorically in our culture, and about how the idea of the "norm" and the "normative" are powerful rhetorical forces socially and politically. I bring into such discussions Kenji Yoshino's use of Erving Goffman's concept of "covering"—or how members of minority groups that seem more closely aligned with the prevailing "norm" are more likely to be accepted by the normative society, despite their minority status. In others words, straight-acting gays are just more acceptable and more likely to be accepted socially (and politically?) than queeny fags. The rhetorics surrounding this phenomenon of covering are rich and complex, and I have found that students seem to thoroughly enjoy talking about them—even as they know I am gay.

Are some uncomfortable with the discussion? Inevitably. But so am I. And we discuss such discomfort as well. We discuss how it is political for me to discuss such topics in the classroom and how it would just as political if I did *not*. Every choice of reading matter or discussion topic is political and ideologically valenced. And the subject of choice itself should always be part of a class's ongoing metadiscussion.

As I have discussed these issues with instructors, some have countered by saying that, as an openly queer man, I have a "natural" reason to want to discuss sexuality issues with students. I am dubious about this because *all of us have sexualities*—not just queers. But I wonder: *is* it easier for an openly gay teacher to talk about sex and sexuality in the classroom than a heterosexually identified teacher? I have no idea, though I suspect students would not think that a nongay teacher teaching a "gay text" or talking about queer sexuality (or sexuality in general) is trying to convert them or liberalize their thinking. Maybe. Maybe not. Regardless, it would be totally disingenuous for me to pretend to be the "heteronormative teacher." I am not that teacher. Specifically, I would be robbing students of my attempt to model an academic who tries to be both fully aware of his own contextualized position *and* grapple with tough stuff from a variety of viewpoints. That is the trick, no? Pretending to neutrality lessens the complexity of the rhetorical task, and lures us into thinking that there *is* a neutral position. There isn't. And I don't think we'll ever come together and rationally hash through our various issues unless we acknowledge our positions—and acknowledge others' positions as part of the process.

Note that the content here is really all about *rhetoric*. And rhetoric is inevitably political. As our students take up a variety of issues as citizens in a pluralistic democracy, it behooves us to introduce students to how issues are cast rhetorically, how they are often falsely binarized in the media, how views about issues stem from complex contexts, and how a greater rhetorical awareness of those contexts provides us a more subtle way of understanding those issues and communicating effectively with those whose views differ from ours. Ultimately, I find myself most strongly agreeing with Patricia Roberts-Miller in *Deliberate Conflict: Argument, Political Theory, and Composition Classes*: "People experience conflict as difficult because it is difficult. . . . A world without any enclaves at all, in which one could never find a comfortable place of agreement, would be exhausting, but a world where people really disagree, where our central assumptions are questioned, can be exciting. The task for any democratic theory is to describe a city where difference is productively challenging, and to persuade people to spend much of their lives there" (2004, 57).

Our students deserve nothing less than an introduction to that complexity. And perhaps, as I have argued throughout, a productive introduction to challenging complexity begins by joining *our students'* conversations about sex and sexuality—and perhaps joining them begins first with *listening.*

ENCOURAGING TRANSGRESSION, ENCOUNTERING RESISTANCE, OR A CASE OF FAILING TO LISTEN

Resistances to our work can occur in seemingly odd, unforeseen ways, particularly when our own agendas, often not thoroughly acknowledged, foreclose on what our students are trying to tell us about their interests, values, and needs. In the final chapter of *Textual Orientations: Lesbian and Gay Students and the Making of Discourse Communities,* Harriet Malinowitz argues that teachers should think fully and carefully about the ways in which the identities that both teachers and students bring to a writing classroom are complicated and varied. More specifically, she asks us to acknowledge the extent to which we might wish to maintain, rather than erase, our differences; as Malinowitz puts it, "though people usually want to leave the margins, they do want to be able to bring with them the sharp vision that comes from living with friction and contradiction" (1995, 251–52). Such "friction and contradiction" can offer a plentitude of critical entrances for "queering the brew," as she puts it, or for critiquing the dominant narratives with which and through which our lives are constructed and lived. Configured as such, the writing classroom becomes a powerful site for developing skills of cultural critique, investigating the social functions of narratives, and examining the construction of personal and political identities through social deployments of language and story.

To promote both inclusivity of viewpoint and a critique of dominant modes of thought, I have tried, like many other compositionists, to encourage students to explore how their outsiderhood, the various ways they simultaneously do and do not fit into our normalizing culture, produces *transgressive* and *critical knowledges* that they can use to critique and potentially subvert their placement within the culture at large. In many ways, as I have argued throughout this book, increasing sexual literacy itself may act as a mode of transgressive critique, as a way of opening a space to think critically and differently about identities, relationships, and normative values.

At the same time, it is important to realize that the role of the *teacher* in this exercise is often left undertheorized—an oversight that enables critical blind spots in our understanding of our pedagogical performances. Most discussions of transgressive pedagogy figure the teacher as an uncomplicated "nurturer" of transgression, who empowers his or her students to think critically and thereby subvert those aspects of the status quo that are oppressive. For instance, Malinowitz, borrowing from Lester Faigley, suggests that "[h]elping students to achieve critical awareness of the ways that definitions of the self emerge from discourse and of 'how definitions of the self are involved in the configuration of relations to power' . . . is the closest we can come to 'empowering' them; it is only when one is self-conscious about position and location in this way that one can act to *re*position and *re*locate oneself in the world" (1995, 72). More specifically, in her discussion of creating writing courses that are friendly and supportive (of lesbian and gay students, for instance, or of those with alternative views), Malinowitz maintains that while "no teacher can completely control [classroom] conditions," a teacher can nonetheless "promote and encourage a classroom environment which, beyond being 'affirmative,' is structured to creatively tap the involvement of queer subjectivities in the class's epistemological brew" (1995, 258).

As promoter and encourager, the teacher's role seems relatively clear-cut and transparent. My experience in the classroom, though, demonstrates that the teacher's subjectivity and identity, particularly in classrooms in which transgressive knowledges are nurtured and developed, offer a few more challenges than has yet been adequately understood. Specifically, the teacher's position in the university and the identities that students—particularly students already drawn to transgressive ideas—construct for her often presuppose that she is neither aware of nor interested in transgression, that her very position in the classroom indicates her support of the status quo. Moreover, we are not immune to the tendency to construct our *students'* identities, to see them as "members of the choir," as fellow resisters, as transgressors of the status quo. Such complex projections can create identifications, misidentifications, and points of resistance that can teach us much about one another, the classroom as a site of learning, and the possibilities and limits of think-ing transgressively.

An example of this complex phenomenon, and the unforeseen resis-tances that can emerge within such complex pedagogical environments, may be useful here, and I'd like to outline briefly a course I codesigned with two of my longtime colleagues, Michelle Gibson and Deborah Meem. Informed by feminist, queer, and postmodern theories, our course had as its primary text Dorothy Allison's *Bastard out of Carolina*. We believed that this book's transgressiveness and insistence on disman-tling traditional, sentimental constructions of family and morality would provide students with a way to begin the process of intellectual and emo-tional self-examination. My colleagues and I designed the course syllabus together, worked together throughout the term, and wrote essay assign-ments together. We also asked our students to interact with one another through e-mail as they read, discussed, and wrote about Allison's book. Our goal was to help students see Allison's process of undermining and transgressing traditional notions about family, friendship, sexuality, gender, and so on in order to help them begin to critique their own long-held beliefs about these issues. In general, we wanted to (1) help students see the transgressive in their reading, writing, and experience; (2) champion the transgressive; and (3) increase students' awareness of transgression so that they might begin to understand its complex rela-tionship to critical thinking, as well as to their own lives. In many ways, this curriculum was among the first I experimented with in trying to help students develop a critical sexual literacy—a literacy that would ana-lyze and interrogate normative constructions of intimacy in our culture. To facilitate these goals, we hoped that a close reading and discussion of the issues in *Bastard out of Carolina* might prompt those in the class with transgressive experiences or knowledges to begin thinking critically about them. Moreover, we hoped that a respectful consideration of such knowledges would serve as an invitation to share them with others, thus further reinforcing the creation of an atmosphere in which transgres-sion could be understood and appreciated—and perhaps even used.

All in all, though, we felt successful in provoking discussion and thought about several thorny issues, and our discussions generally kept students from recasting the novel into "traditional" modes of understanding. However, we found that our own positions as teachers in the university sometimes worked against the goals outlined above— particularly with students who already saw themselves as transgressive before they entered the course. Many of those students were inclined to resist the novel and the transgressive ideas we were espousing because they were presented by teachers and because these students had constructed the teacher's identity as in sync with the status quo. While certainly not all students chose to resist our work, I could see such resistances at play in certain students, most notably a very bright young man named Zach.

I liked Zach immediately. Among all of my students that quarter, he clearly had the most developed—and consciously cultivated—sense of personal style. Dressed every day completely in black, including starkly dyed hair and matching satchel, Zach stood out from the other gener-ally casually dressed students in the classroom. And that was the point, I think. For his style was clearly designed to transgress the norms of appear-ance absorbed by so many of my other students, whose clothing mostly mimicked those worn by the fashion models of Tommy Hilfiger, Ralph Lauren, or their favorite band's neo-grunge lounge wear. But Zach's pen-chant for black was more than just a fashion statement. It announced his attitude—a studied cynicism, a cultivated skepticism. Zach was no *mere* goth. In a way, his black outfit was a metonym for his whole demeanor: he didn't mind standing out, in both dress and beliefs.

This attitude found prime expression in the numerous buttons and pins he had attached to his book bag, which added a bit of color to the black motif. But here again, the pins served a calculated purpose; they often bore political statements, with usually subversive sentiments, such as "Nuke another godless, homosexual baby seal for Christ!" They were clearly designed to "torque off" those who happened to see them—and they were hard to miss. As such, I gathered they were a little dose of the personal (and the political) to counteract the amnesia of conformity surrounding him. The buttons also revealed, subtly but subversively, that Zach was queer. And I could barely contain a bit of pride and admiration in such daring coming from a nineteen-year-old.

All in all, Zach's appearance, pose, and attitude forcefully drew my attention. As a queer teacher, I felt compelled to "watch out" for all of my les-bi-gay students. But more than that, I felt a special affinity for Zach— particularly the button-toting Zach. His "in-your-face" pins reminded me immediately of the kinds of pins I used to wear as a teenager. While I was never allowed to dress all in black or dye my hair (which I desperately wanted to do to mark metonymically the distance between my queer self and my Southern Baptist parents), I would often sport a button with some provocative statement. I wanted to draw attention, disturb, and, in a word, "queer" the surrounding landscape of political and personal conservatism and conformity. I was to southern Louisiana as Zach was to Cincinnati. I could understand his motivations, as they had been—and are to this day—mine as well. So, with Zach's self-presentation and overt queerness triggering my memories of my own longed-for transgressive young adulthood, I couldn't help but *identify* with Zach. He seemed so much what I had hoped to be as a young man, as well as what I still hoped to be from my position within the academy. Moreover, I thought that Zach would be the perfect co-conspirator in this class. He, of all the students, would understand the kind of transgressive thinking I would be encouraging.

But my delight was soon to receive a "reality check," demonstrating to me that my identification with Zach was more a product of my own projections than anything else. I wanted the students' final essay for the class to trace how their engagement with *Bastard out of Carolina* had "queried" the values they wrote about at the beginning of the course. I felt this would be a perfect opportunity for Zach to expound more on his transgressive style and politics, especially since he claimed to have enjoyed the book so much.

But this is not what Zach had in mind at all.

My first moments of dis-identification occurred during a teacher-student conference about the topic of Zach's last essay, in which he wanted to discuss and problematize the relationship between child abuse and the development of homoerotic feelings—a connection that some students in the class were linking causally because Dorothy Allison, a lesbian, had been abused as a child. I was intrigued by the topic, primarily because I thought Zach would transgressively challenge the "received wisdom" of his classmates and argue against such a pathologizing understanding of the queer. Instead, Zach told me that the primary reason abuse and homosexuality shouldn't be linked is because no one in his or her right mind would consciously choose to be homosexual; in his view, homosexuality was inevitably a biological predisposition. The development of a gay identity had little to do with abuse, and everything to do with genetic coding. I was taken aback—and really couldn't believe that somebody who self-presented so transgressively, and seemingly "queerly," could hold such seemingly conservative views. Zach was invested, understandably so, in tolerance for queers.

In our conferences together, I had attempted to challenge some of Zach's essentialist notions, hoping to provoke a bit more transgressive thinking about the value of homoerotic interest not as an identity but as a *possibility*—a position—of critique. Regardless of its "origin," I wanted to help students see an open and celebratory queerness as a critique of heteronormativity; queerness was a celebration of sexual freedom, the choice to be proud of one's desires and intimacies, regardless of their etiology and precisely *because* they were so disparaged by the larger "straight" culture. Instead, Zach ignored my advice and produced an essay that explored homosexuality as a biological given, an essential trait. His was a plea for tolerance, not transgression.

By the end of the quarter, I realized that I had been misreading Zach's self-positioning within the classroom. Despite my identifications, and what I took to be his initial identification with me, we were hardly co-conspirators. And while I initially believed I had "failed" to encourage transgressive thinking on Zack's part, I realized that I had failed to recognize his own investments, his sense of what is "transgressive," in my rush to promote transgressive thinking and critique. So ultimately, Zach certainly transgressed—but not at all in the ways I had intended. His brand of transgression turned out not to be the kind of transgression that I was hawking in the classroom. Rather, his transgression was to resist me—to resist what he saw as unproductive for his life, his world.

Certainly, in creating spaces in which it is safe to transgress, we open up the possibility of having our own cherished ideas, beliefs, and authority (as transgressive as they may be) come under subversive scrutiny. I can't help but feel that it might have been my early identification with Zach that *may* also have contributed to his resistance to my brand of transgression. With my fumbling attempts to make a connection with him, as well as my pronounced interest in letting him know that he had a queer ally in the class, I might have set myself up as someone this student *had* to transgress. In short, my identification with Zach might very well have foreclosed on the possibility of my recognizing transgressions that I had not "authorized" in the context of the class.

Jeffrey Weeks offers some useful thoughts on the nature of transgression that might provide a way to analyze and understand what happens when we attempt to "nurture" the transgressive in the classroom. In *Invented Moralities*, Weeks notes: "Transgression, the breaching of boundaries, the pushing of experience to the limits, the challenge to the Law, whatever it is, is a crucial moment in any radical sexual project. As an individual act it speaks of a self obscured by an ignoble sexual order. For many this act of defiance is the expression of a buried truth. It is the characteristic stance of the individual resister who says 'Here I am, I can do no other'" (1995, 108). In many ways, Zach was telling me his "buried truth," that he could "do no other"—and, as Weeks might suggest, he *was* taking seriously our call to think and act transgressively. Zach, probably for the first time in his life, was confronting large institutions—and their representatives (us)—with his own self-representation, his own self-knowledge; therefore, his initial utterances of self-articulation, hurled at the educational machinery, may have been an attempt to stake out a sense of self, produced as a *defensive* truth about oneself, against the seemingly cold and indifferent institution.

The dilemma, then, of nurturing the transgressive in our classrooms is a complex one. The transgressions we wish to encourage may not be those necessarily shared by the students themselves, who often have their own transgressive agendas. Moreover, the power/narrative of the classroom inevitably positions the student and the teacher in an agonistic relationship, in which the teacher, as authorizing agent, necessarily sets the boundaries of the classroom—boundaries that remain, despite our intentions, invitations to transgression. In other words, my "nurturing" of transgression could be read as an attempt to "authorize" or even "normalize" certain forms of transgressive thought and behavior—normalizations that our students may try to resist. With such knowledge, I can do much better than lament these first tentative steps toward transgressing and critiquing the socially normative; I can—and should—honor such attempts, even if such attempts are not my own. Perhaps they should be honored precisely *because they are not my own*, but someone else's, constructed and articulated to meet an individual's needs. I am not sure there can be any sexual literacy without such a basic appreciation for our differences.

WHAT DO WE DO NOW? OR
FUTURE DIRECTIONS OF SEXUAL LITERACY

Throughout this book, I have offered examples from my own and others' classrooms of pedagogies that both highlight and interrogate intersections among literacy and sexuality—as well as the sexualized nature of literacy throughout the West. My goal has been to emphasize how a significant dimension of literacy education and development in our first-year composition classrooms is being overlooked and can be addressed through engaging, thoughtful, and critical writing exercises.

Granted, my focus has been more on issues of *sexuality as largely related to identity*, and I admit that I have addressed only glancingly a wide variety of "sex issues"—ranging from reproductive freedom to sex education— that should be considered in the composition classroom *as much as* issues of sexuality, sexual orientation, and sexual identity. My only defense in not picking up these issues for discussion is that one book can only do so much. As such, I want in the remaining pages of this last chapter to be *suggestive* of how other sex and sexuality issues can be approached profitably and productively in first-year composition courses.

So, when we ask our students what kinds of sex and sexuality issues are important to them, we might be surprised at the responses. If we have been paying attention to venues such as Facebook, MySpace, student newspapers, or other online forums, we may see that students are invested in exploring not just the mechanics of sex (the "how to") but intersections among sex, discourse, culture, and politics. And as we begin to address sexual literacy in our courses, we must consider its intersections with other literacies. In particular, issues of religion and race intersect sex/uality in powerful ways. I have, for instance, had students who have wanted to write about their experiences with biracial relationships, or with navigating intimacies with people with disabilities. Many readings could augment such explorations, in-class discussions, and writing experiences. The work of Audre Lorde, for instance, offers a rich set of insights into how a thoughtful individual occupies and interrogates intersecting identities. Lorde is a queer lesbian of color who struggled with cancer; her essays in *Sister Outsider* model ways of thinking about the complexity of experience—about the ways in which one's sexuality, one's race, and one's body are simultaneously one's own and not one's own. Our deepest senses of self are both deeply personal and deeply socially imbricated. And experiencing oneself sexually as a white person is not always the same as experiencing oneself sexually as a black person in our culture. Lorde's writing on such subjects could prove illuminating for a wide variety of students, and I wouldn't be surprised if many students have much to *add* to Lorde's initial thinking about the intersections among sexuality, ability, and racial identity. For instance, students could follow the lead of Dwight A. McBride in *Why I Hate Abercrombie & Fitch*, who critically examines how race and class markers, not just clothing, are marketed erotically in the company's sexy advertisements of beautiful young (white) people: "Surely we know that people are not buying 'Abercrombie' for the clothes. The catalog itself isn't even about featuring those, after all. People buy 'Abercrombie' to purchase membership into a lifestyle" (2005, 86). Critically and rhetorically examining view books, catalogs, Web sites, and even A&F stores might stimulate students' thinking about the complex literacies of sexuality put into service to promote particular racial and class values.

But there's so much more. Students are clearly invested in issues of sex education, many of them having just encountered a variety of different sex education experiences in high school. Certainly, the politics of sex education most reveal how deeply personal issues are intertwined with public debates, with the rhetoric of different ideological positions that jockey for influence. And as students move into sexual maturity, they may want to consider the variety of sexual enhancements that are marketed to them. Whose interests are represented in enhancements such as Viagra, or in effective contraception? How are such marketed? What rhetorics are at play in both their marketing and in the public discussion of them? And certainly, what about sexual violence? Discourses surrounding sexual violence, particularly against women and children, reveal significant cultural values and ideologies at play, as women, for instance, are often depicted as agentless victims. What gender politics is working here? What sexual literacies need understanding—and critique?

When thinking about such assignments and the courses I might build around them, I have generally kept a few key questions in mind, a few guideposts for the writing of assignments that keep them flexible, attuned to student interests and needs, and capable of challenging students in productive ways. I always ask myself, what do my assignments assume? What kinds of voices do they elicit? What kinds of voices do they potentially silence? Whoever creates assignments through which others are asked to interrogate their thinking must also be open to interrogation as well. Along those lines, I have posed students the following questions when they are confronting different representations, particularly representations that portend to represent their interests as sexual people:

How does the representation "think" me?

How do others think me?

How am I given to myself in the representation?

How do I *think myself?*

How *could* I think myself?

From here, students can explore the politics of representation, the ways in which rhetorics and discourses touching on our most intimate selves circulate publicly, how possibilities of relationship and intimacy are opened up and foreclosed upon by such discourses, how certain lives are validated, others not.

When considering such questions, I inevitably find myself thinking of the work of Foucault, with whom I largely inaugurated this project in the first chapter of this book. In particular, I am interested in the *ethical* dimension of Foucault's work, because I firmly believe that, more than anything, we are asking students to consider densely ethical questions when we ask them to consider their own literacy practices, not just their sexual literacies. Thinking critically about the comportment of one's body in relation to others, in the representation of one's desires for others, in the stories that we tell about sex, sexuality, sexual identity, and intimacy, we are grappling most profoundly with ethical issues, with relations between selves and subjects. In *The Ethics of Marginality: A New Approach to Gay Studies*, John Champagne characterizes Foucault's relationship to ethics this way: "This care of the self, a theme through-out Foucault's later work, represents the attempt by the (subjugated) subject to work within cultural forms of subject production, countering the practices of modern disciplinary subject formation through what Foucault terms practices of self. . . . Foucault suggests that such prac-tices ought to move toward freedom, which Foucault suggests, after the Greeks, is an ethical practice of self-government" (1995, xxix). Foucault wants us to recover—and further—the Greek philosophical principle of the "care of the self"; or, more specifically, "[t]o take care of oneself consists of knowing oneself. Knowing oneself becomes the object of the quest of concern for self" (231). Along these lines, I have striven to situ-ate my classroom at a curious juncture in Western education, Western philosophy—between "know yourself" and "take care of yourself."

If, as I have maintained throughout this book, knowing yourself in contemporary Anglo-American society is to know yourself sexually, then the furtherance of sexual literacy should be a key goal of critical educa-tion. And indeed, it should be clear at this point that exploring connec-tions among sexuality, language, and literacy is to probe *political* dimen-sions both of language use and of constructions of sexuality. Foucault, a political activist himself, was well aware of the potential for not just scholarly but also political critique present in his work, and he conceived of this political dimension in very personal terms. Perhaps Foucault's most provocative statement in regards to his philosophy is found in a late interview, in which he opted for anonymity: "The movement by which, not without effort and uncertainty, dreams and illusions, one detaches oneself from what is accepted as true and seeks other rules— that is philosophy. The displacement and transformation of frameworks of thinking, the changing of received values and all of the work that has been done to think otherwise, to do something else, to become other than what one is—that, too, is philosophy" (1997, 327).

I believe that inviting us all to explore sexual literacy is an invitation not just to know ourselves better, but to "think otherwise," to push at current "frameworks of thinking" and challenge "received values." I don't know if we will become "other than what one is," but we may at least become more critically cognizant of what we are.

So, as I approach the end of this book, I am asking myself if I will ever teach a first-year writing course with Susie Bright's *The Sexual State of the Union* as the primary course text. Frankly, I am uncertain. That course would be stimulating and exciting—and risky—in ways that I often find hard to resist. (I completely understand Oscar Wilde's sentiment about being able to resist anything but temptation.) But I must admit that I have enjoyed thoroughly the incorporation of issues of sex and sexuality into the writing classroom alongside other issues of literacy, as in the assignments I have described throughout this book. In many ways, such incorporation (as opposed to domination!) seems particularly productive because my students and I have explored sex/uality and their connection to literacy in the context of a variety of literacy issues. Doing so, in a way, normalizes discussion of sexuality. Sexuality isn't something particularly "special" we're going to talk about. It's simply another issue, another important aspect of the human experience that deserves our critical and rhetorical attention. I believe all of us can—and *should*— consider the development of sexual literacy as a significant component of becoming *literate* in our society, and the only way to work with students on such sensitive material is to do so calmly, respectfully, openly, and honestly. Our students deserve nothing less.

NOTES

1. For a fuller discussion of feminism and the teaching of writing, see the wonderful collection *Feminism and Composition: A Critical Sourcebook*, edited by Gesa E. Kirsch, et al. (2003), which anthologizes "classic," early feminist approaches to composition as well as more recent trends in thinking about gender in the writing classroom.

2. Given this distinction, we will nonetheless see gender as an important—and indeed *necessary*—consideration when thinking about sex and sexuality. If anything, and as we will see in chapter 4, sexuality studies in the 1990s and at the beginning of the twenty-first century is beginning to offer us fairly nuanced and sophisticated ways of thinking about the complex relationship between sex, sexuality, and gender.

3. For a more thorough introduction to Foucault, see Annamarie Jagose's *Queer Theory: An Introduction*.

4. Of course, some scholars resist the discursive turn in sexuality studies, claiming that the theorists I have been discussing pay insufficient attention to corporeal or bodily issues. Tim Dean, in "Bodies That Mutter: Rhetoric and Sexuality," takes up the argument that sexuality is rhetorically and discursively constructed, an argument put forward famously by Foucault and extended by Judith Butler and other queer theorists. As he puts it, "[m]y aim is to outline a theory of rhetoric, sexuality, and embodiment that is both immoderately antifoundationalist *and* antirhetoricalist" (2000, 84). More pointedly, Dean asks, "Are bodies purely discursive? Or, to put the question in Edelman's terms, is sexuality purely rhetorical?" (83). While his point is well taken, I cannot help but wonder if his argument is based on a "straw man" fallacy; highlighting the discursive nature of sex and sexuality is not to *deny* the body, but it is rather to underscore aspects of sexuality that have been overlooked or misunderstood in the rush to naturalize sexuality as *purely* of the body.

5. Admittedly, I am glossing over a *lot* of useful feminist theory, and there are good books that consider the development of queer theory and sexuality studies out of feminist thinking, as well as current debates and points of contestation between sexuality/queer studies and feminist theories. See in particular *Feminism Meets Queer Theory*, edited by Elizabeth Weed and Naomi Schor.

6. For more on Habermas and communicative reason, see in particular his chapter "An Alternative Way out of the Philosophy of the Subject: Communicative versus Subject-Centered Reason," in his book *The Philosophical Discourse of Modernity* (1995).

7. As other scholars pick up on this notion of the "reflexive sexual citizen," they attempt to envision how such a conception of citizenship might actually alter our relationship to sex, sexuality, each other, and our own bodies. Marvin M. Ellison, writing in *Erotic Justice: A Liberating Ethic of Sexuality*, for instance, is deeply invested in promoting "[a] liberating social ethic of sexuality [that] places great value on the humanly powerful desire for intimacy and community" (1996, 14). Ellison sees at least three key characteristics of such a "liberating social ethic":

> First, advocating erotic justice in the face of sex-negativity requires honoring the goodness of sexuality as human embodiment

Second, advocating erotic justice in the face of heterocentrism and compulsory heterosexuality involves genuine gratitude for difference and diversity

Third, advocating erotic justice in the face of sexual violence and coercion requires empowering the moral agency of the sexually abused and violated and also requires the eroticizing of equality between persons and among groups (28–29).

Of course, the pressing question for such an agenda is, how? How do people understand the complex intersections between sexuality and citizenry, much less advocate for "erotic justice"? Arguing for "erotic justice" may be a bit beyond the scope of this book, but it is an intriguing concept, worthy of further exploration.

8.   For some additional interesting work on queer language use, see the collection *Queer Words, Queer Images: Communication and the Construction of Homosexuality*, edited by Jeffrey Ringer (1994), which contains a section on gay and lesbian rhetorics, including a rhetorical analysis of Harvey Milk's speeches and the rhetoric of "tolerance."

9.   For a review of such work, as well as examples of methodologies in collecting and analyzing information about such literacies, see my *Digital Youth: Emerging Literacies on the World Wide Web* (2005).

10.   Early in the quarter, I receive written permission from students to quote from their work and to discuss assignments and teaching methods and situations. I offer them the option of being acknowledged, either directly or pseudonymously. In this case, since some students elected to have their real names used and others did not, I refer only to students anonymously and by perceived gender.

11.   As I have discussed this exercise with fellow teachers and other composition scholars, I am inevitably asked if I eventually let the students know that Straightboyz4Nsync is a hoax site—and, moreover, a hoax site authored by their instructor. I did, and their reactions were surprising in a number of ways, though I can only summarize because I did not think at the time (alas!) of collecting written commentary about their responses to being "hoaxed." But to summarize from discussions with them, it seemed that many were unsurprised—itself surprising. What can account for such lack of reaction? Perhaps the following. I had used the Mutant Watch hoax site in an earlier class exercise, and many students had already encountered numerous hoax sites on their own, so I think that the idea of being "hoaxed" was neither estranging nor alarming for these students. In some ways, we as literacy teachers can take comfort from that: these students are not accepting everything they read on the Web at face value, and we can use the Web to foster a sense of critical literacy and information evaluation.

More specifically, I think students weren't surprised because they understand—either intuitively or as part of their experience of Web surfing—that homepages are themselves performances, and that not all performers tell the whole truth and nothing but the truth. Cheung may figure homepages as "emancipatory," but many seasoned Web surfers suspect, I think, that personal homepages can be as much carefully constructed projections of idealized or even fabricated selfhoods as they are revelatory of deep-seated truths. Cheung himself notes that homepage authors engage in "self-censorship" and that the Web is home to an "unavoidable existence of a certain degree of deception and overstatement" (2000, 49, 51). As such, I think, increasingly, many Web surfers view personal homepages with a grain of salt. You can even see such skepticism lurking in some of my students' responses to Straightboyz4Nsync: just who is this guy?!

Despite my students' seemingly relaxed or unruffled response to being hoaxed, using such material raises some interesting ethical questions about "tricking" students. To what extent can I "closet" myself as the author of a site in order to talk about the "closet"—and still maintain my ethos as a teacher, or scholar, for that matter. Put another way, to what extent can any of us use trickery and deceit to talk about the various tricks and small deceits we all commit to protect aspects of our lives from close scrutiny, bigoted attack, and rhetorical, if not actual, violence? Many pedagogues and scholars have talked about the usefulness of "outing" one-self—as gay, lesbian, queer, even straight—in the hopes of alerting students to the presence of both queers in the social sphere and the circulation and construction of sexual and gender identity throughout our culture. In particular, Didi Khayatt has argued well, recently, both pro and con for "coming out," and she maintains that "the decision whether to come out in class and how to come out must remain with the jurisdiction of the individual teacher" (1998, 46). She argues for careful consideration of this so that no instructor is reduced simply to a "sexual category." The emphasis here, rather, is on *disclosure*, on bringing the hidden and marginalized into the open—and doing so in pedagogically productive ways.

12.   For a fuller discussion of why it is "tricky" but nonetheless useful to consider such terms as *trans, transgender,* and even *transsexuality* more broadly, see my introduction to *Bisexuality and Transgenderism: InterSEXions of the Others* (Alexander and Yescavage 2004).

13.   For a good discussion of the more "contentious" aspects of the debate between Butler and some feminist thinkers, see Butler's essay "Against Proper Objects" (1997a) and an interview with Butler, "Feminism by Any Other Name" (Braidotti 1997), both included in the collection *Feminism Meets Queer Theory.*

14.   Kate Bornstein's *My Gender Workbook* has a section entitled "Back into the Classroom: Three Gender Performance Workshops" (1998, 225–42) that may be just as useful as Califia-Rice's questions for inspiring classroom activities to explore the performance and construction of gender narrations.

15.   In "Bi, Butch, and Bar Dyke: Pedagogical Performances of Class, Gender, and Sexuality" Michelle Gibson, Martha Marinara, and Deborah Meem suggest that instructors themselves need to be critically aware of the identities—and the concomitant stories that compose such identities—that they bring into the classroom with them if they are to be sensitive to the many different stories that students bring into the classroom: "Compositionists committed to creating classrooms in which traditional academic power structures are problematized and critiqued must also commit themselves to interrogating their own positions in those classrooms. We must think seriously about the identities we bring with us into the classroom, remain conscious of the way those identities interact with the identities our students bring, and insert ourselves fully into the shifting relationship s between ourselves and our students at the same time that we resist the impulse to control those relationships" (2003, 486).

16.   I have chosen six stories to discuss. Of the ten stories produced, all of which are intriguing and insightful, these six stories generated the most in-class discussion. Students have given me permission to quote from and discuss their work.

17.   Butler herself self-corrects in her book following *Gender Trouble, Bodies That Matter,* maintaining that her formulation of performativity in *Gender Trouble* does *not* mean that gender can be taken on and off like a suit of clothes. More recently, in Kate More's interview with Butler, "Never Mind the Bollocks: Judith Butler on Transsexuality," Butler offers a new articulation: "There's a kind of forward moving effort to reconceive and redefine what counts as real. So for me the performative theory of gender was not about putting on a masquerade that hides a reality, or that is derived from a higher reality, but it's actually about a certain way of inhabiting norms that alters the norms and alters our sense of what is real and what is live-

able. . . . I think I'm interested in disrupting the symbolic in order to rearticulate it in more expansive ways" (1999, 297). If there is one thing that the persistent and nearly pervasive use of stereotypes in the student narratives suggests, though, it is that such "rearticulation" is hard to come by. Certainly, I would like to think that the paired-fiction exercise was an invitation for students to inhabit some gender norms in such a way as to imagine how they might be changed.

18. All students whose work is used here gave permission to me in writing to quote from their work. None elected anonymity.

REFERENCES

Alexander, Jonathan. *Digital Youth: Emerging Literacies on the World Wide Web*. Hampton Press: 2005.

Alexander, Jonathan. "Out of the Closet and Into the Network: Sexual Orientation and the Computerized Classroom." *Computers and Composition* 14.2 (1997): 207–216.

Alexander, Jonathan, and David Wallace. "The Queer Turn in Composition Studies: Reviewing and Assessing an Emerging Scholarship" [article under review]

Alexander, Jonathan, and Karen Yescavage (eds.). *Bisexuality and Transgenderism: InterSEXions of the Others*. Harrington Park Press, 2004.

Alexander, Jonathan, and Michelle Gibson, eds. "Special Cluster: Queer Theory." Special issue, *JAC: A Journal of Composition Theory* 24.1.

Alexander, Jonathan, and William P. Banks, eds. "Sexualities, Technologies, and the Teaching of Writing." Special issue, *Computers and Composition* 21.3 (September 2004).

Altman, Dennis. *Global Sex*. Chicago, IL: University of Chicago Press, 2001.

Berg, Allison, et al. "Breaking the Silence: Sexual Preference in the Composition Classroom." *Tilting the Tower*. Ed. by Linda Garber. New York: Routledge, 1994: 108–116.

Banks, William P. "Written Through the Body: Disruptions and 'Personal' Writing." *College English* 66 (September 2003): 21 - 40.

Barron, Nancy G., Nancy M. Grimm, and Sibylle Gruber. *Social Change in Diverse Teaching Contexts: Touchy Subjects and Routine Practices*. New York: Peter Lang, 2006.

Bartholomae, David. "Inventing the University." In Ellen Cushman, et al. (eds.), *Literacy: A Critical Sourcebook*. Boston: Bedford, 2001. 511–524.

Bell, David, and Jon Binnie. *The Sexual Citizen: Queer Politics and Beyond*. Cambridge, UK: Polity, 2000.

Bennett, William J. *The Broken Hearth: Reversing the Moral Collapse of the American Family*. New York: Doubleday, 2001.

Berlin, James A. "Composition and Cultural Studies." *Composition and Resistance*. Ed. by C. Mark Hurlbert and Michael Blitz. Portsmouth, NH: Boynton/Cook Heinemann, 1991: 47–55.

Berlin, James. "Rhetoric and Ideology in the Writing Class." *Cross-Talk in Comp Theory: A Reader*. Ed. by Victor Villaneuva . Urbana, IL: National Council of Teachers of English, 1997: 679–700.

Berlin, James A., and Michael J. Vivion. *Cultural Studies in the English Classroom*. Portsmouth, NH: Boynton/Cook Heinemann, 1992.

Bizzell, Patricia, and Bruce Herzberg (eds.). *The Rhetorical Tradition: Readings from Classical Times to the Present*. Boston, MA: Bedford Books, 1990.

Bleich, David. "Genders of Writing." *Journal of Advanced Composition* 9 (1989): 10–25.

Boardman, Kathleen, and Jonathan Alexander, Margaret Barber, Pete Pinney. "Teacher Involvement and Transformative Power on a Gender Issues Discussion List." *Meeting the Challenge: Innovative Feminist Pedagogies in Action*. Ed. by Maralee Mayberry and Ellen Cronan Rose. New York: Routledge, 1999: 169–190.

Bordo, Susan. *The Male Body: A New Look at Men in Public and in Private*. New York: Farrar, Strauss, & Giroux, 1999.

Bornstein, Kate. *Gender Outlaw: On Men, Women, and the Rest of Us*. New York: Vintage, 1994.

Bornstein, Kate. *My Gender Workbook.* New York: Routledge, 1998.

Boyd, Danah. "Friendster and Publicly Articulated Social Networking." Paper presented at CHI 2004, Vienna, Austria. (2004, April 24–29). Available online at http://www.danah. org/papers/CHI2004Friendster.pdf.

Braidotti, Rosi. "Feminism by Any Other Name [An Interview with Judith Butler]." *Feminism Meets Queer Theory.* Ed. by Elizabeth Weed and Naomi Schor. Bloomington, IN: Indiana University Press, 1997. 31–67.

Bright, Susie. *Susie Bright's Sexual State of the Union.* New York: Simon & Schuster, 1997.

Britzman, Deborah P. "Queer Pedagogy and Its Strange Techniques." *Inside the Academy and Out: Lesbian/Gay/Queer Studies and Social Action.* Ed. by Janice L. Ristock and Catherine G. Taylor. Toronto: University of Toronto Press, 1998: 49–71.

Butler, Judith. "Against Proper Objects." *Feminism Meets Queer Theory.* Ed. by Elizabeth Weed and Naomi Schor. Bloomington, IN: Indiana University Press, 1997. 1–30.

Butler, Judith. *Bodies That Matter: On the Discursive Limits of Sex.* New York: Routledge, 1993.

Butler, Judith. *Excitable Speech: A Politics of the Performative.* New York: Routledge, 1997.

Butler, Judith. *Gender Trouble: Feminism and the Subversion of Identity.* New York: Routledge, 1990.

Butler, Judith. *The Psychic Life of Power.* Stanford: Stanford University Press, 1997.

Califia, Pat. *Sex Changes: The Politics of Transgenderism.* San Francisco: Cleis, 1997.

Califia, Patrick. "Trannyfags Unzipped." Speaking Sex to Power: The Politics of Queer Sex. San Francisco: Cleis, 2002. 131–136.

Califia-Rice, Patrick. "Family Values." *The Village Voice.* Available online at http://www.villagevoice.com/issues/0025/califia-rice.php. 2000.

Cameron, Deborah, and Don Kulick. *Language and Sexuality.* Cambridge, UK: Cambridge University Press, 2003.

Caughie, Pamela L. *Passing and Pedagogy: The Dynamics of Responsibility.* Urbana, IL: University of Illinois Press, 1999.

Champagne, John. *The Ethics of Marginality: A New Approach to Gay Studies.* Minneapolis, MN: The University of Minnesota Press, 1995.

Cheung, Charles. "A Home on the Web: Presentations of Self in Personal Homepages." In David Gauntlett (ed.) *Web.Studies: Rewiring Media Studies for the Digital Age.* London: Arnold, 2000. 43–51.

Dean, Tim. "Bodies that Mutter: Rhetoric and Sexuality." *Beyond Sexuality.* Chicago, IL: University of Chicago Press, 2000.

Delpit, Lisa. *Other People's Children: Cultural Conflict in the Classroom.* New York: The New Press, 1995.

D'Emilio, John. "Capitalism and Gay Identity." *Culture, Society and Sexuality: A Reader.* Ed. by Richard Parker and Peter Aggleton. LondonL UCL Press, 1999: 239–248.

Dethier, Brock. *The Composition Instructor's Survival Guide.* Portsmouth, NH: Heinemann, 1999.

DeWitt, Scott Lloyd. "Out There on the Web: Pedagogy and Identity in Face of Opposition." *Computers and Composition* 14.2 (1997): 229–244.

Diamond, Suzanne. "When Underlife Takes Over: An Insight on Student Resistance and Classroom Dynamics." *Conflicts and Crises in the Composition Classroom—and What Instructors Can Do About Them.* Ed. by Dawn Skorczewski and Matthew Parfitt. Portsmouth, NH: Heinemann, 2003: 27–33.

Dickemann, Jeffrey M. "Words, Words, Words: Talking Transgenders." *GLQ: A Journal of Lesbian and Gay Studies* 6 (2000): 455–466.

Duggan, Lisa, and Richard Kim. "Beyond Gay Marriage." *Nation,* July 18, 2005 (http://www.thenation.com/doc.mhtml?i=20050718&s=kim).

Durst, Russel K. *Collision Course: Conflict, Negotiation, and Learning in College Composition.* Urbana, IL: NCTE Press, 1999.

Easton, Lee. "'Explain It to Me like I'm a Sex-Year-Old . . . ' The Pedagogy of Race, Sex, and Masculinity in *Philadelphia*." *Inside the Academy and Out: Lesbian/Gay/Queer Studies and Social Action*. Ed. By Janice L. Ristock and Catherine G. Taylor. Toronto: University of Toronto Press, 1998: 244–266.

Ellison, Marvin M. *Erotic Justice: A Liberating Ethic of Sexuality*. Louisville, KY: Westminster John Knox Press, 1996.

Epstein, Debbie, and James T. Sears (eds.). *A Dangerous Knowing: Sexuality, Pedagogy and Popular Culture*. London: Cassell, 1999.

Escoffier, J. "Foreword. In Gagnon, J. H., *An Interpretation of Desire*. Chicago, IL: University of Chicago Press, 2004: xiii–xxvi.

Faubion, James. "Introduction." *Aesthetics, Method and Epistemology*. Volume 2 in *The Essential Works of Foucault*. New York: The New Press: 1998.

Feinberg, Leslie. *Trans Liberation: Beyond Pink or Blue*. Boston: Beacon, 1998.

Feinberg, Leslie. *Transgender Warriors: Making History from Joan of Arc to RuPaul*. Boston: Beacon, 1996.

Flynn, Elizabeth A. "Composing as a Woman." *Feminism and Composition: A Critical Sourcebook*. Ed. by Gesa E. Kirsch, et al. Boston: Bedford, 2003: 243–255.

Foucault, Michel. *Ethics: Subjectivity and Truth*. Ed. Paul Rabinow. New York: The New Press, 1997.

Foucault, Michel. *The History of Sexuality: An Introduction, Volume I*. Trans. Robert Hurley. New York: Vintage Books, 1990 (1978).

Francis, Margot. "On the Myth of Sexual Orientation: Field Notes from the Personal, Pedagogical, and Historical Discourses of Identity." In Janice L. Ristock and Catherine G. Taylor (eds.) *Inside the Academy and Out: Lesbian/Gay/Queer Studies and Social Action*. Toronto: University of Toronto Press, 1998. 72–96.

Freire, Paulo. "The Adult Literacy Process as Cultural Action for Freedom." In Ellen Cushman, et al. (eds.), *Literacy: A Critical Sourcebook*. Boston: Bedford, 2001. 616–628.

Gagnon, John. 1990.

Gagnon, John H., and William Simon. *Sexual Conduct: The Sources of Human Sexuality*. Chicago, IL: Aldine, 1973.

Garton, Stephen. *Histories of Sexuality: Antiquity to Sexual Revolution*. New York: Routledge, 2004.

Gauntlett, David. "Judith Butler." *Theory.org*. Available online at http://www.theory.org.uk/ctr-butl.htm, 1998.

Gee, James Paul. "Literacy, Discourse, and Linguistics." In Ellen Cushman, et al. (eds.), *Literacy: A Critical Sourcebook*. Boston: Bedford, 2001. 525–544.

Gibson, Michelle, Martha Marinara, and Deborah Meem. "Bi, Butch, and Bar Dyke: Pedagogical Performances of Class, Gender, and Sexuality." *Feminism and Composition: A Critical Sourcebook*. Ed. by Gesa E. Kirsch, et al. Boston: Bedford, 2003. 466–487.

Giddens, Anthony. "Intimacy as Democracy." *Sexuality and Gender*. Ed. by Christine L. Williams and Arlene Stein. Malden, MA: Blackwell, 2002.

Giddens, Anthony. *The Transformation of Intimacy: Sexuality, Love and Eroticism in Modern Societies*. Stanford, CA: Stanford University Press, 1992.

Giroux, Henry. "Liberal Arts Education and the Struggle for Public Life: Dreaming about Democracy. In Darryl J. Gless and Barbara Herrnstein Smith (eds.) *The Politics of Liberal Education*. Durham, NC: Duke University Press, 1992.

Goncalves, Zan Meyer. *Sexuality and the Politics of Ethos in the Writing Classroom*. Carbondale, IL: Southern Illinois University Press, 2005.

Graff, Gerald. *Beyond the Culture Wars: How Teaching the Conflicts Can Revitalize American Education*. New York: Norton, 1992.

Hairston, Maxine. "Diversity, Ideology, and Teaching Writing." *Against the Grain: A Volume in Honor of Maxine Hairston*. Ed. by David Jolliffe, Michael Keene, Mary Trachsel, and Ralph Voss. Cresskill, NJ: Hampton Press, 2002.

Halperin, David M., *One Hundred Years of Homosexuality: and Other Essays on Greek Love*. New York: Routledge, 1990.

Halperin, David. *Saint=Foucault: Towards a Gay Hagiography.* New York: Oxford University Press, 1995.

Habermas, Jurgen. *The Philosophical Discourse of Modernity.* Cambridge, MA: The MIT Press, 1995.

Hawisher, Gail. "Forwarding a Feminist Agenda in Writing Studies." *Feminism and Composition: A Critical Sourcebook.* Ed. by Gesa E. Kirsch, et al. Boston: Bedford, 2003: xv-xx.

Herdt, Gilbert, et al. National Sexuality Resource Center's (NSRC) Fifth Summer Institute. San Francisco State University. San Francisco, CA: July 2006.

Hesford, Wendy. *Framing Identities: Autobiography and the Politics of Pedagogy.* Minneapolis: University of Minnesota Press, 1999.

Hochman, Will. "Transactional Dynamics of Paired Fiction Writing." *Wings* 5.2(1998): http://www.daedalus.com/wings/hochman.5.2.html.

Holdstein, Deborah H., and David Bleich (eds.). *Personal Effects: The Social Character of Scholarly Writing.* Logan, UT: Utah State University Press, 2001.

hooks, bell. *Teaching to Transgress.* New York: Routledge, 1994.

Houle, Brian R., Alex P. Kimball, and Heidi A. McKee. "'Boy? You Decide; Girl? You Decide': Multimodal Web Composition and a Mythography of Identity." *Computers and Composition Online* (Fall 2004): http://www.bgsu.edu/cconline/houlekimballmckee/index.html.

Irvine, Janice. *Talk about Sex: The Battles over Sex Education in the United States.* Berkeley: Univ. of California Press, 2002.

Jagose, Annamarie. *Queer Theory: An Introduction.* New York: NYU Press,1996.

Jarratt, Susan C. "Feminism and Composition: The Case for Conflict." *Contending with Words: Composition and Rhetoric in a Postmodern Age.* Ed. by Patricia Harkin and John Schilb. New York: MLA, 1991: 105–23.

Jordan, Jay. "Rereading the Multicultural Reader: Cross-Cultural Composition Readers and the Reconstruction of Cultural Identities." *College English* 68.2 (November 2005).

Katz, Jonathan Ned. *The Invention of Heterosexuality.* New York: Plume, 1995.

Khayatt, Didi. "Paradoxes of the Closet: Beyond the Classroom Assignment of In or Out." *Inside the Academy and Out: Lesbian/Gay/Queer Studies and Social Action.* Ed. By Janice L. Ristock and Catherine G. Taylor. Toronto: University of Toronto Press, 1998: 31–48.

Kirsch, Gesa E. et al., eds. *Feminism and Composition: A Critical Sourcebook.* Boston: Bedford, 2003.

Kirtley, Susan. "What's Love Got to Do with It?: Eros in the Writing Classroom." *A Way to Move: Rhetorics of Emotion and Composition Studies.* Ed. by Dale Jacobs and Laura R. Micciche. Portsmouth, NH: Heinemann, 2003: 56–66.

LeCourt, Donna. "Writing (Without) the Body; Gender and Power in Networked Discussion Groups." *Feminist Cyberspaces: Mapping Gendered Academic Spaces.* Ed. by Kristine Blair and Pamela Takayoshi. Stamford, CT: Ablex, 1999. 153–175.

Loffreda, Beth. *Losing Matt Shepard: Life and Politics in the Aftermath of Anti-Gay Murder.* New York: Columbia University Press, 2000.

Lu, Min-Zhan. "Reading and Writing Differences: The Problematic of Experience." *Feminism and Composition Studies: In Other Words.* Ed. by Susan C. Jarratt and Lyn Worsham. New York: The Modern Language Association Press, 1998. 239–251.

Luhmann, Susanne. "Queering/Querying Pedagogy? Or, Pedagogy is a Pretty Queer Thing." *Queer Theory in Education.* Ed. by William F. Pinar. Mahwah, NJ: Erlbaum, 1998.

Malinowitz, Harriet. *Textual Orientations: Lesbian and Gay Students and the Making of Discourse Communities.* Portsmouth, NH: Heinemann, 1995.

McBride Dwight A. *Why I Hate Abercrombie & Fitch.* New York: NYU Press, 2005.

McComiskey, Bruce. *Teaching Composition as a Social Process.* Logan, UT: Utah State University Press, 2000.

Meyerowitz, Joanne. *How Sex Changed: A History of Transsexuality in the United States.* Cambridge, MA: Harvard University Press, 2002.

Middleton, Sue. *Disciplining Sexuality: Foucault, Life Histories, and Education.* New York: Teachers' College, Columbia University, 1998.

Miller, Richard E. "Fault Lines in the Contact Zone: Assessing Homophobic Student Writing." *Lesbian and Gay Studies and the Teaching of English.* Ed. by William J. Spurlin. Urbana, IL: National Council of Teachers of English, 2000: 234–252.

Miller, Richard E. "Teaching after September 11." In *Composition Studies in the New Millennium: Rereading the Past, Rewriting the Future.* Ed. Lynn Z. Bloom, Donald A Daiker, and Edward M. White. Carbondale: Southern Illinois University Press, 2003.

Monson, Connie, and Jacqueline Rhodes. "Risking Queer: Pedagogy, Performativity, and Desire in Writing Classrooms." *JAC* 24.1 (2004): 79–92.

More, Kate. "Never Mind the Bollocks: Judith Butler on Transsexuality." *Reclaiming Genders: Transsexual Grammars at the Fin de Siècle.* Ed. by Kate More and Stephen Whittle. Londgon: Cassell, 1999.

Nussbaum, Martha. "A Defense of Lesbian and Gay Rights." *Sex and Social Justice.* New York: Oxford University Press, 1999.

Pinar, William (ed.). *Queer Theory in Education.* Mahwah, NJ: Erlbaum, 1998.

Plummer, Ken. *Intimate Citizenship: Private Decisions for Public Dialogues.* Seattle: University of Washington Press, 2003.

Plummer, Ken. *Telling Sexual Stories.* New York: Routledge, 1995.

Pollack, William. *Real Boys: Rescuing Our Sons from the Myths of Boyhood.* New York: Henry Holt Publishing, 1998.

Pratt, Mary Louise.

Prosser, Jay. *Second Skins: Body Narratives of Transsexuality.* New York: Columbia University Press, 1998.

Ramdas, Lalita. "Women and Literacy: A Quest for Justice." In Ellen Cushman, et al. (eds.), *Literacy: A Critical Sourcebook.* Boston: Bedford, 2001. 629–643.

Regan, Allison. "Type Normal Like the Rest of Us: Writing, Power, and Homophobia in the Networked Composition Classroom." *Computers and Composition* 9.4 (November 1993): 11–23.

Rhodes, Jacqueline. "Sexualities, Technologies, and Literacies: Metonymy and Material Online." *Computers and Composition Online.* (Fall 2004).

Ristock, Janice L., and Catherine G. Taylor, eds. 1998. *Inside the Academy and Out: Lesbian/Gay/Queer Studies and Social Action.* Toronto: University of Toronto Press.

Ritchie, Joy S., and Kathleen Boardman. "Feminism in Composition: Inclusion, Metonymy, and Disruption." *Feminism and Composition: A Critical Sourcebook.* Ed. by Gesa E. Kirsch, et al. Boston: Bedford, 2003: 7–26.

Ringer, R. Jeffrey (ed.). *Queer Words, Queer Images: Communication and the Construction of Homosexuality.* New York: New York University Press, 1994.

Roberts-Miller, Patricia. *Deliberate Conflict: Argument, Political Theory, and Composition Classes.* Carbondale, IL: Southern Illinois University Press, 2004.

Romano, Susan. "On Becoming a Woman: Pedagogies of the Self." *Feminism and Composition: A Critical Sourcebook.* Ed. by Gesa E. Kirsch, et al. Boston: Bedford, 2003: 447–465.

Rubin, Henry. *Self-Made Men: Identity and Embodiment among Transsexual Men.* Nashville, TN: Vanderbilt University Press, 2003.

Ryden, Wendy. "Conflict and Kitsch: The Politics of Politeness in the Writing Class." *A Way to Move: Rhetorics of Emotion and Composition Studies.* Ed. by Dale Jacobs and Laura R. Micciche. Portsmouth, NH: Heinemann, 2003: 80–91.

Sedgwick, Eve Kosofsky. *Epistemology of the Closet.* Berkeley, CA: University of California Press, 1990.

Seidman, Steven. "From Outsider to Citizen." *Regulating Sex: The Politics of Intimacy and Identity*. Ed. by Elizabeth Bernstein and Laurie Schaffner. New York: Routledge, 2005: 225–246.

Selfe, Cynthia L., and Gail E. Hawisher. *Literate Lives in the Information Age: Narratives of Literacy from the United States*. Mahwah, NJ: Lawrence Erlbaum, 2004.

Shanley, Mary Lyndon (ed.). *Just Marriage*. New York: Oxford University Press, 2004.

Shor, Ira. *Empowering Education: Critical Teaching for Social Change*. Chicago, IL: University of Chicago Press, 1992.

Showalter, Elaine. *Teaching Literature*. Oxford: Blackwell, 2003.

Sinfield, Alan. *Cultural Politics—Queer Reading*. London: Routledge, 1994.

Sirc, Geoffrey: *English Composition as a Happening*. Logan UT: Utah State University Press, 2002.

Skorczewski, Dawn M. *Teaching One Moment at a Time: Disruption and Repair in the Classroom*. Amherst, MA: University of Massachusetts Press, 2005.

Skorczewski, Dawn M. and Matthew Parfitt, eds. *Conflicts and Crises in the Composition Classroom— And What Instructors Can Do About Them*. Portsmouth: Boynton/Cook-Heinemann, 2003.

Smith, Lauren. "Staging the Self: Queer Theory in the Composition Classroom." In Calvin Thomas (ed.) *Straight with a Twist: Queer Theory and the Subject of Heterosexuality*. Urbana: University of Illinois Press, 2000. 68–85.

Spellmeyer, Kurt. "Education for Irrelevance? Or, Joining Our Colleagues in Lit Crit on the Sidelines of the Information Age." *Composition Studies in the New Millennium: Rereading the Past, Rewriting the Future*. Ed. by Lynn Z. Bloom, et al. Carbondale, IL: Southern Illinois University Press, 2003.

Spigelman, Candace: *Personally Speaking: Experience as Evidence in Academic Discourse*. Carbondale, IL: Southern Illinois University Press, 2004.

Spurlin, William, ed. *Lesbian and Gay Studies and the Teaching of English*. Urbana, IL: National Council of Teachers of English, 2000.

Street, Brian. "The New Literacy Studies." In Ellen Cushman, et al. (eds.), *Literacy: A Critical Sourcebook*. Boston: Bedford, 2001. 430–442.

Stryker, Susan. "Transsexuality: The Postmodern Body and/as Technology." *The Cybercultures Reader*. Ed. by David Bell and Barbara M. Kennedy. London: Routledge, 2000. 588–597.

Sullivan, Patricia A. "Feminism and Methodology in Composition Studies." *Feminism and Composition: A Critical Sourcebook*. Ed. by Gesa E. Kirsch, et al. Boston: Bedford, 2003: 124–139.

Teunis, Niels and Gilbert Herdt (eds.). *Sexual Inequalities*. [manuscript in preparation]

Thomas, Calvin. *Straight with a Twist: Queer Theory and the Subject of Heterosexuality*. Urbana: University of Illinois Press, 2000.

Tobin, Lad. *Writing Relationships: What Really Happens in the Composition Class*. Portsmouth, NH: Heinemann, 1993.

Turner, William B. *A Genealogy of Queer Theory*. Philadelphia, PA: Temple University Press, 2000.

Twitchell, James B. *Branded Nation: The Marketing of Megachurch, College, Inc., and Museumworld*. New York: Simon & Schuster, 2004.

Wallace, David L., and Helen Rothschild Ewald. *Mutuality in the Rhetoric and Composition*. Carbondale, IL: Southern Illinois University Press, 2000.

Warner, Michael. *The Trouble with Normal: Sex, Politics, and the Ethics of Queer Life*. New York: The Free Press, 1999.

Weed, Elizabeth, and Naomi Schor, eds. *Feminism Meets Queer Theory*. Bloomington: Indiana University Press, 1997.

Weeks, Jeffrey. *Sexuality and Its Discontents: Meanings, Myths, & Modern Sexualities*. Boston: Routledge & K. Paul, 1985.

Weeks, Jeffrey. *Invented Moralities*. New York: Columbia University Press, 1995.

Wolff, Bill. "Reading the Rhetoric of Web Pages: Rethinking the Goals of Student Research in the Computer Classroom." Currents in Electronic Literacy Fall 2003 (7). Available online at http://www.cwrl.utexas.edu/currents/fall03/wolff.html.

Young, Morris. *Minor Re/Visions: Asian American Literacy Narratives as a Rhetoric of Citizenship*. Carbondale, IL: Southern Illinois University Press, 2004.

Yoshino, Kenji. *Covering: The Hidden Assault on Our Civil Rights*. New York: Random House, 2006.

INDEX

ABOUT THE AUTHOR

JONATHAN ALEXANDER is Associate Professor of English at the University of California, Irvine, where he also serves as Campus Writing Coordinator. His previous books include *Digital Youth: Emerging Literacies on the World Wide Web,* the co-edited collection *Role Play: Distance Learning and the Teaching of Writing,* the co-authored textbook *Argument Now, a Brief Rhetoric,* and the co-edited book *Bisexuality and Transgenderism: InterSEXions of the Others.*